CAVAFY

Cavafy

a biography

Robert Liddell

SCHOCKEN BOOKS · NEW YORK

à Bernard de Zogheb
et
aux autres amis alexandrins

First published by SCHOCKEN BOOKS 1976

Library of Congress Cataloging in Publication Data

Liddell, Robert, 1908-
  Cavafy: a critical biography.

  Bibliography: p. 212
  Includes index.
  1. Kabaphēs, Kōnstantinos Petrou, 1863-1933.

[PA5610.K2Z74 1976]   889'.1'32 [B]   76-9135

Manufactured in the United States of America

Contents

Illustrations

Great masters who have shown mankind
An order it has yet to find,
What if all pedants say of you
As personalities be true?
All the more honour to you then
If, weaker than some other men,
You had the courage that survives
Soiled, shabby, egotistic lives,
If poverty or ugliness,
Ill-health or social unsuccess
Hunted you out of life to play
At living in another way;
Yet the live quarry all the same
Were changed to huntsmen in the game,
And the wild furies of the past,
Tracked to their origins at last,
Trapped in a medium's artifice,
To charity, delight increase.
Now large, magnificent, and calm,
Your changeless presences disarm
The sullen generations, still
The fright and fidget of the will,
And to the growing and the weak,
Your final transformations speak,
Saying to dreaming 'I am deed.'
To striving 'Courage. I succeed.'
To mourning 'I remain. Forgive.'
And to becoming 'I am, live.'

W. H. Auden *New Year Letter*

Apology

It was while George Seferis was dying that I received an invitation to write a life of Cavafy, and I felt more than usually sensitive to what he had said. 'Outside his poems Cavafy does not exist. As it seems to me, one of two things will happen : either we shall continue to write scholastic gossip about his private life, fastening upon the *bons mots* of provincial witticisms; and then, of course, we shall reap what we have sown; or else, starting from his basic characteristic, his unity, we shall listen to what is actually said by his work, this work in which, drop by drop, he spent his own self with all his senses.' With these words in mind, I wondered whether a life of Cavafy ought to be written, even a critical biography.

It would be a pioneer work. The most complete 'life', that by Michael Peridis, is only a sketch. The invaluable studies by Mr Timos Malanos are only in part biographical; he has tended to ignore dates. Mr Stratis Tsirkas has been occupied with the social background rather than with the poet's life. Moreover very much more material is now available.

A study of these, the leading Cavafists, revealed great discrepancies in matters of fact as well as in interpretation. Michael Peridis, who probably wrote without any particular prejudice, was (though a most intelligent man) without much literary training. 'Anyone who wants to study the poet's work below the surface,' said John Mavrogordato, 'must begin by reading the investigations of Mr Malanos, even if he does not always like them.' Probably for Mavrogordato, as for others, Freud raises his ugly head too often in the very sensitive work of this critic. But in the work of Mr Tsirkas – where great industry and energy are displayed, to which we must feel indebted – the ugly head is that of Marx, whose intrusion is far less relevant, as the following pages will show.

It may not be the case that an accurate life of the poet can do very much to illuminate his work. But it must be probable that his critics will fare better if they are delivered once and for all from contradictions, from a confused tradition, from guesswork, fiction and misrepresentation. There is then a case for a biography, and this must be my apology to Seferis' dear and honoured shade.

A book on Cavafy in English, and without Greek citations, can only pretend to biographical definitiveness. Presently we may hope for Mr Edmund Keeley's work, after which we shall know a great deal more about Cavafy's poetical development. We are also to await publication of fragments and of the poet's notes by Mr George Savidis.

Criticism, however, is never finished, and many thesis subjects will probably remain. The sources have been admirably studied by Mr Malanos, but others may have something to tell us about literary influences – the Phanariot poets of the nineteenth century, the French Parnassiens and Symbolistes, the English romantic poets and Browning, and finally Cavafy's discovery of himself as an Alexandrian poet and heir to Callimachus – but an heir to Callimachus enriched by many other legacies.

Of his language Messrs Keeley and Sherrard, authors of the best and latest English translation – and perhaps we may hope for a complete translation from them – have well written: 'Cavafy's Greek, even with its deliberate archaisms, is closer in crucial ways to the spoken idiom than is the language of other leading Greek poets of his time.' It is not *katharevousa*, the artificial language, nor yet the pedantic and limited demotic of those who will not admit into their writing the scraps of *katharevousa* syntax and vocabulary that are commonly heard in conversation. A thorough examination of his language – and of its debts to Alexandria and Constantinople, and even to his years in England – needs a linguistic expert, but one who is also sensitive to literary values.

English was Cavafy's second language, and that most commonly used in his family and with many of his friends. A number of his notes, in English, has for some years been in print, though not very accessible. The generosity of Mr George Savidis has enabled me to study a great many unpublished letters and papers in English and Greek, which contribute materially to our knowledge of the poet's life and background. A book that should make these English texts available in their original form needs no further justification.

I do not quite know what Seferis meant by 'the *bons mots* of provincial witticisms'. If the witticisms of Alexandria are 'provincial' because not metropolitan, they need be no worse for that. Some of those who have talked about Cavafy – notably Pieridis and Sareyannis – have done much to create our picture of him. Only too little gossip of the right kind has been preserved, but, as one of Ivy Compton-Burnett's characters observed: 'It has a frail hold on life like all precious things.' Cavafy was much addicted to it; he said to his friend Christopher Nomikos: 'These things, my dear, make life bearable.' I am happy to remember that George Seferis himself was far too amusing a conversationalist to despise gossip.

Acknowledgements

I am grateful to Mrs Kyveli Singopoulou for granting me permission to quote published and unpublished texts by Cavafy.

Thanks are also due to: Mr W. H. Auden and the executors of T. S. Eliot (and Messrs Faber and Faber); the executors of E. M. Forster (and the Hogarth Press); the executors of Sir Maurice Bowra (and Messrs Macmillan); the executors of John Mavrogordato (and Messrs Chatto and Windus); Mr Rex Warner and the executors of George Seferis (and The Bodley Head); Messrs Edmund Keeley and George Savidis (and the Dial Press).

Above all, I wish to express my profound gratitude to that great Cavafy scholar, Mr George Savidis, who has shown me every sort of generosity at all stages of my work. He has given or lent me valuable publications and photocopies, and above all has granted me access to the rich Cavafy archive which is fortunately in his possession. Without his help this book could not have been written, and I wish to thank his son Dimitri for the photographs.

A happy consequence of this undertaking has been the renewal of my friendship with Mr Timos Malanos, the most authoritative critic of Cavafy. Years ago, in Alexandria, he encouraged my first steps in Cavafian studies. Now, by the waters of Leman, he has had the goodness to read these pages, and to make invaluable suggestions and corrections. I must not, however, allow him or Mr Savidis to be thought responsible for any error into which I may fall.

Mr Basil Athanassopoulos, an intimate friend of the poet's. and a frequent visitor in the Rue Lepsius, has helped me with his wonderful memory. I am also indebted to Mr Christian Ayoub (now of Montreal) and his probably unrivalled knowledge of Alexandrian society, and to Dr Alan Bird who has kindly supplied me with information about Liverpool.

Note on Translations and Greek Names

The translations of poems (except where indicated) are my own, though I may quote a line or phrase from Mavrogordato. I have normally used the best edition of the 154 poems of the 'canon', that edited by George Savidis (Athens, 1963). Nevertheless I have thought it proper to refer the English reader to the translation by John Mavrogordato, at present the best complete version in the language : every one of the poems of the 'canon' is therefore given its number in that translation, which follows the order in the memorial edition published by Alexander and Rika Singopoulos (Alexandria, 1935). The bibliography of Cavafy's works is fully discussed in Chapter VIII.

In the translation of ancient names I have preferred the Latin forms traditional in England, e.g. Caesarion, Seleucides, etc. I have even ventured to quote Mavrogordato in this spelling, instead of in the 'Grotesque' forms (as they have been irreverently called after the great historian) Kaisarion and Seleukides. Nor (sincerely as I admire their work) can I imitate the phonetic 'Selefkidis' of Messrs Keeley and Sherrard. My general principle has been that if Cavafy is to be rendered into English, it should be into English that he must be rendered.

In the transliteration of modern Greek names I have followed the method in general use, while avoiding the ugly unnecessary *dh* and *gh*. There will be some inconsistency, especially where the name of a family has been differently spelt by their acquaintance (e.g. Benaki or Benachi, Zervudachi, Zervoudachi, Zervudaki).

Women's names have not always been put into the genitive form practised in Greece : I refer e.g. to Alexander and Rika Singopoulos, rather than to Alexander Singopoulos and Rika Singopoulou. Nevertheless Penelope Delta and Mme Zelita are mentioned by the form of their names by which they are generally known.

I   Before the Bombardment

Of ancient Greek Alexandria nothing survives but the name and the site, and the Romans have only left inconsiderable remains behind them. The conquering Arabs, who were to build so magnificently elsewhere, here did nothing but destroy. A miserable village stood during the centuries where had been the city of Alexander and the Ptolemies; of the poets Theocritus, Callimachus and Apollonius Rhodius; of Antony and Cleopatra; of saints and heresiarchs such as St Athanasius and Arius; of learning and philosophy, of the Mouseion, of Plotinus and Hypatia. The Venetians went off with the head of St Mark, the apostle of Egypt. The Greek patriarch lived in Cairo – when he did not live in Constantinople – and in Cairo was the patriarchal library, home of the Codex Alexandrinus of the Gospels, until this was given to Charles I of England.

The present Alexandria, the creation of the viceroy Mohammed Aly, is an entirely new city. This son of a Cavalla tobacco merchant not unnaturally favoured the Greeks among the other colonists whom he attracted thither. These were largely (though not exclusively) Greeks of the dispersion, from various parts of the Ottoman empire : Greeks by name, language and religion, if only in part by blood. The new Greek colony had no continuity with the great past. But Airs, Waters and Places have powers, as Hippocrates has taught us, and there is still greater power in the Greek name and language. In this banausic, commercial city, where the Greeks had only come to make money, one voice was to arise, to claim a spiritual descent from the ancients, the voice of Constantine Cavafy.

Like many people whose families have seen better days, Cavafy was interested in his genealogy. During his years in Constantinople (1882–5) he amused himself by making notes of what he could collect of his father's family from his paternal aunt, Roxandra Plessos, and of his mother's family from his maternal grandfather, George Photiades. Several manuscripts are in

existence: there is a little notebook in English, written for his
brother John; there is a Greek paper (incomplete) that has been
printed,[1] and a much fuller unpublished document in English.
It is upon the last of these that I shall mainly rely in this chapter,
for it contains much information that can only have come to him
from other sources, probably including his mother and some of
his brothers. It is written with the poet's characteristic abbreviations of words (more often suspensions than contractions); these
are generally easy to expand, being obvious in themselves or
rendered obvious by the context. As this is not a literary text I
shall quote boldly from my reading of it (when it is beyond
reasonable doubt) and inflict on no one the ugliness of a diplomatic transcript. It appears to be a later compilation than the
Genealogy that has been printed, and sometimes corrects it.
Nevertheless, the poet is not always quite accurately informed
about his father's earlier life, about which we have lately
acquired definite information from the researches of Mr Kyriakos
Metaxas, who has published *inter alia* the application for British
nationality made by Peter Cavafy in 1850.[2]

The name Cavafy derives from the Turkish word for 'shoe-
maker'. The family possibly had its origin on the Persian-
Armenian border,[3] but it had been known in the Greek community of Constantinople as early as the beginning of the
eighteenth century: it had property at Hypsomatheia, and
tombs at Balukli. John (1701–1762) was governor of Jassy in
Moldavia; he later lived in Vienna and is said to have received
an Austrian title. When he was asked by a niece why the title
was not still used in the family, the poet said (surprisingly)
'Greeks don't like all that', and (very sensibly) 'clerks should
avoid that sort of thing'. The title may not have been authentic;
John may not have been a direct ancestor; and if he were, his
heirs would be a senior branch of the family. Another eighteenth-
century 'notable' was George Cavafy (1745–1792) archpriest of
the church of Antioch.

We are on surer ground when we arrive at John Cavafy
(1779–1844), the poet's grandfather, a substantial merchant of

1. *Genealogy.*
2. Article by Mr Kyriakos Metaxas in *Eleutheros Kosmos*, Athens, 6 May
1973.
3. Malanos, *Cavafy*, p. 12; *Cavafy 2*, p. 80.

Constantinople who married Phevronia (1783–1868), daughter of Michael Scarlatus Pandus (or Pangiotis) of Constantinople and Jassy. John was of moderate height and wore a Constantinopolitan costume with a fur calfak on his head: he was known for straight dealing, but inclined to weakness. So was not his wife, a tall self-willed woman with hard and severe features surmounted by a sort of turban, though in later life she affected European dress. Her daughter told Constantine many stories of her acrimoniousness; in her widowhood she had lived with Roxandra and her husband, and had dominated them.

John Cavafy was able to give his sons what was considered a good education at that time, but he could not start them with much capital. His eldest son George (1806–1891) went to London about 1827 and worked as a clerk in the office of Nicolas Thomas and his partners Ikplitsis Ionides and John Argenti in Tokenhouse Street near the Bank of England. In 1829 the company moved to Finsbury Circus, and was known as A. A. Ionides and Co. In March 1834 George Cavafy married Mariora, daughter of Nicolas Thomas, in London; Spyridon Trikoupis, then Greek ambassador, was present. Two years later his younger brother Peter John (born in Salonica in 1814) followed him to England. He lived three years in Manchester, two in London and a further five years between Manchester and Liverpool, returning to London in 1846. At first he worked for Ionides and Co., and then (after 1844) with Cassavetti, Cavafy and Co. In 1849 he and his brother commenced as Cavafy Bros.

Peter John travelled a good deal, and often stayed in Paris for pleasure. It is possible that he made an earlier and childless marriage. In 1849 he revisited Constantinople, and was staying at his mother's house in Pera when he married Haricleia (1835–1899), the poet's mother, at Neochori (or Yeniköy) on the Upper Bosphorus, in April of that year.

Haricleia was the eldest daughter of George Photiades (1800–1891), a diamond merchant, and member of a distinguished family of Chiot origin established in Constantinople by 1680 in the Phanar, the old Greek quarter beside the Orthodox patriarchate and near the Golden Horn. Among other notable sons, the Photiades family produced an archbishop of Caesarea in the eighteenth century, and a Prince of Samos in the nineteenth (i.e. a Christian governor of the island, appointed by the Porte).

This family, at one time called Tarag-Hanadji because of an office held by one of them in connection with the mint, now owned a villa at Yeniköy and was well-to-do, in spite of occasional ups-and-downs. It has been related by one of his great-grand daughters that when bills became troublesome and creditors too pressing, the Tselebi George Photiades was wont to take refuge in a hospital (of which he was one of the founders) and to go to bed, forbidding all visits, and only reappearing when the family fortunes had improved.

Nevertheless, while the Cavafys were gentlefolk (though we need not take seriously their legendary descent from the imperial house of Ducas, nor yet the very bogus-looking home-made crest that sometimes adorned their writing-paper : a helmet of strange design, floating about, and not fixed on a wreath), the Photiades were almost aristocratic. It was perhaps not purely out of affection for their grandfather (though they may have hoped to be remembered in his will) that for some years Constantine and his brother Paul wrote Φ or F, instead of Π or P, for their middle initial; they were thus choosing their mother's maiden name instead of their father's Christian name (the normal Greek practice) for their own middle name. It is possible that as young men first going into society they liked to remind the world of their Phanariot kindred. Constantine seems to have abandoned this practice in the year of his grandfather's death (1896). George Photiades had left him nothing. Mr Malanos[4] has suggested that the change of middle initial allowed the poet to disown some early poems signed 'Constantine F.'. Possibly he no longer cared to boast of a Phanariot background, and was, in a way, choosing his native Alexandria for his city rather than Constantinople. Probably not too much should be made of it : Paul continued to address letters to his brother as 'Constantine F.' until 1912.

After their marriage, Peter John took his young wife to his mother's house, and it seems that he left her there for some months while he went to manage the Liverpool branch of the firm. His brother Dimitri was also living in the house, with his wife Smaragda, with whom he was always quarrelling. Their sister Roxandra was another inmate. 'The sojourn of the young bride was not a pleasant one in her mother-in-law's house,' wrote her son; and we can well believe it. There the poor girl gave

4. Malanos, *Cavafy*, pp. 41–2.

birth to her first child, George, in January 1850. Her husband was with her on this occasion.

In the following month he received a letter from his brother George in London (16 February 1850) asking him to go to Alexandria to found a branch there. George declares himself much opposed to Peter John's plan of bringing his family to England. He thinks one of his brothers is needed in Alexandria, and believes that one should not hesitate to go there on account of the climate. He asks Peter John to go at present to Cairo, as joint manager with Emmanuel Pittaridis (husband of their sister, Maria Cavafy), and to visit Alexandria to examine the possibilities, after having settled things in Constantinople – where the branch must have been closed at this time. Peter John so far prevailed that he had his family in England till 1854 or 1855.

In 1850 he went to England with his wife and son. On their way they made a long stay in Paris, which naturally made a great impression on the girl, who hitherto knew nothing but Constantinople. In August Peter John applied successfully for British nationality, dating his application from 8 New Broad Street in the City of London. The whole Cavafy family was at 47 Stamford Hill when on 12 March 1851 Haricleia gave birth to her second son, Peter John II (whom we will call Peter, as his brothers did). He was baptised in London on 24 August, Mariora Cavafy being his godmother.

In 1852 the Cavafys settled in Liverpool at 33 Bedford Street South.[5] There they lived 'a quiet and retired life, not by any means agreeable to a girl of eighteen'. Peter John got his wife teachers of English, Greek and drawing, and she was acquainted with the best Greek families of the place, her friends being Mrs John Schillizzi and Mrs Costa Ralli – one cannot help hazarding a guess that they had been chosen for her. Here she gave birth to her third son, Aristides, on 9 April 1853.

It was not until late 1854 or early 1855 that the Peter John Cavafys moved to Alexandria, though Peter John himself may have visited it before that date.

The family first established itself in the 'Okelle Zizinia', a house rented from the Zizinia family, in the Place des Consuls (later Place Mohammed Aly), then the centre of Alexandrian society. This house, such was the manner of the time, consisted

5. This is the address in Gore's *Directory*, 1853.

of offices and warehouses on the ground floor, and the dwell-
ing-house above. It became known as the 'Okelle Cavafy'.

Peter John 'soon became one of the most prominent merchants
in Alexandria if not the most important of all'. He went up the
Nile – sailing, no doubt, in a felucca – and opened a branch at
Minia in Upper Egypt for the corn trade. In 1860 he founded a
cotton-ginning factory at Kafr el Zayat, in the Delta, and he
had a warehouse at the cotton exchange at Miniet el Basal, a
suburb of Alexandria. He was a lively and cultivated man, and a
busy, energetic merchant. Like other Alexandrian merchants he
benefited by the steep rise in price of Egyptian grain during
the Crimean war. Fortunately for him he had British nationality,
for Greece was on the Russian side, and its diplomatic relations
with Egypt were broken off. Michael Tositsas, president of the
Greek community in Alexandria, left the country, committing its
care to the vice-president, a French subject: an illustration of the
conflict between race and nationality that has continually
occurred among colonists in Egypt.

In the Okelle Zizinia four more children were born to
Haricleia: Helen (1855–6), Alexander (1856–1905), Paul I
(1858–9) and Paul II (1860–1920). There they were visited
by George Cavafy from London, and his wife and son. John
(1861–1923) was born during a visit to Constantinople.

Peter John moved to the new and smart Rue Cherif. Again he
did not buy a house, but rented the Okelle Zogheb; there again
he had the offices and residence in this new 'Okelle Cavafy',
now the head office of the firm. Its main business in Egypt was
wheat, but it dealt also in cotton. The designation of the firm
was 'P. J. Cavafy and Co.' in Alexandria and London – where
the offices were in Threadneedle Street – and 'Cavafy and Co.'
in the other places, including Liverpool, where the offices were in
Fenwick Street. In Cairo the offices were in Mouski Street.

The Phanariot poet Alexander Soutsos came to stay with Peter
John and Haricleia in the Okelle Zogheb in 1862 and wrote
frigid little epitaphs for their dead babies which were inscribed
on the family tomb in the Greek cemetery at Chatby, first acquired at Helen's death. Haricleia was not so easily consoled.
Paul II perhaps replaced Paul I, but she never had the daughter
for whom she longed. In each pregnancy she hoped for another
Helen, and in her last spoke of the unborn child by that name.

When this child, the future poet, was born on 17 (Old Style) or 29 (New Style) April 1863, he was given the name Constantine. Perhaps this was regarded as the masculine equivalent of the name Helen, as SS. Constantine and Helen have the same feast day. Haricleia kept Constantine in frocks and allowed his curls to grow as long as she could; he was always her darling and her Benjamin.

He was baptised more than a year later by the priest-in-charge of the Evangelismos, the church of the Greek community in Alexandria. The sponsor who received him from the font was his first cousin Amalia Pittaridis (later Mme Pappos); her father was now manager of the Minia branch of Cavafy and Co. Her sister Thalia had been godmother to his brother Paul.

When the Cavafys first settled in Alexandria the Greek colony was still small, only some three thousand souls; but Greek was generally spoken, for many of the Dutch, English, French and Italian settlers had come from Smyrna or Constantinople. 'Alexandria was very gay as most of the settlers were prosperous financiers and merchants. Balls and dinner-parties were frequent.' Peter John lived in grand style: 'his furniture, carriages, silver and glass were of a fine quality then rare among the Greeks'. The house in the Rue Cherif was 'the rendez-vous of the best Alexandrian society'. It was a society of wealth, that knew nothing of landed proprietorship or of political influence; few of its members were titled – and this was a rather later development when Catholic Syrians bought titles of the Pope, or when consuls or bankers were ennobled by Powers to which they had been of service. The British, not wishing to create for themselves hereditary law-givers in Alexandria, only conferred knighthoods. Some people acquired the Egyptian designation of Pasha or Bey. Though the early settlers, from 1830 onwards, were proud of their early arrival, there was, as an authority on Alexandrian society[6] reminds me, 'no Mayflower'. The Cavafys were very well established towards the end of the first period of revived Alexandria: their position was excellent and their origins (particularly Haricleia's) were more than respectable. Even after they had lost their money they remained, as the same authority tells me, *nice*, and would always be considered as belonging to the upper classes, though fallen into social obscurity through

6. Mr Christian Ayoub.

poverty, and rendered (some of them) unattractive by self-pity.

Their *floruit* was short but brilliant. We are told that Haricleia was soon recognised as one of the most beautiful women in Alexandria. This is hard to believe from a photograph in which she looks like a ball of black suet. An earlier photograph taken in London (probably about 1851) shows the profile of a charming nose, and the mouth is pretty – she was already inclined to embonpoint, but that would render her no less attractive under eastern eyes. She must have made a striking contrast with her tall, fair husband. It is related that people used to stop to gaze at her with admiration as she came out of her house in the Rue Cherif 'swaying charmingly' on the very high heels that she wore to add to her diminutive stature, to take her place in her carriage behind her Italian coachman and her Egyptian groom. The poet told one of his nieces that he had rarely seen his mother on her feet, and she imagined it was when her grandmother 'alourdie par les plaisirs de la table et le luxe de l'oisiveté' was going from her divan to her victoria for a leisurely drive by the Mahmoudieh canal. Her son affectionately addressed her (in English) as 'Fat One'.

Said Pasha, the viceroy, distinguished Haricleia by his attentions, and 'very often offered her his arm'. His successor, Ismail, was a friend of Peter John, who often attended the Vice-Regal court. In 1869 Ismail, then Khedive, decorated Peter John with the Mejidieh order, on the opening of the Suez canal.

Peter John made a great deal of money, and spent it freely : there were several Greek servants in his house, and his children had an English nurse and a French tutor. Apparently the three eldest sons, George, Peter and Aristides, were sent abroad for their studies : their brother records that they were educated in England and France. Peter John and Haricleia travelled every summer and visited 'most towns in Italy and France', also Malta and Corfu. On one journey, soon after his birth, they took Constantine to Paris with his nurse. In the winter Peter John frequently visited Cairo. He was unfortunately improvident, spending as much as £4000 a year, and 'he never seems to have been in enjoyment of really good health'. When he died, on 10 August 1870, 'his property was small, and he did not leave much at his death'. It has been suggested that his youngest son was speaking relatively : his father left little in comparison with the vast fortunes left by other men of his world. It is, however, likely that the provision left for his widow and her large family was very inadequate. Shortly afterwards they were to lose it, such as it was. The poet, only seven years old in 1870, had 'but a vague memory' of his father, whom he described as 'a rather tall man, of a pleasing and distinguished countenance'. But he seems always to have been aware that he was born a rich man's son.

Haricleia lived the first two years of her widowhood in great seclusion in Alexandria. Aristides seems to have gone to London in 1871 to work in the office of Cavafy and Co., and George also almost certainly went at much the same time. Their mother and the rest of the family followed in 1872. After brief pauses each in Marseilles, Paris and London, Haricleia went to Liverpool, where she settled in 1873 at 12 Balmoral Road, Elm Park, Fairfield,[7] with Peter and her four youngest sons. George remained in London, and Aristides went back to work in the family firm in Alexandria.

The family occupied an eight-room house with a small plot of garden in front; the annual rent did not exceed £65, but in Liverpool at that date this was not a meagre sum. Peter and Alexander worked in the office of the family firm and the former, when still far too young and inexperienced, soon became manager. Haricleia still led a secluded life, and her only frequent visitors were her neighbours, members of the Seriades and Notaras families, and relations of Mariora, her brother-in-law's wife. It is probable that she did not much care for Mariora, much her senior, whom Constantine describes as a woman 'of irritable temper and fond of money'.

We are to ' that Paul, John and Constantine were studying – but not whether or where they went to school. There is one piece of evidence about John and Constantine. John (1 October 1882) wrote to Constantine: 'Poor Stopford!' He must (he thought) have been 'our schoolfellow', his father having been 'pastor of Dawlish'.[8] This suggests that they went to an English school,

7. This is given as their address for 1873 in the *Post Office Guide*, whereas the house is marked empty in Gore's *Directory*. No doubt they settled during that year.

8. I had conjectured that 'poor Stopford' had shortly before died a hero's death at Tel el Kebir, but Army Records forbid that supposition. It

whether in Liverpool or London or elsewhere. Much as one would
like to identify it, it might not be more than a name to us, if it
were a short-lived private school, which is probably the case.
There is no other record of their having English friends or acquaintances.

George Cavafy, the eldest brother, now manager in London,
was 'led astray by the temptations of London life' and 'engaged
in unhappy speculations' which 'proved his ruin and contributed
to the speedy liquidation of the firm'. But he was 'by no means
responsible for the actual loss of the family's surviving fortune.
The management of that fortune was entirely in the second
brother's hands, Peter John's, who lost it in unfortunate speculations, mostly in United Bonds and Sugar.' His mother was aware
of his transactions, though Constantine does not throw blame on
her. Peter, he says, though 'owing to inexperience he did not act
for the best still acted entirely in an honest spirit'. Nor had
George done anything dishonest. By the time he wrote this, Constantine had already suffered from the dubious activities of
Aristides and Paul.

In 1874 the family fortunes seem to have taken a turn for the
better; perhaps the 'unfortunate speculations' began by paying
dividends. Peter went into lodgings in Liverpool, while Haricleia moved to London, to 15 Queensborough Terrace, Hyde
Park, a ten-room house, at a rent of £220 per annum. She now
led a more cheerful life, going occasionally to the parties of
Greek merchants and to the theatre. She had 'two well-filled
drawing-rooms' and 'kept up visiting relations' with the leading
Greek families of London. In the summer she went to the sea: in
1875 to Harper's Hotel, Dover, and 1876 to West Cliff Hotel,
Folkestone.

Then the crash came; their speculations failed, and they had
to sell their furniture and part of their plate and return to Liverpool, where they lived at 45 Huskisson Street (probably in
lodgings) for nearly a year. At the same time the liquidation of

does not appear that anyone of that name was vicar of Dawlish, but perhaps
John was as ready as Jane Austen's Robert Ferrars to locate people there.
So far he defies identification. The Rev. Frederick Manners Stopford,
rector of Tichmarsh in Northamptonshire, had a son Albert Henry (b. 1860)
whose age fits. But the name originates in Lancashire and there might be
others of that name at school in Liverpool.

Cavafy and Co. began, and they lost the last £3000 of their private fortune in 'unlucky ventures'.

On 24 July 1877 a passport was issued to 'Mrs Harriet Cavafy, widow of Mr Peter John Cavafy, a naturalised British subject – (certificate of naturalisation dated August 13, 1850) – travelling in Europe and Africa accompanied by her three sons, Paul, John and Constantine, aged respectively 16, 13 and 12 years.' In fact they were respectively 17, 16 and 14 years old.

Aristides (who had come to England at the time of the liquidation) and Alexander went back ahead of the others to Alexandria. Peter accompanied his mother and young brothers, and George remained in London 'earning his livelihood as clerk and sometimes manager in the offices of Greek merchants trading with the Levant'.

When the Cavafys left Liverpool in September 1877 'all the money the family possessed was about £300'. They spent three days in London at the Charing Cross Hotel, two in Paris at the Hôtel du Louvre and fourteen days at Marseilles at the Grand Hôtel. Haricleia had some thought of settling there, and tried to find a place as broker for Peter with Greek merchants of the town with whom she was acquainted. Her efforts and Peter's were unsuccessful, and towards the end of September they proceeded to Alexandria.

After a brief stay at the Hôtel de l'Europe on the Place des Consuls, they rented an eight-room flat on the third floor of the Okelle Debbane in the Rue Mahmoud Pacha el Falaki. Their rent was £70 per annum, but they had only one servant; life was dull and poor, and the earnings of the sons were small. The furniture that they purchased was 'very poor', but they may have brought some relics of their former splendour out of storage. We know that oil paintings, portraits of Peter John and Haricleia executed in Italy by a 'good' painter in 1860, were among the things destroyed in the events of 1882. Haricleia received 17,500 gold francs (£875) compensation in 1885, so that she must have lost more than the 'very poor' furniture – and some family furniture has survived the death of the poet, who was the last of the family. At this time, 'though she had some acquaintance and was occasionally invited to parties, Haricleia Cavafy's life was a life dull and of poverty', for the family 'barely managed to make two ends meet'.

The one advantage of their flat was the privilege of using the Debbane garden where 'the present writer' (says Cavafy) used to play with his neighbours, Stephen Schilizzi and John Rodocanachi. It was about this time, or a little earlier, that he set to work on a historical dictionary; he got as far as the name *Alexander.*

We know little else about his studies, except that he was certainly a pupil at the 'Hermes Lyceum',[9] a commercial school run by Constantine Papazis, for the academic year 1881–2. There he got to know the third of his early friends, Mikès or Michael Ralli, and also had Stephen Schilizzi as a fellow-pupil. John Rodocanachi had gone to school at Uppingham.

Papazis, a native of Chios, had returned to his island after having obtained a German doctorate, to teach history, and to be an assistant in the Koräis library. The earthquake of 1880 sent him to Alexandria, where he had relations. The subject of his specialised study had been Demetrius of Phalerum. That peripatetic philosopher and elegant rhetorician, appointed 'overseer of Athens' by Cassander of Macedon, fled after his death (297 B.C.) to the court of Ptolemy I Soter at Alexandria, where he organised the Mouseion on the lines of that of Athens. Ptolemy II Philadelphus banished him to Upper Egypt, where he died from the bite of an asp in 283 B.C. Demetrius, who was ready to sell himself to every side, was the sort of historical character to intrigue Cavafy; it is therefore not impossible that he may have found something congenial in Papazis, though it is much to see in him a real influence on the poet. It is an all too frequent occurrence that pupil and teacher never discover a common interest until too late, especially when they are not in sympathy with each other. We only know, for what it is worth – and perhaps it is not worth much – that neither Stephen nor Mikès ever speak of Papazis with respect or affection in their letters to Cavafy. It is ironical that Papazis should have pronounced a funeral oration over Mikès (afterwards printed) when his forty days' mind was celebrated in the church of the Evangelismos in November 1889.

The events of 1882 were to be of great importance to the Cavafy family, whose life was disrupted for the next three years.

9. Tsirkas, *Epoch*, pp. 133–8.

While the historian of modern Egypt should above all things desire the truth, the biographer of Cavafy need only be concerned with what he certainly (or probably) believed, whether true or false, and with his reactions to public events. Historical justice (if it could be found) is not here of importance. When we come to the poem *Thermopylae* it will be unnecessary to waste time over the strategy of Leonidas, of which rather more can now be reasonably conjectured than in his day; we shall only be concerned with what Cavafy supposed, as a reader of Herodotus. Arábi Pasha, the prime mover of the events of 1882, is, perhaps, a more controversial figure, for the army-backed revolutionary government of Egypt made grants to his descendants a few years ago. To a student of Cavafy Leonidas and Arábi are both one with Nineveh and Tyre, and it is not here the place to weigh the pompous officialdom of Lord Cromer against the romantic libertarianism of Wilfrid Scawen Blunt, the representatives of the two extreme points of view.

A brief and untendentious account of the catastrophe of 1882 is to be found in E. M. Forster's book *Alexandria: a History and a Guide*. It does not pretend to be more than a summary of events, but it is at least a version of those events certainly known to Cavafy.

'Arábi, the founder of the Egyptian Nationalist Party . . . then Minister of War, was endeavouring to dominate the Khedive Tewfik, and to secure Egypt for the Egyptians. Alexandria, which had held a foreign element ever since its foundation, was therefore his natural foe, and it was here that he opened his campaign against Europe . . . The details – like Arábi's motives – are complicated.' He is generally thought to have been a 'stooge' used by people far more clever than himself.

'For some while past the population of Alexandria had shown unusual effervescence. Europeans had been hustled and spat on in the streets. A sheikh had been crying aloud in the public thoroughfares, "O Moslems, come and help me to kill the Christians!" '[10]

The western powers were anxious about the situation, and in May an Anglo-French fleet was stationed off Alexandria.

A riot on 11 June, which began with a fight between a drunken Maltese and an Arab donkey boy in the Rue des Soeurs, quickly developed into a situation where the city was under mob

10. Cromer, vol. I, p. 287.

rule. Such a state of things, dreaded by Egyptians and Europeans alike, has occurred from time to time in modern Egypt and has always been an odious possibility.

The riot of 11 June 1882 was later referred to as 'the massacre of the Christians' and in later Greek school books the xenophobia and pillage of the occasion were cited as the cause of the subsequent British intervention. Forster says that about a hundred and fifty Europeans were thought to have been killed that day 'but we have no reliable statistics'. Mr Tsirkas thinks only thirty-five Christians were killed, out of whom only two were Greeks.[11] 'The Egyptian troops in the city [says Forster] refused to intervene without orders from Arábi, who was in Cairo. At last a telegram was sent to him. He responded and the disorder ceased. There is no reason to suppose that he planned the riot. But naturally enough he used it to increase his prestige.' Attempts to blame the riot on the Khedive Tewfik were also based on no sort of evidence; it was a fortuitous explosion of a kind to be expected. Nevertheless some indirect responsibility rests upon Arábi and his colleagues. 'For a long time past, they had done their best to arouse the race hatred and fanaticism of the cowardly mob at Alexandria.'[12]

British men-of-war under the command of Admiral Seymour had been in the harbour during the riot; they took no action, but their future action was to be foreseen. The British residents of the city (who included Mrs Peter John Cavafy and her sons) were ordered to evacuate the place by their consulate. Sir Charles Cookson, the British consul, had been seriously wounded on 11 June. There were rumours of a coming bombardment. It was, of course, the time of year when many Europeans leave Egypt on account of the heat; on this occasion the exodus was particularly large.

It had begun even before the riot, Cavafy's friend John Rodocanachi had written to him on 5 June, from England: 'I see in the papers that all the Europeans are running away from Egypt, and I cannot help roaring when I imagine you and Michael running away with an umbrella in one hand and a sac in the other and with a couple of hundred barbarians after you ... Is that fool Arábi Pasha kicking [up] such a row as they say?

11. Tsirkas, *Epoch*, pp. 101 ff.
12. Cromer, vol. 1, p. 288.

Confounded cheek of him, he wants his head smaked [*sic*], and I can't either make out Gladstone who keeps on saying that it is impossible to do something, or some other rot of the kind, if d'Israeli was here he would manage it *tambour battant.*' That is to say, with a 'Blimpishness' not uncharacteristic of Egyptian Greeks, he sighed for a strong Tory government that would be (in the language of later times) 'tough with the Wogs'. We do not know what Cavafy thought, but very likely his sentiments were much the same, living as he did in an atmosphere where the 'Rumi' ('Romans', i.e. Greeks of the Eastern Empire) were in perpetual opposition to the 'Arapadhes'.

Michael Ralli and Stephen Schilizzi were already in Athens by 17 June. Thence they went to Tinos and Syra, where they were plunged in boredom. They were thankful to return in the autumn to scarred Alexandria.

'By June 17, 14,000 Christians had left the country, and some 6,000 more were anxiously awaiting the arrival of ships to take them away.'[13] Early in July Haricleia, and the six sons with her, left by an Austrian Lloyd steamer for Constantinople. 'Their precarious situation made them be of the very last to leave the town.' The family had been living upon the sons' earnings: Peter was a clerk to the Board of Health, Aristides a broker, and John a clerk in the agency of R. J. Moss. By their departure they were hazarding their jobs. Peter and John returned after a month's absence, and Aristides followed them early in October.

On 11 July Admiral Seymour, at last ready, picked a quarrel with Arábi, declaring that he would bombard Alexandria if any more guns were mounted in the forts. Arábi would not agree, and a violent bombardment followed, in which the French took no part. It was successful, and in the evening Arábi and his forces left the town by the Rue Rosette, and took up a position further east.

'The town' (says Forster, perhaps relying upon too partial a source) 'was scarcely damaged, as our gunners were careful in their aim.' On the contrary the town was left a shambles, and much of the destruction seems to have been caused by the bombardment, and not only by the catastrophic riot and fire of the following day.

There was only one piece of artistic damage to be deplored,

13. ibid. p. 289.

and it is extravagant to call it an act of 'vandalism'.[14] though it meant the end of the one beautiful monument in Alexandria. When Fort Kait Bey (which occupied the site of the ancient Pharos) was bombarded, the minaret of its fifteenth-century mosque was seen 'melting away like ice in the sun'. The two exquisite minarets erected by Kait Bey in Cairo may console us, for we may be sure it was exactly like them. Nevertheless we must grieve that Alexandria should have lost so lovely an ornament. If there were a bombardment at all, Fort Kait Bey must have been a target, and the destruction of its minaret inevitable. The bombardment has, however, seemed to many people a futile atrocity.

If it were futile, it was of course an atrocity, The futility lay in the mistake of not following it up immediately by a landing-force. In consequence the city was given up to fire – the work of deliberate incendiaries – and to pillage. Not unnaturally a riot broke out far more destructive than that of the previous month. It would now be impossible to tell (even if it were our concern to do so) what damage was done by the mob, and what by the British guns.

By the middle of the month, 'reinforcements having arrived, effective possession was taken of the town and something like order restored. On July 15, Europeans and Egyptians began to return to Alexandria.'[15] It was not until a month later that the military expedition under Sir Garnet Wolseley was to arrive; this finally defeated Arábi at Tel el Kebir, and put Alexandria out of further danger.

14. Tsirkas, *Epoch*, p. 114.
15. Cromer, vol. II, p. 297.

II Constantinople

For Cavafy's life in Constantinople the main sources are the manuscript already quoted, and the letters he received from his brother John and from his three friends, Michael Ralli, Stephen Schilizzi and John Rodocanachi – these are all in English. Unfortunately his own letters do not survive (though John Cavafy says that he carefully preserved every one that he received – it is possible that Constantine destroyed them after his death). There is some indication that the letters to the friends were not always very interesting, though more than one was read to the Schilizzi family to the general admiration. He does not seem to have been a very good letter-writer for (as Forster once said of his correspondence with him) other people were more interested in him than he in them. Moreover from his friends he had two things to hide : homosexuality and acute poverty.

Haricleia, says her son, relapsing into Greek idiom, 'had nineteen years to see her family' : she had been in Constantinople on the occasion of John's birth. Her mother was now dead, but her father was still alive; he does not appear to have been very prosperous at this time.

One of the poet's nieces (who owned that she was frequently inattentive to her uncle's talk, said that he used to speak with enthusiasm of Constantinople. 'C'était aussi la vie brillante des ambassades où sa mère et ses tantes avaient brillé, c'était aussi les mariages dans le monde diplomatique.' Haricleia, who married at fourteen, can hardly have shone in any embassy : but of her sisters, Sevastie married the Belgian chargé d'affaires at Constantinople, Léon Verhaeghe de Nayer, and Amalia (widow of Alexander Psilliary) married Callinus, interpreter to the Belgian legation.

Amalia was now in Constantinople, also another sister Efvoulia (or Evelyn) Papalambrinus. 'They welcomed her affectionately', but do not seem to have done much else for Haricleia.

It appears that she went first to spend a few days at Therapia, for Cavafy wrote some English verses dated 18 July 1882 :[1]

> Goodbye to Therapia and joys of the hotel—
> Good dinners that make you exultingly swell . . .

The second stanza opens :

> However Calikioy's opposite shore
> I must hail tho' by far more simple and poor . . .

He must mean that he is going to Kadiköy, that is, near Haydar Pasha – on the Asian shore and near the mouth of the Bosphorus – where his grandfather had rented a small house for the summer, having let his villa at Yeniköy to the Persian consul. There he received the refugees.

When the lease of the villa at Yeniköy expired, Haricleia went there with Alexander, Paul and Constantine – the others having by that time returned to Egypt. John writes (20 November, in reply to his brother's letter of 12 November): 'I note that you write from Aunt Plessors' house [this was in Rue Taxim, in Pera], but a short letter from Paul today gives us to understand that you have moved to Yenikeuy.' Very likely they had moved, but Constantine was staying on for a time with his aunt in the city.

This is of interest, because years later Cavafy gave Mr Malanos[2] to understand that in Constantinople he stayed with two distinct families of relations, that these lived in different neighbourhoods, and were not on good terms, and that he was presently to exploit this situation, which permitted him to spend a night out from time to time without his movements being controlled. Yeniköy is some way up the Bosphorus; there might often be a legitimate excuse for staying the night near the centre : a party, a lecture or a concert. His mother, restored to the bosom of her own family, may have had no close touch with her husband's relations with whom she had once lived so unhappily; we are told that, though fond of her own sisters, she never got on well with them. If Constantine did not come home, she might imagine him with 'Aunt Plessos', with whom she was unlikely to

1. Cavafy, *UP*, p. 195.
2. Malanos, *Cavafy*, pp. 14–15.

compare notes in an age which scarcely knew the telephone. We know that Constantine was intimate with Aunt Plessos, for it was she who furnished him many facts about his father's family. It was care of Alexander Stoyannovitch, husband of her daughter Coralia, that Constantine had his letters directed by his three friends. This might be a protection against curiosity at home, or merely the easiest way of receiving them, Yeniköy being out-of-the-way.

Haricleia and her sons were not the only inmates of her father's villa; beside the old man himself, there were her brother Photios and his wife and two children. Her father seems to have given her no more than house-room, for we are told that she lived on the little that the sons working in Alexandria were able to re-mit to her. Even the roof over her head seems to have been pre-carious, for John writes (31 March 1885): 'Your news of the failure of the renting of grandfather's house relieved us of an intense anxiety. We only hope that negotiations of a similar nature will continue to fail for at least two months yet – because undoubtedly, ere that period shall have elapsed, you will be once more in Egypt.' John was optimistic; the family remained in Yeni-köy till the following October.

John's letters show that their poverty was real. He had been staying for a few days in comfort with his chief, R. J. Moss, at the Hôtel Beau Séjour in Ramleh, and had been afflicted by the con-trast: 'To think of mamma and you so miserably lodged at Yenikeuy was sadly distressing' (4 December 1882).

Later (referring to a letter from Alexander to Peter): 'You cannot imagine how the perusal of the latter had grieved and pained me – It is evidently impossible that mother and your-selves can continue to lead this miserable existence, and I do think Aristides' proposal to borrow £200 is the only way out of the difficulty' (17 April 1883). They were to borrow on their claim for war indemnities.

On the following 28 August John writes: 'I can well sym-pathise with all mother writes about your position in Constanti-nople at present and entirely agree with her in thinking that the best thing to be done is that the family should return here as soon as it can well be effected. Though we shall certainly labour under many difficulties, we shall always manage to scrape along better than we are doing now.'

And in September. ' 'Tis really very unjust that we three should be leading comparatively speaking, so easy a life when you in Constantinople have so many disagreeables to put up with; and have to live on the miserable pittance we send you.' And yet no one would have said that their life was easy, certainly not their young brother. They had to scrape painfully to send about £13 a month between them to their mother and brothers.

In December 1884 John went to stay with Moss at the Beau Séjour, but was miserably embarrassed at the state of his wardrobe : 'ragged shirts, that are well-nigh bare at the sleeves and collars with constant manipulation of the scissors to cut the shirtings : the knee-bulging trousers, the stained and glittering coat'. Worst of all, he found the temptation to a 'shabby–genteel mentality' which he had to resist. But though enduring all this, and the 'dogged wretchedness of office life', he could write : 'You are three times worse placed than I.' When 'Aunt Sevastie' passed through Egypt on her way to Shanghai with her husband Verhaeghe de Nayer – an agreeable visit for 'all mother's family have such an affectionate, enticing manner' – she showed their mother's photograph. 'I am indeed sorry', wrote John, 'that mother cannot afford to send us one.'

Their only relief could be the payment of the indemnity, and this was miserably delayed. 'You cannot imagine how our misfortunes (which are a good sample of those of many another) have made me hate the English' (he wrote, on 27 August 1884). 'They, and their pomp and grandeur, are a great fallacy, a living humbug. No other nation in the world would have occupied a country for two years, and then, as they, have nothing to show of work done, of good effected. There is a general outcry against them and they richly deserve it.' And in September : ' "Oh," say the English, "these foreigners can wait," in their selfish exclusive stupidity.'

There is however no sign that John disapproved of the intervention, though he was naturally distressed at the sight of poor, blasted Alexandria. 'You cannot imagine what a sad sight the old house was to me when I saw it for the first time !' – thus he wrote in his first letter, and he speaks of 'blinding clouds of lime dust' in the streets. Nevertheless there is no sympathy for Arábi. 'They say they are going to bring Araby here – the scoundrel will put a long face on, when he is driven about in the streets as a rebel, where, if you remember, three months ago he passed with the bearing of a sovereign. He will meet his just reward – as it is, he was never worth anything – Fortune led him on not genius.'

And later: 'I read in *The Times* the other day, that there is only one procedure with Araby left to England, i.e. to hang him.' This was because there was a popular belief in Egypt that he had escaped capture. 'I hope they'll do it here. What a sell if they let him go scot free! It is not unlikely – the English are such fools sometimes!'

John's personal (and no doubt well-grounded) objection to the army of occupation was on account of its commonness. At the Beau Séjour he met vulgar English officers, 'all fearfully conceited and egotistic', who were 'revelling over B and S [brandy and soda]'. Their women, as often, were even more objectionable. There was the virago of a colonel's wife 'who eats . . . as woman never ate before'. When, on account of his Agency, he had professional dealings with the Military he found himself up against arrogance 'generally accompanied by the most intense stupidity and ignorance – ignorance of the country, ignorance of commercial etiquette, ignorance of languages, even (believe me) their own, ignorance of everything.'

There is no difficulty in believing him. Though Michael Ralli found the English soldiers 'very amusing when drunk', Stephen Schilizzi had been discouraged by an elder brother from making acquaintance with English officers and soldiers: 'My brother did not approve it and told me they are not people of my class.'

Those who love Cavafy must have a warm feeling for John, so devoted to his 'little mentor', to the little brother, 'the dearest little fellow', whose powers he recognised as so much greater than his own. It was to be his glory to have recorded Constantine's deeds, and Constantine was to be the greatest glory of the imperial house of Ducas. John, perhaps, was making a pleasant literary joke, remembering what Gibbon had written about *Tom Jones* and the house of Hapsburgh, from which Fielding's descent was equally bogus.

Constantine was indeed a general favourite: 'Cossetted and protected by all his family, he was the youngest child, and there were all those brothers to look after him. His intelligence, moreover, manifested at a very tender age, was the pride of the whole

family. His brothers in their letters (these are no longer extant –
but she may have seen some) often repeat that they ought to be
able to make him financially independent, so that he could
devote himself to writing. And they were not ordinary people,
who get excited when one brother writes ten lines; they were all
cultivated . . .' So wrote Rika Singopoulos (in her unpublished
notes) and the same authority speaks of Constantine's especial
affection for Alexander. But their niece Madame Valieri (who
had been particularly near to John) believed that he was the only
one of the brothers who really understood Constantine. John,
indeed, writes with amusement that Alexander (reading Herodotus with Constantine) had written that he found that author
'rather lax in his descriptions of morals' : his does not sound a
mind likely to be altogether congenial to the poet, but perhaps
Constantine found him restful, because he was the least intellectual member of the family. Paul (the only homosexual brother)
may have been too fond of society to come near to Constantine
(not that Constantine by any means disliked the world);
Aristides – always quoted by John as an authority on social events
in Alexandria – was also *mondain*. The extreme vulgarity of
Paul's journalism and of Aristides' drawing makes us think that
Rika Singopoulos was too generous about the brothers. Peter, by
twelve years the poet's senior, seems remote : 'Circumstances
warped his temper,' wrote Constantine. He had an especial pity
for Peter, who returned to Alexandria as a clerk in 1877, having
only a year previously been manager of Cavafy and Co. in Liverpool. 'His feelings must have been very bitter; he must have felt
his humiliation very acutely (more especially in so small a place
as Alexandria was then, and is even now . . . His feelings must
have been very bitter every day he mixed with his fellow clerks.'
John, near to Constantine in age, was like him in temperament,
reserved and saturnine. Their niece, Madame Valieri, never saw
either of them laugh; at most they gave a rare smile that quickly
vanished. 'Il est certain que les "murs" qui isolaient Constantin,
isolaient aussi Jean et qu'une invisible barrière se dressait entre
lui et ses contemporains.' John had not the sexual barriers that
shut Constantine in (or out),[3] and there were no political or social
barriers in John's case.[4] Perhaps it is Madame Valieri who is right

3. Malanos, *T.*, p. 120.
4. Tsirkas, *Epoch*, p. 213.

about the *Walls*. It is natural that, back in Alexandria, John should have missed Constantine intensely. He would retire to his room after a dull day's work 'to think, to think of you mostly whose voice is always ringing in my ears'.

Constantine's letters to John seem to have been equally endearing, but the brothers had little good news to send each other. John had a life of routine and a series of disappointments about the indemnities to record, and badness of business, and the financial struggles of Aristides; and Constantine a history of family illnesss. Haricleia was ill in 1883, and in the next year had a 'first attack of the complaint from which she died' – which was then called haemorrhage of the brain. Alexander's health was precarious, Constantine was seriously worried about his eyes, he also had chilblains; the Bosphorus can be cold and dank, especially on the European side where the sun sets early; very likely the villa at Yeniköy was ill-heated – part of their privations.

Nevertheless it does not appear that the brothers whined about their lot. Constantine is always exhorted to keep up Haricleia's spirits, and not to let her worry about the cholera epidemics in Egypt; while John acknowledges heartening letters from his brother. And they kept up literary pursuits. John occasionally improved Constantine's Greek, and his English too. He ought not, for example, to say that the dinner at his cousin Coralia's consisted of four 'plates'. They exchanged views on French and English literature: La Fontaine, Balzac, Thackeray, Tennyson, Browning, Swinburne. It was a satisfaction that they were acquainted with the son of the clergyman who had buried Anthony Trollope. John stinted himself still further in order to send Constantine the *Queen* and the *Gentleman's Magazine*.

Constantine was badly off for books in Constantinople, and often applied to John for information. He had begun a translation of *Much Ado about Nothing*, and John could help him to explain 'recheat', but was stumped by 'cinque-pace'. There Michael Ralli (to whom application had also been made) was able to find the explanation. Perhaps Constantine never got much further than that, early in the second act: he translated the song *Sigh no more, ladies* in the following scene.[5]

5. Cavafy, *UP*, p. 3.

He and John exchanged their own poems, and read each other's with brotherly partiality. John wrote post-Shelleyan English verse with a good deal of facility, and already by 1880 he had composed a series of poems which he called *The elegy of life*; now he was writing *The death of Phocas*, a narrative poem of some eighty lines about a Christian martyr in Corinth. Later on he was to refer to his 'distractingly untutored verses'. Constantine was later to express a similar (and not unmerited) contempt for his own early verse; but by a kindly disposition of Providence the young are able to view their own work and that of their fellows with a complacency that prevents premature discouragement. Constantine was working on a version of *Auld Robin Gray*,[6] in a Greek island setting, and in the Greek fifteen-syllabled ballad metre; the theme of a supposedly dead lover returning from the sea attracted him, and he wanted to read *Enoch Arden*.

John might still be called the more accomplished writer. At their age his two years' seniority still counted, and his command both of Greek and English seems to have been more perfect: what he admired in his younger brother was his keen intelligence and his 'lore', by which he probably meant his erudition. It is not certain that at this date he was at all sure of the way in which Constantine was to distinguish himself, though later we find him lovingly translating his poems into English, with the author's collaboration. His own ideals for poetry were very different, for he wrote: 'The themes I like best to deal with are such as can hardly be discerned through the surrounding imagery – and which, though unapparent on the whole – here and there with a word or a simile are made forcibly palpable, and indicate the key of the entire poem.' Nothing could be less like Constantine's aims.

John is less dull when he attempts light verse.

> Fly letter, fly! God speed thee home!
> Mind not the winds nor lashing seas;
> Knowing thine errand, strive with these
> And prove that love hath masterdom.

6. Dalven, pp. 178–80.

I hope you will not call this gam-
mon, for the metre's fault – if any –
Is rapid rhymes. Have you read Tennyson's poem 'In Memoriam'?

So he wrote (7 November 1882), and he went on :

The Zervoudachis have some while
Been here, I meet them pretty often :
I bow – and their grim faces soften
In what is meant to be a smile.

This family was frequently the butt of Michael Ralli and Stephen
Schilizzi. It is strange that Mr Tsirkas, who chooses to dismiss
their contempt of Papazis as schoolboy fun, should take them far
more seriously when they mock at people who went out of their
way to curry favour with the Army of Occupation.[7] Any sort of
lion-hunting is rather comic, even in the eyes of people who have
no objection to the lion.

Michael Ralli spoke of 'Papazis' beastly hole' (8 December
1883), than which even the boredom of office life was prefer-
able. 'That honourable gentleman, on his leaving Alexandria,
left most of his masters unpaid and the best of it is that he has
no intention of paying them at all.' In the summer of 1882
Michael had met one Negroponte; 'a thorough degenerate Greek
as Papazis would call him, though according to me the best and
jolliest fellow alive. He's been in England, and hardly knows a
word of Greek, and looks down with the greatest contempt on
everything belonging to Greece.' It is unnecessary to suppose that
Michael felt like Negroponte – though he found such students of
the University of Athens as he met 'a pack of boobies'. But he
does not seem to have thought much of Papazis' exclusive sort of
Hellenism, and Stephen Schilizzi (18 October 1882) wrote of
'the reverend D.Ph.', who was 'continually plaguing our ears with
his sonorous orations on Homer and Thucidides [sic].'

Mr Tsirkas[8] has blamed Michael Peridis for having 'scissored'
this correspondence with 'unforgivable pitilessness' in his book.

7. Tsirkas, *Epoch*, p. 139.
8. ibid., p. 138.

'Who,' he asks, 'will persuade me that it is simply due to critical inadequacy?' It is not. It is due to critical good sense (when what Cavafy's friends have to say is of no interest), and to good manners. Twenty-five years ago there must have been living people who might have been pained by passages that cannot now cause reasonable offence.

Michael Ralli particularly laughs at Sir Constantine Zervudachi and his wife. New-made knights who are 'only moderately genteel' have been a joke since long ago, even before Jane Austen's Sir William Lucas was knighted, and 'the distinction had perhaps been felt too strongly'. I remember in my childhood that Glasgow used to be called 'the City of Dreadful Knights', and no doubt it still goes on.

'You are wrong in thinking Sir Constantine's dinners such aristocratic affairs. He often gives dinners to English officers, and the last one was a decided fiasco, all the meats being brought in cold and badly cooked. Such things however must be overlooked in the appreciation of his character, as, having past [sic] most of his youth in a *bakaliko* [grocer's shop], it should not be expected that he should know more on these subjects than the generality of *vakalides* [sic].' So Michael writes (13 March 1884), and goes on to talk of the knight's meanness: 'I suppose you know he has very good carpets on his stairs, and he is so fond of them, that on entering his house he takes the greatest care possible *not to tread on them* for fear of their being spoilt. This piece of information was communicated to me by the boab [concierge]. It is so characteristic that I cannot help believing it.' He also tells of Sir Constantine's haggling over tomatoes, and of his care not to overpay a shoeblack.

'Lady Zervudachi goes regularly to the théâtre' (he writes a month later) 'and decks her ugly person with a good lot of jems [sic] and dress. During the entreactes [sic] her box is always full of English officers. Zervudachi gives lots of dinners to them ...' (A week later) 'Sir Constantine has not given a dinner for some time. It seems he finds it too expensive to give a good one; besides rumour says he does not like bringing out his champagne.'

From these passages it can quite clearly be seen why Peridis exercised a little censorship in 1948 which cannot now be necessary, and that the 'Sir' with his 'baccalic air', and the 'Lady' who behaved like a *parvenue*, though she ought to have known better (she was a Mavrogordato), were a natural laughing-stock to these high-spirited and engagingly snobbish young men. There was no objection to the entertainment of English officers as a thing in itself.

No one had any qualms about meeting the Army of Occupation; the nineteenth century in general, and nineteenth-century Alexandria in particular, were refreshingly free from that modern priggishness which allows politics to influence private life. In those days people were far more intolerant about 'sinners' than we are today, but they had a far larger tolerance for 'publicans' and their congeners. When you were invited to a party you went, if you were *mondain*, and stayed away if you were not; if you had not been invited you ran down the entertainment. No pretence of principle entered into it.

Thus, when the Zervudachis gave a ball, and invited the Cavafys, Peter said that he would not go on any account (and, no doubt, 'humiliated' as he was, the society of the *nouveaux riches* would have irritated him); Aristides, of course, went, because he liked that sort of thing. John went, perhaps for a change, and perhaps (not a little) because it would give him material for a letter to Constantine; moreover he was able to borrow Peter's frock coat. It was all very splendid : the English officers glittered with decorations, and 'all the Greek community was present, and all the Greek "jeunesse dorée" (! !)' Stephen and Michael were too young to be invited.

'The supper' (said John), was nothing extraordinary – a perpendicular one – a cold one – (nothing like Menasce's) . . . when the gentlemen's turn came there was little or nothing left.' Poor old Mr Synadinos, who had fasted for two days, promising himself a blow-out, was sadly disappointed. Stephen Schilizzi, on the other hand, had heard that the ladies were starving; and one of the officers remarked to John that 'the wines were very poor'.

Mr Tsirkas[9] has tried to build up a picture of Michael Ralli as a progressive spirit, because he enjoyed the novels of Georges Ohnet. It is not necessary to find ideological reasons for a young man's enjoyment of inferior fiction. At one time he and Constantine had greatly enjoyed the novels of Mrs Henry Wood; now

9. Epoch, p. 139.

he was selling them off to pay gambling debts and what he owed at the beer-shops.

Of course there is mention of the sad straits of Alexandria, Rue Cherif in ruins and trade bad; but there is no suggestion of blame directed against the occupying power. The boys write a great deal to Cavafy (and Peridis has very properly 'scissored' them) about the newly learned adult pleasures of smoking and fornication.

If the student's aim is not to fit a person to a Procrustean theory, but simply and humbly to find out what little one can about him from letters addressed to him, the results will be meagre. We learn, for example, that Cavafy had a sweet tooth. Michael – in the new Ralli house near the Porte de Rosette, in that Greek colony that the English nicknamed 'Peloponnesus' means to 'smuggle in drinks, jams, biscuits and cigars' into his room : 'though I know well you will not like to partake of brandy or cigars, you may like the ginger biscuits and raspberry jam'. As a true son of Haricleia, we may imagine Constantine sticking two ginger biscuits together with raspberry jam. And Stephen gives us to understand that he was interested in ornithology.

Stephen, indeed, does give us some glimpses of Cavafy in Constantinople. 'Your brother Aristides told me that every letter that he receives contains some amusing thing or other and he told me an anecdote of an eccentric Englishwoman, the wife of a Greek. She liked extremely literary conversation and indulged in it so much with others as to make her husband sleepy – You never told us neither that you put questions in an examination without getting a right answer. You never told us of the Greek master who in his discussion with you was unfortunately always on the wrong side, but who set himself right after consulting books on the subject.

'You never told us neither that you found yourself in a visit you paid, face à face with a Samian prince.'

There was no reason for Michael Peridis to tell us about John Rodocanachi's dog-fancying, or Michael Ralli's quail-shooting; he had, however, reasons for mentioning the sex life of Alexandria as we see it in letters from Michael and Stephen. 'You *must* accompany us on Sunday night down to the Arapina to see Arab and Turkish women dance naked,' wrote Michael. No doubt the 'Arab woman' kept a disorderly house. 'You write me nothing about your private life,' complained Stephen. 'How can you be so secret? Don't you put confidence in us, or what the devil? Not a word is to be taken from you in any way.' And again: 'I see that notwithstanding your strong objections you give us some glimpses of the secret of your private life. You talk of your "amusements de jeune homme" which shows that you partake of such and further on you say "that a prudent young man with nothing but "bonnes fortunes" in the "demi-monde" . . . Prudence is not a quality in which you are wanting so, my dear, this phrase "vaut un aveu". I hazard myself on this subject at the risk of displeasing you. But I am not to blame, the temptation is so much greater as such mentions are rare on your part.'

Stephen had indeed little to go on, and there can be no doubt that his friends found Constantine shy about such things; and indeed he seems always to have had some delicacy in talking about sex. But it is most reasonable to conclude (with Peridis) that he did not want to reveal his homosexuality. His friends might not have been tolerant. Stephen wrote of their acquaintance, Léon Scanavis, that he was 'ridiculed even by the donkey boys. He has been accused and is suspected to do a very dirty business with them. At least he has such a reputation.' And: 'rumours are current about him and nicknames given which I dare not mention for fear to spoil the whiteness of my paper.'

We learn from the manuscript notes of Rika Singopoulos that Cavafy's homosexuality 'began to manifest itself in Constantinople, with his cousin George Psilliary' in 1883. The latter was the son of his maternal aunt, Amalia Callinus, by her first marriage. We also learn from the same source that at this time Cavafy also had some heterosexual experience. These, no doubt, are the facts, and the only facts of the kind known to us about this period in his life. We do not know if his cousin were his lover or his confidant, or both; and for all we know it was he who first led him to a brothel. There is no record of any sort of emotional involvement with anyone. Years later an elderly lady in Constantinople was known to boast that she had been wooed by 'the poet Cavafy', but it is almost certain that she meant John – who had then published verses.

The poems written at this time tell us nothing; they are exer-

cises in verse, no more revealing than those of the young men in
Proust who wrote such lines as :

> Je n'aime que Chlöe au monde,
> Elle est divine, elle est blonde,
> Et d'amour mon cœur s'inonde.

One called *Dünya Güzeli*[10] is not without interest. The veiled
Turkish beauty says :

> Ah, if I were a Christian and if I had the right
> To show myself to everyone whether by day or night,
> Then men would see me and admire, women with jealousy . . .

Here we see a simple form of the dramatic monologue that he was
to use so often, a touch of irony – in the impish reference to
Christianity (which he sometimes mocked, but never repudiated)
– and an interest in the juxtaposition of different civilisations.

A poem written years later, in September 1915, tells us more
about his youth. *And I leaned and lay on their beds*[11] is about a
visit to the homosexual rooms of a mixed brothel :

> I went into the secret rooms
> And leaned and lay on their beds.

In a manuscript[12] of this poem these two lines are followed by
two others :

> Which even when I was still a boy
> Indefinitely my body desired.

If this poem be autobiographical (and it looks like it) it seems
to say that Cavafy was congenitally homosexual, and that he had
no very early experience – that is to say, it is completely in accord with such evidence as we have.

If Cavafy (and it may well be so) had made only bungling
and unsuccessful heterosexual experiments, he might not wish to
be speaking of them. He certainly hinted in later life to young

10. cit. Tsirkas, *Epoch*, p. 141; Dalven, p. 176.
11. Keeley and Savidis, pp. 46–7.
12. Cavafy, *UP*, p. 245.

admirers like Mr Malanos[13] of homosexual experiences in Constantinople. We know that his homosexuality continued to influence his life and work, and that in the latter there is no trace of heterosexual interests. It is therefore most likely that he felt embarrassed at the idea of accompanying Michael and Stephen to the 'Arapina', and that it was not only modesty (though he was modest) that kept his 'private life' out of his letters. Mr Tsirkas[14] thinks that he learned this modesty in England; but John Rodocanachi was writing from Liverpool that 'the governor' allowed him to smoke and now and then, to go 'you know where and what for' – and there he caught 'a common clap'.

About his poverty Cavafy was equally reticent, for Michael and Stephen continually ask about his return to Alexandria, and give no signs of knowing that this was a matter in which he had no choice.

Nevertheless, he always had fond recollections of Constantinople; on this all witnesses seemed to be agreed, though he never revisited it (as his brother John did). He was wretchedly poor there and, though no doubt he read extensively, he was often hard up for books. It would not seem likely, from all we know of him, that he could have been particularly sensitive to the visual beauties of the Bosphorus, which he celebrated in two very poor poems – the English verses (already quoted) written on his arrival, and a more graceful little poem in Greek on Nichori (Yeniköy)[15] written before his departure in 1885 – surprising when one is aware how much many of his family hated 'cette affreuse Yenikeuy'. There is no sign that he appreciated the splendours of Ottoman architecture.

Once he wrote to Michael Ralli that he hated Alexandria: we need not take this seriously, as Michael evidently did not. The three friends, when they went to Liverpool, preferred the Greek society there, and felt no desire to return. There was still something 'small town' about Alexandria. There is no reason to suppose that Cavafy shrank from a return to occupied Egypt – and no reason why he should have done so. But in Constantinople he had had his first taste of freedom. In Alexandria he must live all the time under his mother's roof, and in a town where he

13. Malanos, *Cavafy*, p. 15.
14. Tsirkas, *Epoch*, p. 241.
15. Cavafy, *UP*, p. 15.

might expect to pass the rest of his days. He tells us that Haricleia's greatest pleasure in Constantinople was to pay a visit of a few days to her sister Amalia Callinus. It is possible that Constantine also enjoyed occasional and pleasant hospitality, of which we have no record, perhaps with Amalia Callinus' son, George Psilliary.

III   Return to Alexandria

The family was reunited in October 1885 when Haricleia Cavafy came back from Constantinople with Alexander, Paul and Constantine to a house in the Rue Tewfik, the 'Okelle Spanopoulo', rented and meagrely furnished by the other three sons. At some time some rather better furniture must have come into their hands. Madame Valieri, the poet's niece, speaks of the 'meubles de famille que ses frères lui avaient abandonnés'. She found in his flat 'plus évocateur des rives du Bosphore que de l'Egypte moderne'. Some of the things may have come from Yeniköy – though it hardly seems likely – some may have been salvaged from the house in the Rue Falaki. Mr Malanos tells me that Cavafy once said to him : 'The furniture, and everything here, is part of the relics of a great house'; he naturally supposed that the Okelle Cavafy in the Rue Cherif was intended.

They came back to a city still feeling the effects of the catastrophe, but not too severely : 'The Alexandrians', as Stephen Schilizzi had written, 'are exceedingly light-hearted and take things as they come.'

It would have been more agreeable, in a book designed for English readers, to make no mention of Mr Tsirkas' mistakes about the next six and a half years of Cavafy's life; they will be refuted by documentary evidence. But as he is named as an authority by Miss Dalven in the Preface to her translation,[1] and his theories may thus (or in other ways) be indirectly known to some people who do not read Greek, it seems wiser to point out where he is at fault – particularly as there is always some foundation for what he says.

He states that in October 1885 Cavafy ' "returned" to Greek nationality, abandoning the English protection that his father had obtained "about 1850".'[2] It is not impossible that, after the

1. Dalven, *acknowledgements*.
2. Tsirkas, *Chronology*.

Alexandrian manner, Constantine and the two brothers who came with him from Constantinople, obtained additional Greek passports at this time. But a document dated 11 December 1890, copied in the poet's own hand, describes him as 'an English subject'. He therefore was far from abandoning British nationality, and it is idle to conjecture if he disapproved of British policy in Egypt. He was, however, coming more and more to feel and think as a Hellene (he did not care for the word 'Greek' for himself).

Mr Tsirkas also believes that Cavafy was at this time maintained by his family so that he might give himself up to study in preparation for a literary life, and that he held no salaried post. It is true that some of his work was haphazard, and that he worked for three years unpaid in the office which ultimately gave him paid employment.

The theory of a deep division in Alexandrian society at this time is derived by Mr Tsirkas from an Alexandrian schoolmaster, John Ghikas, of the preceding century, but he has very much elaborated it.[3] Briefly, the 'protoclassatoi' were earlycomers, anti-British, and in favour of Deliyannis in Greece; the 'deuteroclassatoi' were later comers, pro-British and in favour of Trikoupis. This hard and fast distinction is artificial. Some of Mr Tsirkas' 'heroes' (e.g. Averoff) were for Trikoupis, and indeed Averoff was, if indirectly, of great help to Kitchener. In a commercial society like that of Alexandria new people soon became *nice* if they had enough to commend them, while those who had been *nice* retained that distinction, though they might drop into comparative social obscurity through poverty or other causes. The Greek colony as a whole had no reason to regret the British occupation, for the British policy towards foreign communities in Egypt was much the same as that of Mohammed Aly. If some business houses suffered by the influx of British capital, others profited. Families such as the Salvagos, Benachis, Zervudachis, Antoniades became immensely rich, and were large benefactors of the Greek community. The historian of that community[4] calls the last fifteen years of the nineteenth century one of its most brilliant periods. The Cavafys, having lost their money before the bombardment, and entirely because of their own imprudence,

3. Malanos, T., pp. 37 ff.
4. Radopoulos, p. 52.

might be expected to face the new situation without prejudice. Though it was not unnatural that they regarded the 'nouveaux riches' with envy.

Alexander's daughter, Mme Coletti, said to Mr Malanos:[5] 'My father and my uncles, after the Cavafy family had lost its place, lived out of the way, were ashamed and felt déclassés. Because in Alexandria anyone who loses his property is déclassé. It's not like Europe where a man can work and keep his place . . . if my uncle hadn't written, the name Cavafy, once one of the first in Alexandria, would have been forgotten today.' I am informed[6] that this is rather a pessimistic view of Alexandria. The difficult years seem to have made defeatists of the Cavafys: they also seem to have had an exaggerated idea of their former grandeur, of which Constantine can have known so little.

The poet says of his mother, after the return to Alexandria: 'Her life was by no means happy. None of her sons had become wealthy. And there were domestic troubles, on which I need not enter here' – these may have included the very peculiar behaviour of Aristides.

Nevertheless, soon after they had settled down, Constantine had apparently written an optimistic letter to his aunt, Sevastie de Nayer. She replied: 'Ma pauvre soeur avait assez souffert dans cette affreuse Yenikeui pour être un peu tranquille auprès des enfants aussi excellents que vous tous.' She recalled with pleasure her passage through Egypt: 'tes trois frères . . . cet excellent Pierre avec son expression si douce. Aristide, avec son zèle de rendre service à tout le monde; et le ravissant petit Tzoníko.' Two years before, writing to Paul about her stay in Constantinople, she had said: 'Certes c'est fort malheureux que C . . . fut si extraordinaire alors.' We do not know if she meant 'Costi', but of course she might.

Peter was still in the Sanitary Council, Aristides was a broker on the Exchange. Alexander worked for Thomas Cook and Son, Paul for the municipality of Alexandria, and John was still with the Moss agency.

Constantine states that he first worked as a journalist in Alexandria. In 1883 he had written to his godmother Amalia Pappos that he was finishing his studies and contemplated a

5. Malanos, *Cavafy 2*, p. 74.
6. By Mr Christian Ayoub.

career in political journalism; she had discouraged him, telling him that a study of Law was a prerequisite for that profession, and rightly judging that he was not cut out for it.

Next, he tells us, he worked as a broker, employed by his brother Aristides. Rika Singopoulos noted that he worked at the Cotton Exchange in 1888. In February 1889 Aristides married Marie Vouros, and went into partnership with her brother Dimitri. While Aristides was on his honeymoon in Cairo, Constantine wrote him a brotherly letter, but obviously that of a close business associate. 'Thanks for the details concerning the lost memorandum. Here business is rather slack.' He speaks of the marked decline of cotton seed. 'Cotton is weak also . . . we have received no letters from the interior . . . Almost all the office furniture has been removed to our new quarters.'

In late August in the same year Aristides deserted his wife and absconded with £80 cash, boarding a French steamer for Marseilles. Before leaving he posted letters to his family, to his wife – promising to return at once if she would undertake to 'mend' – and to her brother, Dimitri, asking for £90 to settle business that he had left in suspense, and confessing the loss of his wife's dowry. The letters were dated from Suez and Tantah, and in the heat of late summer his brother John scoured those two depressing places for him in vain.

When the truth of the departure was known, the upright John was in despair: he wrote to his brother George (then in France) a letter of which a copy survives, partly in the hand of John and partly in that of Constantine. They beg George to make Aristides return at once, even if he should be ill. The Vouros family threatened to institute divorce proceedings, and even to lay a criminal charge – they were anxious to protect Marie's good name, for there was another daughter to be married. The Cavafys had to make considerable sacrifices to cover up some of Aristides' debts, secretly selling things to raise the money. Aristides wrote a reasonable letter, but remained abroad.

'You asked for £80, we wired "Argent impossible",' wrote Constantine on 14 October. 'The Vouros family will back you up when they see you back. They won't send you a grosi . . . If you've no friend to borrow *sell all you can*.'

A fortnight later he writes again (in English, the words in italics are translated from the Greek): 'You tell me to manage to

send out £12! *Are you joking?* Do you know poor Mama can't
go out to get a little fresh air in Ramleh because she can't pay for
her ticket? Do you know that John, that fine young man who is
the support of the family has nothing left in his pocket? Paul also
has nothing. Peter lost the little he had. You speak of the ten days'
worry you passed about the telegram from Vouros : what are we
to say about the two months of agony we have passed?' He tells
him to sell his ring, watch, chain and sleeve-links.

The matter seems ultimately to have been settled, though
Aristides took some kind of nerve cure in Europe before returning. He continued to be a broker in Alexandria till 1894, when
he removed to Cairo, where he was manager of the Laurens
cigarette company. Aristides died in Cairo in 1902 as a 'négociant
connu et estimé'. His daughter spoke of her mother's dowry
as having been dissipated to prevent some scandal in the
family.

Mr Malanos, in his notes (which on one or two points are
inaccurate), wrote : 'When he lost his money, he worked in a
DAIRA⁷ (Gérance de Biens); later he went into the Government.'
Cavafy had no money to lose, but we need not on that account
doubt this information.

As early as 1889 Cavafy was also doing unpaid work in the
Irrigation Office in the hope of getting a salaried post. Such an
arrangement was by no means uncommon in Egypt at that date,
and we need not suppose him to have done a full morning's work
every day – indeed his other obligations would hardly have allowed
this.

An unsigned letter (copied by Cavafy), dated 11 December
1890 and addressed to the Inspector General of Irrigation, runs
as follows :

'Now that it is improbable the Atfeh pumps will be used again,
Selim effendi Ibrahim the Assistant controller will no longer be
required . . . I have the honour to request you will provide for him
elsewhere . . .

'I also urgently request that you will sanction the increase of
my English office . . .

'Mr Constantin Cavafy unpaid clerk to be given a salary of £7
a month . . .

'Mr Constantin Cavafy (Greek by birth but an English sub-

7. Malanos, *T.*, p. 169; Tsirkas, *Politikos*, pp. 67-9.

ject) is of a highly respectable Alexandrian family. He has worked in my office as an unpaid secretary for a year, and though I did not give any hope of gaining a salary, yet I have found him so useful, showing so much intelligence and working so diligently that I do not know how the work in the office would be done without him. He writes a very good hand, knows French, Greek and Italian, the two former as well as he knows English. He has copied most of the reports submitted this year, calculated or checked most of the estimates and has made some very important translations . . . He can, of course, talk Arabic, though he does not read or write it.'

This appointment was contrary to regulations, and nothing was done. On 11 April 1892 Edward Foster wrote to Cavafy from the Cairo office: 'Although you came to my office on the distinct understanding that no salary was granted or any prospect offered I certainly hoped to get you in.' He thanked Cavafy for 'much help during the last three years'. A permanent post had been vacated by Selim Ibrahim; it could not be held by a temporary, but Cavafy might occupy it as a salaried official until a permanent official was appointed. He remained in the Third Circle of Irrigation for thirty years.

In the interests of the whole truth an odd and as yet unexplained piece of evidence must be stated. The manuscript of a strange early poem in English,[8] *More happy thou, performing member*, bears a signature of apparently later date: *C. P. Cavafy, formerly of the Sanitary Council.* We know that his brother Peter was a member of this, but there is no record of Constantine's connection with it.

It has been seen that Constantine's employment before he was finally taken on by the Irrigation Circle seems to have been rather unsatisfactory, but there is no reason to suppose that he did not work – and it was through no fault of his own that his appointment was so slow in coming. It is likely that he was in perpetual expectation of a post, and that may be one of the reasons for his rejection of other offers. It is perhaps not surprising that he should have failed to take up the suggestion of Sevastie de Nayer that he should get a job in the Customs at Shanghai – that seems too far outside his world – though she told him that there was a future in it and he might end up as grand as 'Sir et Lady C' (which

8. Cavafy, *UP*, pp. 249–50.

shows that the Zervudachis were a family joke). 'N'écrivez sur-
tout rien à Constantinople,' she adds, for jobs in the Turkish
customs were a poor affair, and the family then might make the
comparison.

He refused his brother George's offer of a post in London – in
spite of his occasional impatience with the small town world of
Alexandria. He also declined a post with the 'cotton kings',
Choremi and Benachi. Probably the Irrigation Office offered him
greater freedom.

It would have been an extraordinary thing that Constantine
should have been supported through six years by his family for
the sake of his literary career. One is tempted to quote Ivy
Compton-Burnett: 'People do not know about families', when
they say that sort of thing. Moreover his literary career was as yet
quite inglorious, and not even promising; and his wretched
juvenilia would not earn him a grant even today from the most
generous of those bodies that squander public funds on literary
aspirants. He never did serious research, nor took a university
degree. The finances of his family would not have permitted such
an arrangement, even had it been justified. It seems however (on
the testimony of Alexander Singopoulos)[9] that Constantine may
have received small 'tips' from his family; they may have given
him a little help while he was waiting for a paid post, and in any
case he was almost certainly less well off than the others. It would
appear from accounts that some of his brothers were at times
able to put him in the way of small paid jobs. It is unlikely that
his mother could have helped him when till 1885 she lived on
remittances from her sons, and we have seen how poor she was
at the time of Aristides' scandal. Perhaps her family later did
something for her: she had a little money to bequeath as well as
some diamonds, and (it will be seen) indulged in 'will-shaking'
in the last year of her life.

We cannot, therefore, believe in the picture which Mr
Tsirkas wants to offer us, of a Cavafy entirely devoted to study
and contemplation during the years 1885–1892, training to be a
poet with the dedication of a Milton or a Goethe. Not only does
he deny him work, but almost all recreation, whether in the

9. Rika Singopoulos seems to correct this, for she says he had 'savings'
in 1897. Perhaps it is safer to trust her memory, as she was writing nearer to
the time.

world or the underworld. He is to be exclusively devoted to letters, and to the affairs of the Greek colony in Alexandria (for which there is no evidence that he cared anything).

Michael Peridis[10] tells us that Constantine accompanied his mother to the Khedivial court, and to the villas of notables where they were invited with a 'personal invitation' for him: no doubt Peridis had seen such invitations. Paul stuck those which he received into an album: 1883–1897 is stamped on the cover, though he was not back in Alexandria till 1885. Some of these are addressed to 'Madame Cavafy et ses fils', and the rest personally to Paul. They are numerous, and probably Paul was more *mondain* than his brother, and known to more people on account of his position. Nevertheless Constantine said that he had once been *mondain*, that he liked to be well-dressed, and that he had played tennis.[11]

In his valuable researches in the newspapers, Mr Tsirkas has found the account of a ball at the Zizinia theatre in November 1885. Haricleia Cavafy was present, so were Lady Zervudachi, and a great number of people in Greek or Levantine Alexandrian society, as well as many British officers. Mr Tsirkas comments: 'The presence of Mrs Cavafy at this gathering, resplendent with the names of English officers of the occupation should not astonish us. Haricleia had just returned from Constantinople. She was vain and *mondaine*, even though over fifty. And, as we shall see, she did not at all agree with the racial ideas of her youngest son.'[12]

No one will be astonished at her presence; our astonishment is all for the attribution of such ideas to her son. For all we know he may also have been present. Haricleia was probably accompanied by one or more of her sons. Young men are in demand at a ball, though they may not be socially important enough to be named in a newspaper.

Mr Tsirkas thinks Constantine might have consented to accompany his mother if she called on Riaz Pasha, to whom she had an introduction from Callinus to whom she was related by marriage. 'All the same,' he says, 'I hesitate to believe that the poet went to receptions of other notables or to the court of the

10. Peridis, pp. 56–7.
11. ibid., p. 92.
12. Tsirkas, *Epoch*, p. 183.

Khedive. He, who to show his disagreement with the English policy repudiated the nationality of the occupier, when it would have been very useful to him, must have shown the same intransigence in his other demonstrations.' But we have seen that this 'repudiation' had not taken place. When those British subjects Mrs Peter John Cavafy and her sons Paul and Constantine were invited to a Khedivial Ball at the Palace of Ras el Tin in July 1887 it is unlikely that they disobeyed this quasi-royal command, or that they had any wish to do so.

There may have been some improvement in the family fortunes, as the sons' earnings increased. In 1887 they moved to the Boulevard de Ramleh where they lived for the rest of Haricleia's life. Aristides' peculiar behaviour was a set-back, but the £3000 that he lost or squandered was paid out of his wife's dowry. It was the noble John who was to look after his widow and his little daughter after his early death.

Haricleia was in failing health; for three years she had a very trying twitching in the face, and after 1889 recurrence of her trouble in the head. Her only change of scene in these years was a visit to Cairo late in 1893 with Constantine. She was, however, still fond of society and liked (so Rika Singopoulos tells us) going to the Casino at San Stefano and to the races. Aristides, the bald little dwarf, was 'much liked by women of the demi-monde,' says his brother, and was one of the gay young men about Alexandria at this time; and Paul had a great social success.

At some time in 1886 or 1887 Constantine seems to have written to Spyros Kondoyannis, a young naval cadet, that he was ill from an overdose of pleasure. The young man answered: 'This seems a little odd to me, for when I was in Alexandria you didn't seem to me so fond of pleasure.' Over this little bone Cavafists have wrangled. 'No, he wasn't fond of pleasure as the young cadet understood it,' said Michael Peridis,[13] thinking of the 'Arapina'. But this, he said, did not prevent him from taking part in social joys, going to the Khedivial court etc.

It is not unreasonable to connect the overdose of pleasure with the excesses of which the poet speaks eleven years later – excesses of a sort that he would almost certainly have wished to hide from Kondoyannis.[14]

13. Peridis, pp. 56–7.
14. see pp. 66 ff.

The cadet also wrote: 'I know that you follow the slightest movements of the fair sex with the greatest interest.' Perhaps Cavafy really still did so, perhaps he had managed to impose upon a simple sailor. There is a third and more likely explanation. Cavafy may very well have been quite 'a ladies' man' in a social sort of way. We know that Paul was – we have only to glance at his full dance programmes. It is easy to imagine Constantine handing ices and coffee to ladies at parties full of British officers – he may have gone there half in hope of seeing the officers. He may (for all we know) have been quite a favourite with Lady Zervudachi; hers was the first name on Haricleia's visiting list.

In July 1889 Michael Ralli returned to Alexandria: Stephen Schilizzi and John Rodocanachi remained in Liverpool. Michael died at his father's house in Ramleh on 1 October, apparently of typhoid fever – for Mr Tsirkas England was the source of all evil, and he thinks that there Mikès picked up the microbes from which he died: a long incubation.[15] Cavafy left a chronicle in Greek, in the form of a journal, of Mikès' illness and last days; it was obviously written up after the event.[16]

He begins: 'Sunday 15 September 1889 I went as usual to Ramleh to the house of my dear and only true friend Mikès Ralli. It was fine. I remember that Pericles Anastassiades was there.'

It is a pathetic document, full of the anguish of waiting for the doctor's report. 'I asked Tottis [Mikès' brother Theodore] to telephone me the result of the consultation at the *Pharmacie Française*. As we'd finished dinner at home I went to the chemist's at half-past eight and waited till half-past ten, but no telephone call was heard. I had a frightful *presentiment* that the doctor's verdict was unfavourable. I went home again, and decided about eleven to go to Dr Makis to get information from him how Mikès was. About eleven I went out, and Aleko [his own brother, Alexander] went with me. By half-past eleven the doctor hadn't come back. Aleko went home, but I decided to go to the station and wait for the midnight train [the Ramleh train, later replaced by the tram]. With it in fact came Dr Makis. I asked him and he answered: "He is in a very bad state – typhoid

15. Tsirkas, *Epoch*, p. 140.
16. Cavafy, *Prose*, pp. 253 ff.

state", and it seemed that he had no hopes of his recovering . . .
That night I didn't sleep.'

This was Cavafy's first real grief, and he is thought to have
celebrated it in his poem *Voices* (2)

> Ideal voices and dearly loved
> Of those who have died, or of those who are
> To us lost like the dead.
>
> Sometimes in our dreams they speak;
> Sometimes in thought the brain hears them.
>
> And with their sound return for a moment
> Sounds from the first poetry of our life –
> Like music, at night, far off, that fades away.

Here are echoes of Shelley :

> Music, when soft voices die,
> Vibrates in the memory . . .

And of Tennyson :

> Oh, for the touch of a vanished hand
> And the sound of a voice that is still !

And of Verlaine :

> L'inflexion des voix chères qui se sont tues.

The poignancy of his grief shows Cavafy more capable of non-
sexual love than has sometimes been supposed. But the journal
neither proves nor disproves any other hypothesis, for it is confined to its subject-matter. On the first day (the last when he saw
Mikès in health) he speaks of meeting 'David Septon' – probably
a member of an Alexandrian Jewish family – and 'Evans', to
whose identity we have no clue. Two days later he saw Mikès for
the last time at the Exchange; he does not say what he himself
was doing there.

On 17 March 1891 Peter, the second brother, and the eldest in

Alexandria, died suddenly. 'He was of a strong constitution', says Constantine, 'but careless of his health.' He had become head of his department and was decorated by the Egyptian government with the Medjidieh and Osmanieh orders; he also held an Italian decoration.

The funeral was impressive: the four-horse hearse was followed (says the newspaper report) by a great number of the 'best people of the highest society among us', and the pall-bearers[17] (so Mr Tsirkas says, and he alone is capable of making the distinction) were of the 'first class'. He thinks the paragraph must have been written by the poet himself, because of the literary skill in placing at the end, and out of chronological order, this affecting detail: 'At the moment when the body was to be carried into church his colleagues at the Council would not allow others to carry the coffin, but themselves carried it on their shoulders as a last sign of friendship for him.' One is glad that poor Peter, for all his bitterness, won so much affection. Among Haricleia's jewellery was a silver cross 'engraved with the date of dear Peter's death'.

Mr Malanos,[18] with reason, doubts that Constantine would have rushed straight from the cemetery to the newspaper office to record that his brother's funeral had been such a social success, when he ought to have gone home 'to console his inconsolable mother' – ladies did not at this time attend funerals, though many were present forty days later at the memorial service. Internal evidence would in any case make us hesitate to ascribe the notice to Constantine. Peter's age is given as thirty-six, while he was in his forty-first year, and the last sentence contains a repetition of the verb that is even more inelegant in the original. Of course Constantine did not write it, and no doubt he went back to the Boulevard de Ramleh to offer coffee to those who paid visits of condolence.

Mr Tsirkas thinks that the family sank socially and financially after the death of Peter. There is no evidence of this, or any suggestion that they sank so low as after Aristides' scandal in 1889. Peter's salary (his brother tells us) never exceeded £27 a month, and the other sons were beginning to do better. There are no grounds for saying that 'hard necessity' drove Constantine to

17. Tsirkas, *Epoch*, pp. 194–5.
18. Malanos, *T.*, p. 47.

accept a post in the Third Circle of Irrigation in April 1892, because he had lost Peter's support. There is no connection between
the two events. As we have seen, the office was at last able to
offer him the salaried post that he had been seeking for three
years.

IV   The Cavafy of the Letter 'T'

'This evening it went through my mind to write about my love. And yet I won't do it. Such power has prejudice. I have been freed from it, but I think of those enslaved under whose eyes this paper may pass. And I stop. What pusillanimity! Let me note one letter – T – as symbol of this moment. 9.11.1902'[1]

The letter 'T' has, since the discovery of this text, meant to his readers the homosexual Cavafy. We do not know exactly what the letter meant to him; it probably stands for a name, as it almost certainly does in the list of those who received the 1910 volume.[2]

Mr Malanos[3] has preferred to see it as the initial letter of ΤΕΙΧΗ (*Walls*, no 15).

> Without forbearance, without pity, without shame
> They built big walls and high, and compassed me about
> And now I sit here helpless, reasoning in despair.
> It wears away my heart and brain this cruel fate
> Because outside I have so many things that wait.
> O why, when they were building did I not take care!
> But I never heard them build, never knew them
>   when they came.
> Insensibly they closed the walls and shut me out.

This rendering is by John Cavafy – and that is its sole merit, as being, in a sort, authorised by the poet. He could not, of course, reproduce the homophonous rhymes with which his brother experimented as in *Prayer* (3); but he could have produced something more like the *ababcdcd* rhyme scheme. The poem is

1. Cavafy, *Prose*, p. 303.
2. Savidis, *Bibliography*, p. 220.
3. Malanos, *T.*, p. 63.

dated 1 September 1896, and John's version 16 January 1897. It was first published as a four-page pamphlet, probably in the latter year. There was an epigraph from Aeschylus: *'How do I suffer unjust things'* – the cry of Prometheus Bound.[4]

Mr Malanos[5] hears in this poem the cry of the homosexual, trapped by his temperament. He reminds us that the poem was written in 1896 and refers us to *Days of 1896* (133) when:

> The community was
> Extremely puritan.

He is of course well aware that that poem cannot be autobiographical: its hero is *nearing thirty* (Cavafy was then thirty-three), he has lost his money and his job, and it is *compromising* to be seen with him. There may have been a model for this poem, but it is probably a fiction, like many of his ancient stories.

Yet the cry is surely a more general, universal cry: a cry against the solitude which is the human situation, and those barriers which we create for ourselves, or allow to form around us – perhaps the reserve which was common to John and Constantine, and cut them off from their kind. They were probably the most sensitive members of the family, and perhaps had never wholly recovered from the years of poverty – and loss and disgrace had lately seemed to threaten again with the defalcation of Aristides. The feeling that we have spun barriers out of ourselves is analogous to that expressed by George Herbert in *The Collar*:

> Forsake thy cage,
> Thy rope of sands,
> Which pettie thoughts have made, and made to thee
> Good cable to enforce and draw
> And be thy law,
> While thou didst wink and wouldst not see.

It is the feeling of being shut up alone that is behind Eliot's use in *The Waste Land* of the story of Ugolino of Pisa:

4. l. 1093
5. Malanos, *T.*, p. 112.

Ed io sentii chiavar l'uscio di sotto
all'orribile torre.

Moreover Cavafy has written[6] : 'Besides, one lives, one hears and
one understands and the poems one writes, though not true to
one's actual life, are true to other lives – [he cites, among others,
Walls and *Thermopylae*] – not generally, of course, but specially
– and the reader to whose life the poem fits admits and feels the
poem : which is proved by Xenopoulos' liking (*Walls, Candles
. . .*' Again : 'If even for one day, or one hour I felt like the man
within "Walls", or like the man of "Windows" the poem is based
on a truth, a short-lived truth, but which, for the very reason of
its having once existed, may repeat itself in another life, with
perhaps as short duration, perhaps with longer.'[7] The claustrophobia of *Walls* must repeat itself in many lives, and it is the theme
of *Windows* (11) also. It is connected with the boredom behind
Waiting for the Barbarians (16); it is certainly the inspiration
of *The town* (23).

You said : 'I'll find some other land, I'll find some other sea :
Somewhere there must be, surely, a better town.
My every attempt here is like a charge written down
Against me, and my heart – like a corpse – buried away.
In this swamp is my mind always to stay?
Wherever I look, wherever I turn my gaze,
I see black ruins of my life, and of the days
That here I passed, wasted and lost utterly.'

You'll not find another place, you'll not find another sea.
This city is going to follow you. You'll stray
In the same streets. In the same suburbs you'll grow grey;
Amid these same houses you'll reach old age.
You'll always find this city. Another? – it's a mirage.
There is no ship for you, there is no road.
And just as in this hole you have destroyed
Your life, through all the world you have lost it utterly.

6. Cavafy, *U. Prose*, p. 50. This text is in English. The title given to it by
its editor, *Ars Poetica*, is unfortunate.
7. ibid., p. 54.

1. Haricleia Cavafy, *c.* 1884. Pera

2. George Psilliary (?). Photograph inscribed 'To my respected
Aunt Haricleia'. Pera

There is some excuse for attributing this poem to the Cavafy of the letter 'T' because of his own comment:[8] 'The man who has ruined his life will try in vain to live it again better, more ethically – The city, an imaginary city, will prevent and follow him and wait for him with the same streets and the same quarters.' He added, however, that the poem was not of universal application: he did not mean that no one who had destroyed his life in one place could ever remake it elsewhere.

'More ethically' – these words invited Mr Malanos to suppose that the poet was referring to his own sexual tendencies, and it might be so. He might rather be thinking of the excess, ugliness or dissimulation into which they had led him, or more generally about abuse of energy and waste of time. Behind the poem is a universal sentiment:

Caelum non animum mutant qui trans mare currunt.

It is not only the homosexual who at times finds the modern, industrial city frightful. And in Alexandria – built on a narrow limestone ridge, cut off from Egypt by salt lakes, from Europe by the sea – there is every encouragement to *taedium vitae* and claustrophobia. A better commentary is provided by some words of T. S. Eliot's. After defining the 'poet' as 'one who not merely restores a tradition which has been in abeyance, but one who in his poetry re-twines as many straying strands of tradition as possible', he continues: 'In the case of Baudelaire, this ability to go beneath appearances to the recurrently pervading elements in life was the result of the peculiar dogged strength with which he felt the torturing impact of the great modern city upon the lonely individual.'

Cavafy's homosexuality is of course well known, even too well known, for it can be exaggerated and read into work where it is not present. Nevertheless, it is important to his readers as being not only part of the whole man, but also of his writing self (as it is perhaps not important in the writing self of, e.g., Sophocles and Oscar Wilde). It modified the 'slight angle' at which his friend E. M. Forster[9] observed him standing, and the angle at which Cavafy stood to the universe modified his vision of the

8. Lehonitis, p. 49.
9. Forster, *Pharos*, p. 75.

present and the past and was a cause of its unique quality. If he were for a time bisexual – and there is reason to think so – his heterosexuality never touched his writing self and is therefore of no interest to admirers of his poetry. His homosexuality obviously became predominant early. Had he allowed a psychiatrist to interfere with him, it would have been an outrage on his mind worse than any that those who wish to change their sex can allow to be inflicted on their bodies.

It is wisest to consider his tendency simply by the light of common sense, and not to invoke any of the sciences or pseudo-sciences : Cavafy is not present for examination, and any psychological or biological explanation must be guesswork. Two out of Haricleia's seven sons were homosexual – this is nothing extraordinary, and we may leave it at that. In either case the tendency was probably congenital. She had an intense mother love for Constantine, her Benjamin, but there is no evidence that Paul was particularly a favourite – rather the reverse.

Rika Singopoulos had noted that 'homosexuality first manifested itself in Constantinople with his cousin George Psilliary'; and we have seen that there Cavafy had great opportunities for nocturnal adventures.

It was also noted by Rika Singopoulos that Cavafy had some heterosexual experience : she gives no date for it, and it probably did not amount to much, but there is no reason to doubt it. There is no other evidence on the subject, though it could probably be shown that his 'normal' friends thought that he did as they did : no other conclusion can fairly be drawn, for example, from a letter from his friend Kimon Pericles (6 March 1887) which expresses a hope that he makes 'conquests'. The early poems, devoid of personal feeling, tell us nothing. It is not till 1903 that we find directly erotic poems, and these are always homosexual. Woman is hardly ever present in his work except as a mother : Thetis, Cratesicleia, Anna Dalassina, or the sorrowful mothers of Aristobulos or the drowned sailor. Cavafy, however, was no misogynist : as a young man he was *mondain*, and he always valued the friendship of intelligent women such as Penelope Delta or Rika Singopoulos or Marika Cotopouli.

Mr Malanos[10] tells us about Cavafy's early years, after the return to Alexandria. 'An inadmissible passion at the same time

10. Malanos, *Cavafy*, pp. 17–18.

dominates his existence and paralyses his will. Imperceptibly he had found himself involved in suspect relationships. Persons from an infamous underworld are secretly mixed up in his life and have power over it. With what a confused mind must he then think about prosaic questions of earning a livelihood! Sometimes he himself well understands that he has taken the downward path. If the smallest detail of all this became known, a scandal would break out. Meanwhile he fails to master himself. He spends whole nights in disguise away from his home in lower-class neighbourhoods, bribing servants, accomplices who black-mail him. In these nocturnal escapades is the origin of the poem *He swears* (51). Speaking about it when it was first published [1915] he added – I recollect – the following details to what has already been said. At one time one could live in the neighbour-hood of certain isolated quarters of Alexandria, without one's own part of the town, the "good quarter" we may say, know-ing anything about one's way of life. The reason was that be-tween them stretched *terrains vagues* that have since been filled up with houses, giving the city a unity which it formerly lacked. So in one of those isolated quarters, slave to his temp-tations, he passed his nights. Nevertheless in the morning, realising how low he had fallen at night, he repented, and wrote in large letters on a piece of paper: "I swear I won't do it again." And yet, when night came again he went back to his "fatal joy", disregarding his oath.'

No dates are given, but the testimony of Mr Basil Athanass-opoulos makes it clear that this refers to the years immediately following the return from Constantinople: Cavafy, under greater difficulties, was trying to continue the life he had begun there. 'He bribed the servant to ruffle up his bed in the Rue Tewfik', my informant told me – thus accurately dating the beginning of these escapades before the family moved to the Boulevard de Ramleh in May 1887. Haricleia might therefore imagine that Constantine had slept at home, and had gone out early.

In later years Cavafy took Mr Athanassopoulos on a nostalgic tour of his old haunts. 'Our race doesn't produce beautiful women,' he said, 'but beautiful men.' At that time poor Greek boys came from Europe to work in bars and grocers' shops. They were wretchedly paid and abominably overworked, and only those with a strong physique could endure the conditions. They only had one holiday, *Shem el Nessim* – the Egyptian Spring Holiday that falls on the same days as Greek Easter Monday. The hours of work were intolerably long. One boy had two toes eaten off by mice, while he lay in the sleep of exhaustion on a pile of sacks.

There, in the Rue d'Anastasi, in small shops and cafés were the young men of Cavafy's poems. In the same quarter, on the corner of the Rue Mosquée Attarine, was a house built in the old oriental manner (it has long since been pulled down) with its upper storey projecting and supported on struts. There were shops on the street level, and above was a *maison de passe*. The boab collected boys and girls – and many must have been glad to earn an extra 'talliro' (about four shillings) by prostitution. Some of them may even have found a little comfort in human contact. All night the house resounded with shouts and cries. Cavafy had a room there (and it would have cost him next-to-nothing). There he sometimes slept with Greek boys – occasionally he and his partner got drunk first in one of the little bars nearby. One morning he picked up a piece of chalk and wrote on the dirty window : 'You're not to come here again, you're not to do it again.' And yet the next night or some other night saw him again in old clothes, muffled with a scarf, making his way to this sordid quarter.

Years after were to be written : *'The lines of strength that here had their beginning* (99). Here, *over a disreputable tavern*, he *had the body of love* (53). *There on my body Love had taken hold with his marvellous strength* (83). There, perhaps, he had met such people as the beautiful boy out of the blacksmith's shop (140) *destroyed by suffering and cheap debauchery*, or the other boy – out-of-work – who revealed a perfect body when he had peeled off his shabby cinnamon-coloured suit and his mended underclothes (153). If Cavafy sometimes said, thrasonically, that he had sacrificed his life to his art, we cannot believe it; but out of the mess and squalor that occupied part of his life he has created a unique order and beauty. Homosexuality was no doubt a disadvantage to Paul Cavafy, who was *mondain*, and at one time hoped to make a marriage of convenience; but it made Constantine what he was. He admitted this in Perception (79).

The years of my youth, my life of pleasure –
How clearly now I see their meaning.
What superfluous, what vain remorse . . .
But then I didn't see the meaning.
Amidst the loose life of my youth
The projects of my poetry were forming.
The circuit of my art was being drawn.
Therefore my remorse was never lasting
My resolutions to control myself and change
Held good for two weeks at the very most. [1918]

Mr Tsirkas wishes to throw the responsibility for Cavafy's sex-life upon the British occupation. He admits that the young Constantine may have been narcissistic as a result of the devotion of his mother and brothers. He believes (on no evidence at all) that he learned 'mechanical homosexuality', i.e. mutual masturbation, in England. An Alexandrian need not go far to learn that practice. If he did learn it in England it might as well have been from some Alexandrian friend as from 'poor Stopford' or any other English school-fellow.

The same theorist thinks that Constantine may have acquired an aesthetic feeling for Greek ephebes while he sat at the feet of Papazis; but he does not believe that in Constantinople he did more than gaze at naked boys in baths. We do not know that he went to the baths, but we do know (and so does Mr Tsirkas, for he mentions him in his *Chronology*) about the cousin George Psilliary. Mr Tsirkas does not believe (he has a great capacity for disbelief) that Constantine wandered so far in search of pleasure after his return to Alexandria. At the corner of the Rue de l'Ancienne Bourse and the Boulevard de Ramleh, nearby, were the beer-shops which (a French writer tells us) the licentious and brutal soldiery of the Army of Occupation had turned into a 'Bazaar of Love'. Four hundred 'red-coats' were (according to the same authority) in hospital with venereal disease. An Alexandrian friend of a later generation has told me that at one time prostitutes paraded up and down the Boulevard, male on one side and female on the other. With all this richness at hand, why should Cavafy go further? Perhaps just for the sake of being further from home.

It is rather naif to maintain[11] that Cavafy was at this time plunged in intellectual pursuits : these can easily produce accidie, a state of mind very propitious to the tempter. Moreover, as we have seen, Cavafy was not entirely so occupied. It is true that he lived at home, but knowing Haricleia's habits and engagements, and having a servant as his accomplice, he need not have found this an insuperable difficulty. And that charming woman, mother of seven sons, may have developed something of that 'negative capability' of mothers who, for all their intelligence, can contrive to know no more than they wish. She did indeed write to John and Constantine in 1897 : 'Paulitios stays at home in the evenings, but I'm sure it goes against the grain and isn't at all to his liking. He's not like you, my precious children, who forsake everyone to keep your mother company, above all, you Tźoniko, because already my sweet little one forsakes me when some of his friends are in question.' If she thought she was talking about their social lives she may not have been much mistaken : Constantine may now and then have gone out with a friend such as Pericles Anastassiades. His sexual adventures probably began long after her bedtime, which was at ten or half-past. It is true that he had to get up early to go to work next day, but like other Alexandrian office-workers he had time for a long siesta in the afternoon in which to make up for lost sleep.

The brothers may have been more of a problem. But Aristides married and left the house in 1889, and Peter died in 1891. Constantine might have thrown dust in their eyes, disguising the nature of his escapades. It may not even have been necessary with the three that remained : Alexander and John were particularly close to him, and Paul was homosexual. Nor need we conclude that all always went well in the Rue Tewfik or the Boulevard de Ramleh : we are told there were 'domestic troubles'.

Mr Tsirkas (whose faculty for believing what he chooses rivals his powers of disbelief) thinks that Cavafy's homosexuality was in part due to segregation from the other sex. This is a very odd suggestion : Cavafy was never (as far as we know) at a public school, in prison or in a monastery, he was never a seaman and did no sort of military service. We are told that the Cavafy family 'received', but that it was an all male *salon*.[12] This is unthinkable.

11. Tsirkas, *Epoch*, p. 175.
12. ibid., p. 300.

Haricleia was indeed the only woman in the family (apart from Marie, Aristides' wife) but her visiting-list contains the names of some hundred and fifty Alexandrian ladies. Some of these must have returned her calls on her 'day' (the second and last Friday in the month) – we know they did. Several might be accompanied by their daughters. Moreover Haricleia and her sons went to the Casino at San Stefano and to the Sporting Club, as well as to parties. Constantine could certainly have met young women had he wished to do so, and must indeed have met them whether he wished or no.

It is possible that (as Mr Tsirkas says)[13] it was Haricleia who found for Aristides a bride of 'first-class' family and with a dowry of £4500; it is unlikely that it was she who made the marriage for Alexander with Thelxiopi Theodorou (with £6000), for this did not take place till two years after her death.

Very likely well-dowered brides of 'first-class' family were rare, and were snapped up by the 'second class'; we may however doubt if the Cavafys were quite so particular about family. Mr Tsirkas writes as if they were noblemen of the Holy Roman Empire, careful about their *seize quartiers*. For this reason, he says, John, Paul and Constantine remained unmarried. This, of course, was from choice or chance; all bachelors are not homosexual, John was not. Nor are all married men heterosexual: Paul was trying to arrange a marriage with Barbette Valieri in London. He consulted Marigo Cavafy (wife of his cousin John) about this project. She thought he would make an excellent husband – he was such a good house-keeper, so careful to put the sheets in camphor – but the match came to nothing because he was rather exacting about a dowry: he wanted £10,000, untrammelled by trustees. Knowing Paul, we may be sure that he would have lost it. It is pleasant to know that Barbette Valieri, a saintly woman, later made a very happy marriage. She was much too good for Paul.

To suppose that Constantine was driven to despair by the state of the Greek community in Alexandria (where the Schilizzis and the Rallis and other families of his friends were doing very well), and by the absence of a 'first-class' bride with a portion, is to credit him with a fantasy so extraordinary that it was easier to attribute it to Mr Tsirkas' highly class-conscious imagination. He

13. ibid.

believes that it was not till 1892, when Constantine got a job
(for he will not believe that he worked before that date), that in
despair, and to dull a conscience which reproached him for having
conformed so far to the establishment as to accept this post
(which we know he had been seeking for three years past), he
let himself go, and followed the example of Paul, who 'passed all
bounds', like a bad character in Charlotte Yonge. There is no
evidence of Paul's influence, and we have seen there is every reason
to believe that Cavafy's homosexual life, which began with
George Psilliary nine years before, had continued ever since.

It was at this moment (according to Mr Tsirkas' theory) that
the real perfidy of Albion made itself felt. The permissive society
of Alexandria, hitherto most tolerant about every form of sex-
life, became influenced by British puritanism and hypocrisy, and
was policed by minions of the Satrap. Cavafy was thus forced
into homosexuality by the British occupation just at the time when
it was making it more difficult for him to seek in such pleasures
the distraction that his tormented conscience required. A very
sad story – it is a mercy that we cannot believe a word of it.

Confessions and resolutions written on rough pieces of paper
remain. They are, however, less obvious in meaning than they may
at first seem. It is natural to connect them with his nocturnal ex-
peditions, to which some of them undoubtedly refer; and we may
remember similar, pathetic documents cited in English police
court reports. And yet it is not quite so simple.

The confessions are written in English, and though Cavafy
did not employ any system of cryptography, his abbreviations
here are more violent than usual. Having wrestled with a number of these myself, I am full of admiration for the work of
Michael Peridis and his helpers, though I cannot always feel entirely confident in the accuracy of their transcriptions (here
translated back from the Greek), while having no greater confidence in my own transcriptions of others, which I also quote.
We may be still more doubtful about the interpretation:

'And yet I see clearly the harm and confusion that my
actions produce upon my organism. I must, inflexibly, impose a
limit on myself till 1 April, otherwise I shan't be able to
travel. I shall fall ill and how am I to cross the sea, and if I'm
ill, how am I to enjoy my journey? Last January I managed

to control myself. My health got right at once, I had no more throbbings. 6 March 1897.'

'I'm pale and ugly, while the three first days people congratulated me on looking so well. 5 August 1897.'[14]

'I dragged on shaky for 4 days then there came the stomach derangement on the 28th and a strong one! Will this cure me of my folly??? 28 October 1900.'

'Awaking in the morning. Terror! Terror! 7 January 1901.'

'Ah! Ah! Ah! Ah! Shivering with cold I write. I went $2\frac{1}{4}$ to bed. It is $4\frac{1}{2}$ ... I* at last ... 25 January 1901.'

'Up from bed shivering in the cold. Help! help! . . . the agony, the agony, the agony.

'I'm going through a martyrdom. Now I've got up to write. What am I to do? What's going to happen? . . . Help, I'm lost. 19 November 2 a.m.'

Mr Tsirkas[15] truly observes that some of these documents seem to show a man alone in his room, wrestling with temptation. It might sometimes be a temptation there on the spot, to alcoholism or masturbation. It looks as if (on some occasions at least) Cavafy is admitting to an immediately precedent failure, and most of these documents (there are exceptions) are far from having a drunken appearance. He feels that he has been ruining his health; this points to masturbation, so much more habit-forming and so much more easily indulged in than any other form of sexual pleasure. He may not improbably have believed in the exaggerated accounts of its ill-effects which used to be current. He had had a partly English education, and in Egypt the name for this practice '39' is popularly explained by the myth that it is thirty-nine times more exhausting than any other sexual act. Several leading Cavafyists are persuaded that, like Ruskin, he was a victim to this habit, and some of them have seen its influence on poems where he remembers things past – e.g. *Grey* (60), *Body, remember* (75) etc.

14. Peridis, pp. 43–54.
15. Tsirkas, *Epoch*, p. 297.

Mr Malanos scornfully asks why a man should bother to go out in the small hours and cross Alexandria, in order to indulge a passion for alcohol or masturbation: the first might be satisfied in a neighbouring bar, the second in his own room. But if we do not try to connect every one of the poet's confessions with his sorties, we can form a picture more in accordance with the total evidence. Certainly he visited these low haunts and there enjoyed homosexual pleasures; certainly he sometimes repented. But he seems also to have practised masturbation – and who knows if this were not the consequence of forcing himself to stay at home? This last vice caused him shame (as it frequently does). There is less reason to believe that he regretted his homosexual proclivities which (to judge from his later poems) he eventually came to regard with complete tolerance, though he might reasonably be ashamed of the occasional drunkenness, and of the sordid persons and places involved. He speaks of the 'infamous house'. There is no reason to suppose that he was an obsessional homosexual, the slave of his appetites.

Cavafy seems never to have had confidants, and unfortunately we do not know whether his emotions were in any way involved in his sexual life. No names of lovers have come down to us from the early period. Mr Basil Athanassopoulos has related that, years later, Cavafy told him that at one time he worked as a dishwasher late at night in a tavern or café near the Custom-House, to keep a job for a friend who was sick. Mr Athanassopoulos has, most graphically, imitated for me Cavafy showing him how he washed out the ouzo glasses. This looks like a genuine affection: it also looks like the action of a very young man, and a very poor young man who could not afford to pay a substitute. It is probably another memory of the years 1885–7.

Of more consequence is the note of 25 November 1903:[16] 'No poems were sincerer than the "2 Ms" written during and immediately after the great crapulence of libations succeeding on my departure from Athens. Now say that in time Ale. Mav. comes to be indifferent to me, like Sul. (I was very much in love with him before my departure for Athens), or Bra.: will the poems – so true when they were made – become false? Certainly,

16. Cavafy, *Prose*, pp. 55–6. Cavafy wrote 'cr. of lib'—a more acceptable transcription than 'crapulence of libations' will be offered later, see p. 106.

certainly not. They will remain true in the past, and though not applicable any more in my life, seeing that they remind me of a day and perhaps different impression, they will be applicable to feelings of other lives.'

Alexander Mavroudis, who received a copy of the 1904 poems,[17] has reasonably been identified with 'Ale. Mav.'. He was a smart young man who frequented intellectual circles in Athens when Cavafy was there in 1903. He is said to have had eyes like a sheep, and when he appeared in a thick green overcoat it was thought amusing to say, 'The sheep's in the meadow.' He published some trivial little verses in 1904; some have dedications, but there is none to Cavafy. Later he settled in Paris and wrote French farces under the name of Alex Madis.

Mr Savidis expands the '2 Ms' into '2 Months'[18]: *September 1903* and *December 1903*: these and a third poem, *January 1904*, have the initials 'A.M.' pencilled on the manuscript.

September 1903[19]

At least let me now gull myself with illusions
So that I may not feel my empty life.
And yet I was many times so near,
And how paralysed I was, how cowardly;
Why did I stay there with closed lips,
And inside me my empty life was weeping,
And my desires put on mourning?
So many times to be so near
To the eyes and the lips of love,
To the dreamed of, the beloved body.
So many times to be so near.

It looks as if Cavafy never told his love, and when he sent Alexander Mavroudis the 1904 volume there was nothing in it to give him away.

It is perhaps not too fanciful to imagine Cavafy, a man of forty, accustomed to paying for his sexual pleasures (and cheaply too), awkward and shy with an attractive young man of

17. Savidis, *Bibliography*, p. 217.
18. Keeley and Savidis, p. 63.
19. ibid., pp. 18–19.

his own world. We do not know who 'Sul.' and 'Bra.' were –
'Bra' might be the beginning of many Greek surnames, but
'Sul.' looks like 'Suleiman'. It is hard to imagine Cavafy giving
his affections to a Turk or Egyptian – though it is known that he
had made love on occasion with Egyptians, in spite of his preference for his compatriots.

At this period, apparently one of emotional disturbance, his
poetry seems to become closely autobiographical. At the head of
the touching poem *On the stairs*[20] he has written *Unknown*, in
English, and evidently this refers to the other person in the poem.
This is some of his most poignant writing about the anguish of
the flesh – *soul and body have no bounds* – and we feel that here
not only the bodies have spoken. Sympathy is present as well as
Lust, and some people have called that combination Love. The
poet has no horror of his temperament, only of the *infamous
house* that panders to it.

> As I came down the infamous stairs
> You came in at the door, and for a moment
> I saw your unknown face, and you saw me.
> Then I hid, so you shouldn't see me again, and you
> Came in quickly, hiding your face,
> And plunged into the infamous house, where
> You couldn't find pleasure, as I didn't find it.
>
> And yet, the love you wanted, I had to give you,
> The love I wanted – your eyes told me so,
> So weary and suspect – you had to give me.
> Our bodies felt it and searched for each other;
> Our blood and skin understood.
> But in confusion the two of us hid from each other.

At the theatre,[21] another poem of 1904, is marked 'S': the
initial, no doubt, of the elegant and corrupt young man in a box,
who drew the poet's eyes from the stage, while he thought about
all that he had heard about him that afternoon.

Into the twenty-four poems of the 1910 collection it seems

20. ibid., pp. 22–3.
21. ibid., pp. 23–5.

quite gratuitous to read homosexuality. The beautiful bodies of Nero (13) and of Sarpedon (18) are emphasised, and they add to the pathos of the situation, and there is nothing erotic about this reference. The unpublished poems of the period, as we have seen, are quite another matter.

V   The 'Other' Cavafy

Those readers who have been tempted to feel that Mr Malanos sometimes lays rather too heavy an emphasis on sex, may have at first felt some gratitude to Mr Tsirkas for trying to diminish that emphasis; but unfortunately his 'other' Cavafy is obsessed with politics. The Cavafy of the letter 'T' may be an exaggeration of a truth; the 'other' Cavafy is a myth.

No one can deny Cavafy's passion for the Hellenic world, but his interest in the current affairs of the modern kingdom of Greece was limited. His friend E. M. Forster wrote:[1] 'His attitude to the past did not commend him to some of his contemporaries, nor is it popular today. He was a loyal Greek, but Greece for him was not territorial. It was rather the influence that has flowed from his race through the ages . . . Racial purity bored him, so did political idealism.' Mr Malanos found that he often spoke more as a Philhellene than as a Greek.

We have seen that there is no evidence at all that he was influenced by the rather starched notions of Hellenism held by Papazis, nor have we reason to imagine that he was in any way indoctrinated by his grandfather, or that his grandfather had any doctrine to teach. 'The experienced Photiades' (in Mr Tsirkas' phrase) 'would have shaken his head.'

We do not know when Constantine, Paul and Alexander 'returned to Greek nationality'. It is natural enough for a Greek to wish his nationality to correspond with his race, and their action more probably showed a feeling for the Hellenic world rather than any antipathy to Britain. We know that Paul seems to have had strong feelings for anything Greek. When Marigo Cavafy (their cousin's wife) wrote from Greece to Constantine (17 February 1902) complaining of the roads, she said in jest: 'Don't tell Paul; on the contrary tell him there are no roads like the *Athens* roads, which is true.' We know that Alexander was no nationalist, for during his last illness Constantine had to curb his

1. Article in the *Listener*, 5 July 1951.

criticism of the Venizelist revolution in Crete in case the nurse was a Cretan.

As Alexander worked for Thomas Cook and Son, and Paul for the municipality of Alexandria, they were fully collaborating with the establishment. The notion that Constantine maintained a 'holier than thou' attitude, refused to 'collaborate' and was content to live on those who did so, is perhaps the most revolting idea that anyone has ever had about him; happily it has been shown to be false.

From about the time of Constantine's return to Alexandria in 1885 the second generation of other Alexandrian families was lavishly spending the fortunes that the previous generation had made. Mikès Ralli had written (for instance) that Sir Constantine Zervudachi was as certainly born to make money as his sons to squander it. The Cavafys, who never forgot that they were the sons of a rich man, seem to have felt the comparison. They were inclined to think themselves above work – and had their father lived and flourished there might well have been a Sir Peter and Lady Cavafy in a grand house in 'Peloponnesus', and seven idle sons. As it was, John wrote in his journal: 'To think that I'm now obliged to unload coals in the sun' – but of course he never soiled his hands, and merely superintended the operation.[2]

They were indeed gentlefolk: 'they knew who they were' and looked down on those who did not. 'Aristocracy in modern Greece?' Cavafy once exclaimed. 'To be an aristocrat there is to have made a corner in coffee in the Peiraeus in 1849.'[3] He and his friends might be caustic about the *nouveaux riches* of Alexandria, or about British officers who were not quite of their class – but there was no ideology involved – nothing more sinister than mild envy and snobbishness.

We do not quite know why Constantine refused a post offered him in the Choremi-Benachi office. He had always known the Benachi family, and was later much indebted to their kindness; and it would have been impertinence in a Cavafy (or anyone else) to look down on the Choremis, a 'first-class' family if there ever were one. Mr Malanos thinks he preferred not to work in a Greek firm, where his private life might be a matter for observation and comment. This may be so; English and Egyptian fellow-

2. Malanos, *T.*, p. 83.
3. Forster, *Alexandria*.

clerks would probably be restrained, the former by decency, the latter by a feeling of inferiority, from attempting to take him with them to the 'Arapina'. However it seems more likely that the hours of the Irrigation Service suited him better.

In 1882 his family and friends evidently assumed that the Nationalist movement had to be put down, and it would be extraordinary that he should have differed from them. At that time a resident member of a foreign community who was in favour of 'Egypt for the Egyptians' would be hard to seek: Wilfrid Scawen Blunt was a tourist. Forster cites an account of the English community in Alexandria in 1757, by one Captain Norden, a Dane: 'They keep themselves quiet and conduct themselves without making much noise. If any nice affair is to be undertaken they withdraw themselves from it and leave to the French the honour of removing all difficulties. When any benefits result from it they have their share and if affairs turn out ill they secure themselves in the best manner they can.'⁴ In a similar way the Greek communities let the Great Powers, France and Britain, settle matters for them in colonial countries. They may not have been actively in favour of the Great Powers, but they have viewed with anxiety any attempt by those Powers to withdraw from their responsibilities (however acquired) and they have wished the native population to be kept well 'in its place'.⁴

Mr Tsirkas attacks the 'Hitlerian' activities of the 'Satrap', Lord Cromer. His tone is more polemical than argumentative, and this is not the place to answer his diatribe. But he asks us how we can believe that Cavafy could have acquiesced in such a state of things – and then he completely answers himself, for he shows how far the Greek communities in Egypt did so. When he attacks the cynical manner in which the British government, pushing the French aside, made Arábi's rebellion the opportunity to occupy Egypt, Mr Tsirkas is arguing from strength; the onus of proof must lie on those who seek to justify a foreign government in a subject country. When, however, he wishes to maintain that Cavafy's attitude differed from that of his family and of the Greek community in general, he is arguing from weakness, and the onus of proof lies on him. Are we to believe that a man, known neither for his courage nor for his perfect integrity, but frequently des-

4. Forster, *Alexandria*.

3. Aristides Cavafy   4. John Cavafy

5. Paul Cavafy, *c.* 1918. Hyères

6. Cavafy, *c.* 1900. Alexandria

7. Cavafy, *c.* 1910. Alexandria

cribed as timid and shifty, should have ventured to raise his voice about something that so little affected him? It could be so; but we should require very solid evidence before we could believe it; and as there is not a shred of documentary evidence, we should look to see if he spoke out in his poems in no uncertain voice. This is not the case : Mr Tsirkas tries to fit his improbable *a priori* theory to them, and cannot do it without torture to the lines.

It is true that Cavafy published articles about the Elgin marbles and about Cyprus,[5] and these have been vexed questions between Greece and Britain. But the choice of subjects was partly topical. The Cyprus question was comparatively new in 1893, and one James Knowles had lately written a foolish article making fun of Frederic Harrison's suggestion that the Elgin marbles should be returned to Athens. Cavafy's articles are calm and reasonable; it may be wished that more people had written as temperately upon these themes, for more might in that way have been achieved. His attitude throughout is more 'Philhellenic' than anti-British – it is symptomatic of his growing Hellenism, which seems to have begun with his return from Constantinople. This is not to affirm that Cavafy was professionally pro-British or to propose him as a posthumous candidate for an M.B.E. There may well have been people – jingoist Englishmen or their toadies – whom he was not sorry to annoy. Sir Maurice Bowra[6] remarked of *In a township of Asia Minor* (125): 'He shows the fundamental indifference of the ruled to their rulers. No doubt he had observed this in Egypt' – and no doubt he had felt it.

It is now the place to consider the socio-political interpretation of some of the early poems.

Thermopylae (7), written in January 1901, is in any case a work that raises problems, and that can by no interpretation be turned into a satisfactory poem.

> Honour to those men who have set the bounds
> Upon their lives and guard Thermopylae,
> Who from their duty never swerve aside,
> Upright and honourable in all they do,
> Yet tender-hearted and compassionate.

5. Cavafy, *Prose*, pp. 9–22 and 81–9.
6. Bowra, pp. 34–5.

When they are rich, generous, and, when poor,
They still are generous in little things,
Giving all succour that is theirs to give,
And never speaking anything but truth,
Yet with no bitterness for such as lie.

And greater honour is the due of those
Who can foresee (and many can foresee)
That Ephialtes rises in the end
And at last the Persians will get through.

Maurice Bowra (who presumably was the author of this translation), thinks that here Cavafy began with an abstract conception, and chose an image to show its significance, but they failed
to cohere into a unity. 'The opening and close, with their vivid
images of heroic defence against helpless odds, have the authentic
touch of poetry, but the rest, despite its nobility of tone, is still
rather too abstract to ring with all that Cavafy feels.' It is better
to see Cavafy thus, working outward from the ethical centre to
the far finer frame that encloses it, rather than to call (as others
have done) lines 3–10 'wretched stuffing'. But the kind of conduct praised in these lines, admirable as it is, can in no way be
compared with the heroism of Leonidas and his men at Thermopylae. There was no question of each of them giving in pro-
portion to his means, for each had one and the same thing to
give : his life. Nor are tender-heartedness and compassion virtues
that we associate with the Spartans. Mr Tsirkas[7] tries to give the
poem a factual basis, which is bizarre in itself, and does nothing
to make it any better.

Averoff, who supported the Greek community with great benefactions, is likened to Leonidas. The Medes are the British,
who robbed the Greeks of 'economic hegemony' in Egypt.
Ephialtes, the man from Malis who sold to Xerxes the pass
over the hills by which the Spartans were cut off, is Constantine
Salvago : he succeeded Averoff as president of the Greek community in Alexandria, but went with Cromer, and only left the
community £1000 in his will.

Elsewhere Mr Tsirkas speaks of Averoff as 'still on the battle-
ments'. That great benefactor, giving generously from his

7. Tsirkas, *Epoch*, p. 418.

abundance, was in no sort of danger, and to compare him to one of the greatest exemplars of heroism in world history is to make him undeservedly ridiculous.

Constantine Salvago was no doubt very properly considering the interests of the Greek community when he endeavoured to get on the right side of Cromer, and the collection that he had made for widows and orphans of British soldiers fallen in the South African war might be regarded as an investment. Although his own legacy to the community was not large, he seems to have commended it to his family, for their subsequent benefactions were on a grand scale. The Cavafy family in their days of wealth never did anything particular for it. There is no evidence that Cavafy was at all hostile to Constantine Salvago, and we know that he was in good terms with his family. In 1901 he saw something of Stephi Salvago in Athens, and in 1926 he took pains to be invited to the wedding of 'Ephialtes' ' grandson. As for Cromer, in 1929 he was to write of him as a 'great statesman'.[8]

The next poem in the canon, *Che fece . . . il gran rifiuto* (8) is also unsatisfactory, but a topical explanation does not improve it. Dante's lines :

Vidi e conobbi l'ombra di colei
che fece per viltate il gran rifiuto (*Inferno* III 59–60)

are generally believed to refer to Pietro di Morrone, elected pope as Celestine V at the age of eighty in 1294. He resigned five months later, out of humility, not out of cowardice : Dante placed him in Hell because he thus made room for Boniface VIII, but the Church has raised him to the altars. Cavafy suppressed the *per viltate* to give the poem greater universality : in his lines he makes it clear that the refusal is not necessarily wrong or mistaken. It seems to be a generalised reflection with no bearing on any refusal that we know of in his own life : it is an unsuccessful work, much inferior to some of the poems he left unpublished. The ever inventive Mr Tsirkas[9] wished to connect it with the Oecumenical Patriarch Joachim III, who retired in 1884, and refused to be a candidate for the patriarchal throne

8. Malanos, *T.*, p. 153.
9. Tsirkas, *Epoch*, pp. 351–7.

of Alexandria in 1899. As Joachim III accepted re-election to his former throne in Constantinople in 1901, and occupied it until the end of his life, his case presents no parallel.

Cromer is alleged by the same theorist to make another appearance, in the noble form of Achilles who shouts in the trench and frightens the *Trojans* (12), who are, of course, the Greek community. Priam and Hecuba have not been identified. The versatile Constantine Salvago, who first appeared in the minor part of Ephialtes, makes another appearance in a nobler form even than that of Cromer, for in *Treachery* (17) he is typified by no less a figure than Apollo. True, it is not one of Apollo's better moments, for he had just allowed Achilles to die, though he had promised him long life; but this is a sufficiently glorious transformation for the grocer's son of Marseilles, on whom the 'first-class' Cavafy is supposed to have looked down. No need for the epigraph from Plato to throw dust in people's eyes, for no one (except Mr Tsirkas) could conceivably have made the identification. We cannot even see it, now that it has been pointed out for us. Salvago comes up yet again in *Walls* (15). *Without thoughtfulness* (and this is perhaps a better translation than John's): old George Photiades had shaken his wise head for the last time in 1896 at Yeniköy.

> And when they buried him the little port
> Had seldom seen a costlier funeral.

But he had left nothing to his brilliant grandson. *Without pity* – the other 'first-class' families had done nothing (but what could or should they have done?). *Without shame* – the second-class families had shut Cavafy out from 'the world' (which does not appear in John's version, so we may think that neither he nor his brother thought it important). This is *le monde*, i.e. that of the Salvago balls. There is no reason to suppose that he was not invited, or that he refused all invitations.[10]

This very singular form of interpretation reaches its apogee when it comes to the great poem, *Waiting for the Barbarians* (16):

10. Tsirkas, *Epoch*, p. 276.

What are we waiting for, gathered in the market-place?
It's the Barbarians who are to come today.
And why such inactivity inside the senate-house?
Why do the senators sit still, not making any laws?
> Because the Barbarians are coming today.
> What laws more are the senators to make?
> When the Barbarians come, they'll make laws.

Why did our emperor get up so early in the morning,
Why is he sitting waiting at the great gate of the city,
High in state upon his throne, the crown upon his head?
> Because the Barbarians are coming today.
> And the emperor is waiting to receive
> Their leader. Moreover he has prepared
> A parchment to hand him. On it
> He has given him by writ many names and titles.

And why have our two consuls, and the praetors also with them,
Gone out today in scarlet robes, covered with rich brocade,
Why have they put their bracelets on, with all those amethysts,
And rings upon their fingers, bright with shining emeralds;
Why are they carrying today their precious staves of office,
So exquisitely chiselled, and inlaid with gold and silver?
> Because the Barbarians are coming today;
> And that sort of thing impresses Barbarians.

Why don't our worthy rhetoricians come today as usual
To spout their speeches at us, and say what they have to say?
> Because the Barbarians are coming today;
> And they're bored by eloquence and public speeches.

Why does there suddenly begin so great a restlessness,
And such confusion – and the faces, look how grave they grow!
> Because night has fallen, and the Barbarians haven't come.
> And some people have arrived from the frontiers
> With news that there aren't any Barbarians any more,
And now what is to become of us without Barbarians?
Those people were a kind of solution.

Paul Petridis[11] (inspired by Cavafy himself) commented on these lines: 'He must have composed *Waiting for the Barbarians* in a moment of black despair and deep reflection. It is a splendid, enchanting vision of the poet who is transported into an

11. ibid., p. 323.

imaginary city, whose inhabitants, having developed a high
degree of civilisation, are seized by a delicious nostalgia for bygone ages whose memory is lost in the night of the past. They
fancy that by returning to the life of a primitive civilisation they
will regain happiness. And their desire is nearly fulfilled . . .The
tidings that there are no Barbarians any more is the poet's conviction. He thinks that colossal organism called civilisation is so
perfect, and that its network has our planet so tightly in its grip,
that any attempt to return to primitive life would be in vain.'

And yet this Rousseauism cannot be the whole story: the city
is bored with itself (and in a nineteenth-century fashion) and
would welcome anything for a change. In the last lines there is a
kind of impish fun. A bored child will wish for the ship to sink
or the house to burn down 'to make a change'. He does not *really*
wish it; an adult will laugh at himself a little ruefully if he enter-
tains such a thought. One must be careful not to read into this
poem all that it has meant in our century in various endangered
cities (I think of Helsingfors in 1939, Athens in 1941, Cairo in
1942 – others will supply other names). It has passed from
mouth to mouth of people 'tired of living and scared of dying',
who have been cheered by its light-hearted spirit. There is even
a note of hope. Suppose that at our frontiers there are, after all,
no Barbarians? One may doubt if it is still much quoted in
Alexandria, since the Barbarians have come.

The poem was written in December 1898. Three months previously Kitchener defeated the last Mahdists at Omdurman, and
until then Egypt still feared an invasion. Mr Tsirkas[12] wants us
to believe that the city is Alexandria, the market-place is the
Place des Consuls, the senators are the representatives of the first
Greek colonists, the praetors are the judges of the mixed courts,
and at the Porte de Rosette sits the Khedive Abbas II ready to
welcome the invaders, and presumably to bestow honours upon
their leader the Khalifa (the original Mahdi had died in 1885).
In view of the sufferings of the Greeks in the Sudan under the
Mahdists, it is not possible to believe that the foreign communities would have been glad to welcome them at the Rosetta
gate. The solutions they had to offer were Islam or death.

It is inconceivable that this, or any other of Cavafy's early
poems, can in any way have shocked the feelings of his colleagues

12. Tsirkas, *Epoch*, pp. 334 ff.

or superiors in the Third Circle of Irrigation. Nor can we imagine him as a sort of *enfant terrible* being submitted to any sort of family censorship in the Boulevard de Ramleh. Haricleia could have felt no need to caution him: 'Between ourselves, Costaki, we can say anything: but if you put that in a poem you'll do harm to Aleko and John, and perhaps to Paul too.'[13]

It has been suggested[14] that Haricleia sent Constantine to England and France with John in 1897 to prevent him rushing off as a volunteer in the Balkan war of that summer. This is, of course, absurd: we know him too well to imagine that he would voluntarily have plunged into danger. Moreover his 'confession' of 6 March of that year proves that the journey was already planned, and the war did not break out until May.

It is extravagant to give a political interpretation to *Satrapy* (24) – published in 1910, but written at an earlier date. Cavafy himself excludes this by his note:[15] 'The poet is not necessarily thinking of Themistocles or Demaratos or any other political character . . . the person intended is entirely symbolic, and we must rather take him to be an artist or man of learning who after failures and disappointments abandons his art and goes to Susa and Artaxerxes, that is changes his life and in another way of life finds luxury (which is a sort of happiness) but it cannot satisfy him. The line in parenthesis is important: *the day you let yourself go, and you give in*, for it is the base of the whole poem because of the hint that the hero too easily lost heart, that he exaggerated the events, and was in too much of a hurry to take the road to Susa.' It is clear that as it is a man of letters or learning who is going, he has no feelings of public guilt; it is no treachery to his country to go to Susa and Artaxerxes: it is self-betrayal, betrayal of his true vocation.

Mr Tsirkas[16] believes that this poem refers to Cavafy's joining the Third Circle of Irrigation in 1892; he believes, mistakenly (as we have seen), that the poet never did paid work before this date, and was now obliged to do so by the death of his brother Peter. 'Hard necessity impelled Constantine to enter the "Irrigation" as a temporary clerk. The poet then lived some of

13. ibid., pp. 213–14.
14. ibid., p. 363.
15. Lehonitis, p. 25.
16. Tsirkas, *Epoch*, pp. 176–7.

the most difficult days of his life, but finally took the decision . . .
Susa, Artaxerxes, that is the Medes. And as for the Irrigation
service, we know to what extent it was directed by the English.'

If Constantine never had any more difficult days he was lucky
indeed. We have seen that there is no evidence at all of the poet's
reluctance to work with the British; on the contrary he had been
seeking this post for three years already – and the small tips he
received from his family become intelligible if we regard them as
assistance to him while he waited for an eligible post, and did
much unpaid work. But it is possible that it was the first time that
he was absolutely bound down to the routine of office life, and
he may have felt some regret. Mr Malanos[17] wins our assent
when he says that a clerkship in the Irrigation was no satrapy,
and that its small salary offered no eastern luxury : more important, Cavafy had chosen an ill-paid job which gave him much
free time, and he never gave up his art. In many ways he was
the antithesis of the man in the poem; and yet some concession
must be made to the other side. Though it is absurd to say that
Cavafy *is* this character, we may say that he may have contributed to it. Though he never attained Asiatic splendour, and
always remained fanatically true to his art, there are indications
that he sometimes felt he had made great sacrifices to bourgeois
comfort.

'A young poet visited me', he wrote. 'He was very poor, lived
by his literary work, and it seemed to me that he was grieved to
see the good house I was living in, my servant who brought him
a nicely served tea, my clothes made by a good tailor. He said :
"What a horrible thing it is to have to struggle for a livelihood,
to hunt subscribers for your periodical, and purchasers for your
book."

'I didn't want to leave him in his delusion, so I said a few
words, more or less as follows. His position is difficult and disagreeable – but how much my little luxuries cost me. In order to
obtain them I departed from my natural course and became a
government servant (how absurd!) and I spend and lose all
those precious hours a day – to which must be added the hours
of weariness and sluggishness that follow – what a loss, and what
a betrayal! While this poor fellow doesn't waste a single hour;
he's always faithful to his duty as a child of Art.

17. Malanos, *T.*, p. 26.

'How often during my work a fine idea comes to me, a rare image, and sudden ready-formed lines, and I'm obliged to leave them, because work can't be put off. Then when I go home and recover a bit, I try to remember them, but they're gone. And it's quite right. It's as if Art said to me : "I'm not a servant, for you to turn me out when I come, and to come when you want. I'm the greatest lady in the world. And if you deny me – miserable traitor – for your wretched 'nice house', and your wretched good clothes and your wretched social position, be content with that (but how can you?) and for the few moments when I come and it happens that you're ready to receive me, come outside your door to wait for me, as you ought to every day." June 1905.'[18]

No doubt every artist who has made a compromise with bourgeois life must sometimes feel like this; at other times he may think of the misery of hunting for subscribers to a periodical or purchasers for a book, and other sub-literary activities to which the 'Child of Art' may be compelled by want, and the worse indignity of living on other people. Perhaps Cavafy had not made such a bad choice, and there are signs that he grew reconciled to it :[19] he was a good and useful government servant, and very likely was better off than the Children of Art are in their cafés or bars; at least he had the 'good' house to take refuge in.

> What a pity ! while you have been made
> For fine and great things, that that bad luck of yours
> Always denies you encouragement and success;
> That low habits should be in your way,
> And pettinesses and indifference.
> And how dreadful the day when you give in
> (The day you let yourself go, and you give in)
> And go off a wayfarer to Susa,
> And go to the Great King Artaxerxes,
> Who kindly admits you to his court
> And offers you satrapies and so forth.
> And you accept them in despair,
> Those things you do not wish for.
> Other things your soul seeks, other things it weeps for;
> The praise of the people and the sophists,

18. Savidis, *Bibliography*, pp. 170–1.
19. ibid., p. 170 n.

The hard-won, the inestimable applause,
The market-place, the theatre and the garlands!
Where will Artaxerxes find these to give you,
Where will you find them in the satrapy?
And what sort of a life will you have without them?

Although in the canon of his work Cavafy never seemed to
recognise the Arab conquest of Egypt, he was not without sympathy for the modern country and its people. Urban though he
was, he could not help seeing some of that green and pleasant
land every time he went up to Cairo. An early poem, which he
did not care to reprint, is called *Shem el Nessim*,[20] that charming spring holiday sacred to excursions into the country. He
writes tenderly of the pleasures of humble people, as no one can
write of a Bank Holiday since the days of mass motor travel.

Moreover he seems on two occasions to have been deeply
moved by the fate of young Egyptians. The first occasion was the
Denshawi episode of 1906: a horrible story, and highly dis-
creditable to the 'protecting power'.

In June 1906 some British officers and soldiers, on their way
between Cairo and Alexandria, arrived at the village of Denshawi where, 'misled by a treacherous or incompetent dragoman',[21] they amused themselves by shooting the tame pigeons
belonging to the villagers. There was a clash, and the British re-
treated. One Captain Boyle (or Bull), hit on the forehead by a
stone, made his way through the broiling heat to the British
camp, where he collapsed and died of sunstroke. It was, pre-
posterously, claimed that he had been murdered. 'The sentences
inflicted by the special court were excessive and mediaeval',[22] and
several of the fellahin of Denshawi paid for Captain Boyle's life
with their own. This event inspired a poem written in January
1908, entitled *27 June 1906, 2 p.m.* Another title given to it was
Yussef Hussein Selim.[23]

20. Tsirkas, *Epoch*, pp. 216–17.
21. Storrs, p. 64. Sir Ronald Storrs twice figures in lists of recipients of
Cavafy's poems (Savidis, *Bibliography*, pp. 247 and 256). His moderate but
frank account of the Denshawi incident is a corrective to the virulent
remarks of Bernard Shaw in the preface to *John Bull's Other Island*.
22. ibid.
23. Cavafy, *UP*, pp. 149 and 240.

When the Christians took and hanged
The innocent boy of seventeen,
His mother, dragged and beaten in the dust
There underneath the gallows
Beneath the fierce, midday sun,
Howled, cried like a wolf, like a bear,
And then, exhausted, the poor martyr lamented :
'You only lived seventeen years for me, my boy.'
And when they went up the ladder of the gallows
And passed over the rope and throttled him,
The innocent boy of seventeen –
And it was hanging pitifully in the void
With the spasms of its black agony
That beautifully made youthful body,
His martyred mother rolled in the earth
And did not lament for years any more.
'Seventeen days only,' she lamented,
'Seventeen days only I had the joy of you, my boy

There is no need to draw a political conclusion from Cavafy's humane reaction to one scene of horror – a reaction not unlike that of many British officials in Egypt at that time. He had, moreover, a particular abhorrence for capital punishment, as a manuscript note of his (dated 19 October 1902) shows : [24]

'I often notice how little importance people give to words. Let me explain. A simple man (by "simple" I don't mean a fool, but someone undistinguished) has an idea, condemns a situation or a generally accepted opinion; he knows the great majority of people think differently from him, and so he is silent, thinking he had better not speak, arguing that he will change nothing by speaking. It is a great mistake. I act otherwise. For example, I condemn capital punishment. Whenever I have the opportunity I declare this, not because I think that if I say this the nations will give it up tomorrow, but because I am sure that by saying it I contribute to the triumph of my opinion. It doesn't matter if no one agrees with me. My words are not in vain. Someone will take them up again and they may reach the ears of people who will listen and be encouraged. And of those who now disagree, someone – in favourable circumstances – may remember them in

24. Savidis, *DL*, p. 11.

the future, and by the coincidence of other circumstances he may be persuaded, or his contrary opinion may be shaken. And so in other social questions, and in some where action is above all required. I know I'm cowardly and can't act. Therefore I only speak. But I don't think my words useless. Someone else will act. And my words – coward though I am – will assist his energy. They clear the ground.' We may also remember that the lamentations for the dead, 'moirologia', were the Greek ballads that Cavafy liked best, and that the *mater dolorosa* occurs again in his work, notably in *Aristobulos* (82); in that poem also the victim was a beautiful boy.

It is not recorded whether Ibrahim el Wardani were beautiful; but in any case it is not impossible that his fate appealed to the Cavafy of the letter 'T' quite as much as to the 'other' Cavafy. The connection between sex and hanging is only too well known : some years ago when a beautiful murderess was hanged she got a much better press than she deserved; and Housman's poems are full of hanged lads.

Wardani, a fanatical young chemist, murdered the prime minister of Egypt, Boutrous Ghali Pasha, an anglophil Copt, on 20 February 1910; he had no accomplice, and the motive of his crime was political.

Cavafy's interest in the case is proved by a collection of newspapers that he preserved. He included a note of his own : [25] 'The Egyptian people showed sympathy for Wardani : out of pity for the individual, not – at least among the more evolved part of them – out of approval for the act. An organ of the Italian press in Egypt wrote recommending him to mercy . . . After the execution of the unfortunate young man, Egyptian demonstrations of sympathy were numerous. Poems in his praise were written, pupils of various schools of higher studies wore black ties for mourning; there were gatherings round his grave and there emotional speeches were made, and the hands of friends brought beautiful flowers.'

The case was heard *in camera*, but the speech of the defending counsel to his condemned client was widely circulated afterwards. 'Go to your death with a brave heart and a firm step. For death may find you tomorrow, if not today, and no one escapes it. Go my son, go to your God who holds the scales of the

25. Tsirkas, *Politikos*, pp. 90–2.

highest justice, free from the needs of time and circumstance. Go, our hearts are with you, our eyes will always weep for you. Go, your death sentence, received from human justice, may more than your life be shown as a great lesson to your people and your country. Go, if men do not pity you, the divine mercy is immeasurable. Farewell, my son, farewell, farewell.'

These words, if improved upon by Plutarch, might well be the stuff of one of Cavafy's historical poems. The situation (*mutatis mutandis*) might have reminded him of some ancient story, such as that of Harmodius and Aristogeiton, and may have had an aesthetic appeal for him. It is very unlikely that – so late as 1910 – he thought of treating a non-Greek subject in a poem. But he was evidently interested in the story – only on one other occasion (so far as we know) did he preserve a run of newspapers about a single event. This was when, in Paris in 1904, there was a homosexual scandal referred to as 'Les Noces blanches', involving an English (or American) painter, variously referred to as 'Lord Boulton' and 'Ernest Bulton'. The appeal of both these subjects to Cavafy is obvious enough; it will hardly be maintained that it was the legal problem in each case that intrigued him, thought this was of interest. Were the 'Noces blanches' really an outrage on public decency, or were they only witnessed by participants – and if they were heard and not seen, did that count? And did the prime minister die as a result of the assassin's bullet or the surgeon's scalpel?

No doubt Cavafy felt some pity for the poor misguided individual, but we may safely suppose him to have been at least as 'evolved' as those Egyptians who had no sympathy for the act. The organ of the Italian press was no doubt trying to flatter Egyptian sentiment at the expense of the British, but Cavafy has never been found doing any such thing.

Another manuscript note of Cavafy's (dated 29 June 1908) seems, like the note on capital punishment, to suggest the existence of a 'social' rather than a 'political' Cavafy – inspired though it probably is by jealousy of the Zervudachi family, and their likes.

'I am pleased and touched by the beauty of the people, of poor young men. Servants, workmen, small employees and shop assistants. One might call it a compensation for all they lack. All that work and movement makes their bodies light and symmetrical. They're nearly always slender. Their faces – white when they work in shops and sunburnt when they work out-of-doors – have a pleasant, poetical colour. It's a contrast with rich young men who are sick and psychologically dirty, or fat and greasy from all their food and drink and soft beds; it is as if their swollen or emaciated faces revealed the ugliness of the theft and robbery of their heritage and interest.'[26]

But there can be little doubt that this passage is about the poor Greek boys of the Attarine quarter who were his bedfellows – the same feeling is present in many of the poems – and the contrast is with the *nouveaux riches* of the Greek world. Cavafy, it will be seen, knew very little Arabic, and had not much contact with *les indigènes* – even if a Suleiman were at one time his lover.

It is regrettable, perhaps, to have dwelt so long on the possible reactions of a dead poet to old, unhappy, far-off things, or on the possible contacts of his body with others, most of which have by now, like itself, probably become 'a small quantity of Christian dust'. But the poems are still living, and it is important that they should not be misinterpreted.

26. Savidis, *DL*, p. 11.

VI Family Life: Journeys and Bereavements

During his leave in May and June 1897 Constantine went with his brother John on a journey to France and England. They sailed to Marseilles, where they received the first of the papers preserved in a huge collection of menus, theatre programmes etc. It is an amusing hand-out of a brothel of which the version in English reads: 'Notice. Beware of drivers who for their private interest take travellers to second-rate houses and to their detriment. It is necessary to call attention to such tricks. Be careful to read "ALINE" on the outside Lanterne and only house enclosed.' It is most unlikely that they profited by his invitation; indeed the collection of papers may have been made to amuse their mother. They probably spent some time in Marseilles with Greek friends, such as George Rodocanachi, to whom Constantine brought a letter from his brother Theodore.

Haricleia wrote charming letters (in her vile handwriting) to her 'dearest, precious, precious little boys': now and then there was a word or phrase in English (here italicised). She addressed particularly to Constantine (as being more interested) news of friends fighting in Crete. She warned them both about food in France where 'sauces cover many things'. England still seemed to her *Hôme sweet Hôme*. 'Costaki, in the zoo, don't go too near your friends the animals, because sometimes they get angry. Eat well there, and a lot of *Beef* and grow fat my dearest children.' The poet was nicknamed the *Thin One*, and she the *Fat One*.

As they kept no journal and their letters have not been preserved, we know nothing about their participation in Greek social life in Paris, and not much about their sight-seeing, except that they went (naturally) to Versailles, and also to the Salon. Theodore Ralli's picture *La Prière* was exhibited; it may be the picture that is said to have inspired *Prayer* (3), though other paintings by Ralli have been suggested, and he executed a number of variations on the same theme. They saw *Faust* at the

Opéra, and Beaumarchais' *Barbier de Seville* at the Comédie Française; they also went to every other sort of theatrical entertainment: the Odéon, the Nouveau Cirque, the Grand Guignol. In London they went to see the Victorian Era Exhibition at Earls Court, and the Royal Academy, and they dined at the Star and Garter at Richmond. They probably visited their cousin John and his family. They saw a Pinero play at St James's, and *Madame Sans-Gêne* (with Ellen Terry) at the Lyceum, and other performances. Back in Paris, they went to the races in the Bois de Boulogne, and saw *Oedipe Roi* at the Comédie Française. They sailed from Marseilles, and were home again by the end of June.

Haricleia seems to have been in failing health; her eyes were not so good as they had been, and it was seldom now that she cared to sit between meals at the dining-room table with her sewing – though she made a hat in the last week of her life. We have pictures of her: standing at the window of the dining-room balcony with one hand on the curtain – trying, no doubt, to see all she could of the life below without the vulgarity of being seen. Boredom, if she could not sew, naturally sharpened her appetite: she would stick two biscuits together with jam and eat them, and she had a passion for cakes. After meals she sat in an armchair, with Constantine often stretched on a canapé beside it. At ten o'clock she would begin to get ready for bed. At that hour Constantine generally ate a 'sweet' he says, probably either a 'sweet of the spoon' – such as a thick roll of candied orange peel, or cherries in syrup – or a 'sweet of the pan', one of those sticky, oriental cakes also dripping with honey or syrup. Haricleia's manuscript cookery-book contains receipts that she had written out for many of these delicacies: Kydonopasta, kitron, moustalevria, galaktoboureko, halvàs semigdali and revani. She left her bedroom door ajar, and she and Constantine went on chatting.

Rosina, her maid, was probably a Triestine, as such servants usually were in good Alexandrian houses at this time; she was something of a confidante. Haricleia in her loneliness once had recourse to her sympathy when Constantine had gone up to Cairo.

'I said I wouldn't write, but I can't help it', wrote Haricleia. 'I can't live without you. The house is frightful without you, and

Rosina said the same thing today . . . Yesterday I got your telegram and saw your enthusiasm. Without money life isn't worth-
while, darling, for I have been without all its pleasures. But if
there is health, and one is a sensible person like you, my precious
little boy, you'll always pass a good life. Only health, darling, is
the first thing. I hope you enjoyed the theatre and the party
yesterday' (9 December 1896).

Achmet the cook was an excellent servant. There was a
dynasty of suffragis, Abdou, Mohammed, Hassan; it is not clear
whether they had underlings or not. Mohammed learned to read
and write, and wanted 'Polis' (Paul) to find him a place in
the municipality. This proved to be impossible, and Mohammed
deteriorated as a servant after that: he quarrelled with Rosina
and came later and later in the morning – presumably he lived
in some sort of servants' quarters at the top of the block. They
had to part with him.

Out of her seven sons Haricleia had successively lost George,
through absence, Aristides through marriage, and Peter
through death; and Alexander was much away, at Ismailia or
Port Said. But she weighed heavily on those that remained.
John, who had been so good, rebelled and took a *chambre
meublée* – this was probably at the beginning of 1898. It is not
always possible to date the events or conversations that Constantine jotted down (often with his characteristic abbreviations)
on odd little bits of paper, probably at odd times too, when little
memories of his mother that he wished to preserve came back to
him after her death. Sometimes they must have come with a
sudden pang of loss – there is often the little pathetic parenthesis: 'My Fat One!' Sometimes the notes are in Greek, sometimes in English. Sometimes they seem to be there for no reason
at all, such as this (in blue pencil): 'The chicken Achmet forgot
to roast, and fried at the last minute.'

In 1898 they had a long visit from George. Early in this year
Haricleia started 'will-shaking' – perhaps, now her father was
dead, she had come into some money of her own; she had certainly some diamonds and other jewellery. 'She said she would
leave a souvenir to each, the furniture of her room to George,
and all the rest to me. It seems Paul pouted. So she told me afterwards . . . When she told me this she began to cry, and to tell me
the frightful scene she made and the hysterics she underwent to

leave me a small sum and now trembled lest after her death they tried to take it from me. "From John," she said, "I fear nothing." I kissed her hands . . .' She then decided to leave more to the others, so that her will should not be contested.

Paul was operated on for a fistula, for the second time, in April. He had suffered for months, and Haricleia was worried : George said that Paul had brought it on himself by late nights and drinking. Mr Tsirkas says that Paul had led a dissolute life from his youth, and that he was still (1963)[1] spoken of in Alexandria under the nickname of Gafafy (presumably one who makes 'gaffes' – which is rather surprising). We are told that Constantine had suffered by his reputation, and had later, in a way, profited by it to make copy for his poems, had even tried to adopt Paul's legend for his own to give an interest to his work in the eyes of admirers.[2] There appears to be no foundation for this very disagreeable and singular theory.

Paul went to England in the summer, and saw a good deal of London-Greek society. *'I feel quite a new man,'* he wrote to his mother, when he was *'still under the spell'* of his London visit. (I italicise foreign words or phrases from his Greek letters.) He seems to have been a little worried about what was being said about him at home. 'Costi hasn't sent the *Réforme* [an Alexandrian paper] perhaps they've said stupid things about me again and you don't wish *that I should make bad blood . . .* there's no fear of that.' He told his mother a lot of London-Greek gossip : what dowries the girls had. There were some fashion notes : he intended to brighten her up. He would bring her (among other things) a white parasol : it wasn't too youthful for her, *quite the other way*; it was for ladies not girls. 'If *any little influence is good for something I shall use it'* – apparently with the Salvagos, and to effect Alexander's transfer from Port Said. He had been to Henley Regatta *one of the events of the season*, and was *full up* with engagements.

He evidently thought a good deal about their past life in England. Everything was still as it was : Porchester Terrace, Queen's Road, Westbourne Grove, Whiteley's. No 15 Queensborough Terrace was to be let. *'I went in at once and saw the old house . . . Il y avait un tel air de tristesse about it . . . I have quite made up*

1. Tsirkas, *Chronology*, 1920.
2. Tsirkas, *Epoch*, p. 179.

my mind not to go near the place again.' He resisted the temptation to go to Folkestone.

To his brothers he wrote about fashions for men. He also exclaimed : '*Quelle belle race* the Anglo-Saxon; it's the place for male beauty.' He had been particularly moved by that of a hansom-cab-driver : 'What *complexion*, what *build* – it's *la perfection.*'

They are interesting, affectionate letters, and naturally Haricleia read them with pleasure, or had them read to her by Alexander (when on leave from Port Said) or by Constantine. Once Constantine's breath failed while he was reading, and this scared her. Alexander told her to finish Paul's letter herself, rather unkindly, for his pin-point writing (like that of his mother and her family) is a strain on any eyes.

Poor 'Polis', he was hardly a favourite son. There is a list of Haricleia's complaints about him. He took her to the Sporting Club, and then left her alone there. When he went to England he seemed glad to be going alone and without her. On his return to Alexandria he went out at once, as if he cared nothing for her. He told her by innuendos that she was old. She preferred Aristides' child to him, and meant to give her everything when she was grown up. He had pouted when she made her will, and this had obliged her to leave him more to avoid disputes.

She was becoming rather possessive : 'When I avoided going out with her, with what a complaining eye the poor thing [looked at me]. She didn't dare say anything since she knew her demand was *anormale*, but all her life was *anormale* and we had to compromise with this abnormality or she would have died!' There was a touching scene at the Casino at San Stefano. She had come with Paul, who wanted to get rid of her. Constantine was already there with a friend, who was exceedingly polite to her; but they left her to her unwilling escort.

In September that year she had an attack of some sort. Sometimes her head made a sound like '*gnous, gnous, gnous*'. She became afraid of being alone, and the sons seem to have established a sort of rota by which one was always on duty in the evenings. Constantine complains that it was almost impossible for him to accept an invitation or make an engagement, for he might have to cancel it at the last moment – there is a suggestion that Paul did less than his duty. Alexander came back from

Port Said and was established in Alexandria in November, and
that was a help. All the same, she said: 'I think the only one
who will weep for me if I die is Costaki.'

Alexander almost at once was rather difficult; no doubt he had
become used to an independent life. All the time he was wanting
them to move house – perhaps to live less cramped up together –
sometimes he talked of taking a flat below with John. 'Almost
every day with the question of the house Alexander used to give
her a shock . . . I used to go and find privately Paul and John
and beg of them to speak to him. In the carriage with John on
the fatal day I told him if mother recovered to tell Alexander to
cease upsetting her – so clearly did I see the havoc he caused.'

There is something like a journal of the last few days of
Haricleia's life no doubt jotted down immediately after her
death, but less connected than the notes on Mikès Ralli.

One day in the week 22–29 January 1899, Aristides' wife
Marie called unexpectedly. Rosina said Haricleia was out, but
Marie 'pushed herself in'. The Fat One put on a mantilla and
sat in an arm-chair.

27 January, Friday. 'Afternoon she had her reception [it was
her day]. I remember Paul had to go to a party. I think
on the English frigate and she was alone and she was afraid
because her head was "howling". In the evening when I saw
her after the reception she said it went quite well.'

28 January, Saturday. 'The morning passed as usual, I was
at the office.' He lunched out (badly) with a colleague, sat with
him in the Café Khédivial, and saw him off at the station for
Damanhour. When he went home at 5 p.m. the 'F.O.'
received him '*à bras ouverts*'.

29 January, Sunday. 'I don't remember if I went out in the
morning.' In the afternoon the 'F.O.' drove out with Paul.
'At 5 I went to John's room and talked – I told John to talk
to Aleko so he shouldn't upset Mama.' Then Constantine paid
a social call, at a house where he found Paul. They went home
and dined, together with the 'F.O.' and Aleko – no doubt at
their usual hour of half-past seven. 'Our last Sunday dinner –
woe is me! woe is me!' They were all much pleased with
Achmet's cooking.

30 January, Monday. Marie was to come to dinner. They had

not enough *pastisakia* and Constantine ('the little one') was sent out for more : these seem to have been very small timbales of macaroni, and one does not know why they sent out for them. The menu consisted of soup, chicken and potatoes, *pastisakia* and other things he could not remember.

31 January, Tuesday. Constantine went to a friend's house in the evening, and ate koulourakia (biscuits) and crystallised fruit. 'I drank a lot of cognac, when I left I was very drunk . . . the F.O. didn't hear me when I got home', and that was very late.

1 February, Wednesday. Haricleia dyed her gloves. In the Rue Cherif she would not have been obliged to such an expedient. This is one of several signs that she accepted the change in her circumstances better than some of her sons, who can only have had dim recollections of better days. 'A young woman who looks as if she never had to wear dyed gloves', Ivy Compton-Burnett once said of another novelist.

2 February, Thursday. She tried on a new hat. Paul said it was ugly. 'When Paul went out she asked me if it were really ugly. I said it was pretty. She said : "I made it myself." I went out and had my moustache cut, met Per[icles Anastassiades] who took me home.'

3 February, Friday. Her small grand-daughter was brought to see her, after luncheon and during the siesta. 'I called : "Fat One, don't be frightened; Anna has come with Aristides' child." ' After some hesitation they woke Paul, and went to his room with the child. 'I think the *seduta* ended 4.30 p.m. I had belly-ache : F.O. concerned. I think because on a full stomach I lifted Aristides' child.' On this last day Haricleia wrote a letter to George, unposted at her death.

Later in the afternoon Constantine went to a café, watched billiards and drank port.

Next day, early in the afternoon, Haricleia had a stroke as she was getting out of her carriage to visit the photographers' in Rue Averoff : she died an hour or two later. Her newspaper obituary reads: 'Enjoying the general affection of the Greek and foreign colonies, to the end of her life she practised benevolence together with a charm due to her high breeding and natural elegances. The sudden and painless death of an affectionate

mother, surrounded by the deep love and respect of her children
is indeed the best end of life that any educated woman can wish.
We trust this thought will be a comfort to her children.'

Paul's chief, Sakour Bey, and John's chief, R. J. Moss, were
pall-bearers; also their neighbour Smith, director of the
Eastern Telegraph Company, and the Greek vice-consul. 'Five
bare-headed sons' followed the magnificent six-horse hearse. Two
porters carried the huge wreath from the Municipality, and Ger-
manos, metropolitan of the Thebaid, pontificated, as he had at
Peter's funeral.

Mr Tsirkas does not attribute the newspaper account to the
poet – and we may be sure that he was much too greatly
afflicted to rush off to the newspaper office: he got several days'
compassionate leave from his own office in order to rally from
the shock. The funeral (Mr Tsirkas thinks) though more
extravagant had less 'class' than Peter's; perhaps the family now
moved in more cosmopolitan circles, and less among the Greek
world of their father. Haricleia's visiting-list hardly gives that impression, for most of the better Greek names are on it:
Anastassiades, Antoniades, Benachi, Choremi, Ralli, Rodocanachi, Scanavi, Sinano, Synadino, Vouros, Zervoudachi,
Zizinia etc. It is true there are also English names: Alderson,
Carver, Charteris, Ebsworth, Moss and others; French names
like Amic, Nourisson and la Poméry; and Syrian and Lebanese
names of those from whom the Cavafys had rented houses:
Debbane and Zogheb.

The eldest brother, George, returned from England with a
'chronic illness'; for some time he seems to have been in Cairo,
where Aristides his next surviving brother was living. Constantine also went to Cairo, probably during his summer leave.
George came back to Alexandria, where he died in the German
Hospital on 5 August 1900.

In 1901 Constantine made his first visit to Greece; he
travelled with his brother Alexander, and his friend Pericles
Anastassiades gave him £100 to pay for the journey. He kept a
journal in English.[3] 'This is intended to be a diary of occurrences,
not of impressions and ideas. It may however become the
reverse; it is in the nature of diaries to turn out quite the
opposite of what is expected or intended.' But it did no such

3. Cavafy, *Prose*, pp. 259–300.

thing. It is the only diary of the poet known to us: the notes on the deaths of his mother, of Mikès Ralli and Alexander were written up after the event.

They left Alexandria on the Khedivial Company's steamer *El Kahira* on 12 June. Next day they had to undergo disinfection at Delos, and to pass two days there in quarantine. 'The island is pretty to look at. The bay most picturesque.' They passed through many islands, of whose names he was not always correctly informed, and on 16 June they landed at Piraeus, 'a very nice little place', helped by Cook's men, Alexander's colleagues. They drove up to Athens, where they stayed at the Hôtel d'Angleterre. 'Towards evening we strolled about the leading streets. A very, very pretty town – quite European, in the French and Italian line. The officers' uniforms I liked very much; and the officers and soldiers look all they should be.'

He did the sort of sight-seeing that Baedeker encourages and that few people seem to do nowadays, walking down the principal streets and identifying ministries, banks and other public buildings. The heat was a trial; there was less shade than in Alexandria where streets were narrower and buildings higher. The brothers visited the principal ancient sites and several Byzantine churches. Constantine found the Acropolis 'sublime', and much admired 'the bust of Antinöus' in the Archaeological Museum.

They seem to have spent a thoroughly urban, Alexandrian holiday – sitting for hours in cafés whose names are a melancholy reminder of the Athens that has left us since the Second World War: Yannakis', Zavoritis', Zacharatos'. There they met a number of Alexandrian friends. They visited their cousin (Constantine's godmother) Amalia Pappos, 'a very good soul', and her sister Thalia. They also went frequently to the theatre. They heard three acts of *La Bohème* rendered by a third-rate company whose café was an oven. The theatres were inferior to those of Alexandria, though the Casino at Phaleron was better than San Stefano. Once after the theatre they went into a café in Omonoia (the down-town square), underneath which was a 'whorish place' called 'Concert Alexandre le Grand'. Constantine glanced in for a minute or two: 'It looks a low place. It had a profusion of German girls.'

They never went further out of town than Kifissia (where they had tea) and Phaleron, where they stayed for a time and went on the beach. Nearly everyone they met was an Alexandrian, except Nicola Giannopoulo, 'a handsome young man', and Alexander Giro : and these were cousins of theirs.

It seems a pity that they were content to leave the scenery as a background, that 'the violet hills in the distance' never tempted them to explore their folds, then so unspoiled. But they probably disliked walking, apart from little strolls in the street, and Constantine (who had no visual sense) was always finding 'things of grace, grandeur or interest' : he even found the monument of Byron expiring in the arms of Greece 'a beautiful work'. Besides, during the six weeks' stay in Greece he was seven times 'unwell' – once 'suffering from terrible colics and vomiting all the time'. The water probably disagreed with him.

The most interesting entries in the journal are those concerned with Constantine's contacts with Greek men-of-letters. At the National Gallery he met Polemis, who was on its staff, a writer of fluent anodyne verse : 'a serious man, a little pompous. Said he knew my name. Very polite.' He certainly knew Cavafy's name, and was perhaps the writer (in the answers to correspondents in the *Attikon Mouseion*, 30 September 1891) of the first published criticism of any of his poems.[4] He bought a copy of Polemis' *Alabasters*, and called again.

He left a poem for publication with the review *Panathenaea* and, more important, he met Gregory Xenopoulos, the eminent author of plays and short stories – it is odd to think that, at the age or thirty-eight, this was probably the first time in his life that he met a distinguished author. 'He said he admired my poems, and I said I admired his "contes". And I sincerely do.' He saw him again, and found him 'a sincere and good man'.

Xenopoulos recorded his impressions of Cavafy, but after another visit. He found him 'very dark, like an aboriginal of Egypt, with the attire of a smart Alexandrian'; he referred to his 'slight English accent' (which others have spoken of as pronounced). Cavafy may deliberately have allowed Xenopoulos to think that he was a merchant, which was smarter than being a minor civil servant. 'Under the exterior of a polite and elegant merchant and linguist is carefully hidden the philosopher and the poet.' He found : 'his speech lively, and almost pompous and exag-

4. Savidis, *Bibliography*, p. 116 n.

gerated, his manner very delicate; and all his ceremonies and politeness strike an Athenian used to . . . the shy naïveté and simple awkwardness of our men of letters.'[5]

There were also literary conversations with amateurs: with Mataranga and Droumbis, 'fanatics for the *"kathaverousa"*,' that is, the artificially 'purified' language. There was also an evening with young men *'de la haute'* : Mavogordato, Melas, Negroponte, Paparigopoulos and Valaoritis. 'Consequently conversation was of society and its doings, of that Greek "upper ten thousand" which has many "groupements" (Athens, Alexandria, Constantinople, London, Marseilles, etc.) but is so closely bound together by marriage and social ties that all the important events and the leading names of one "groupement" are thoroughly known to the others.' His own city was following him indeed.

Constantine and Alexander returned to Egypt by way of Patras and Brindisi. Constantine enjoyed the railway journey to Patras and intensely admired the scenery of Diakophto and the exit of the Vouräikos gorge which he saw on the way. Of course he is recording 'occurrences' not impressions, and it is unfair to quote from this pedestrian journal – but it is difficult not to feel that here all the time is a man from Alexandria, where there is no landscape and where, if you disdain to look at the great *palazzi* of the banks, you have very little left to look at. 'The coast opposite Patras is picturesque' – it is one of the finest stretches of coast in Greece. It is more interesting to read: 'I noticed the very good quality of milk they give you' – a remarkable thing in the Greek provinces in 1901.

They left Patras after a day or two on a wretched ship, the *Scilla* with Prince Nicolas on board. Next day they had a long morning in Corfu. 'We walked about the streets which are narrow but have arcades, a great resource against the heat. So have some of the streets of Patras. We went for a drive up the eminences commanding the town of Corfu and must say that it was the most beautiful scenery that I ever saw.' They were among the first passengers back on the ship – the only indication of character in the journal, whether of Constantine's or Alexander's. We have no sign (nor from the Paris and London tour) if Constantine found his brothers good travelling companions.

5. Reprinted in *NE,* 1948.

This year John was going to France again, and Constantine and Alexander had gone down to Piraeus to spend a few hours with him.

Constantine found Brindisi 'a poor and ugly place'.[6] He records no interest in the Via Appia or the death of Vergil, which must have interested him had he thought about them; but we may recollect that an Alexandrian has plenty of associations at home, whether literary or historical, and very little else. But he did feel that he must 'pen a line about Prince Nicolas' departure. There is a Greek vice-consul (a ship-chandler, I think) in Brindisi, M. Cocotos by name. This personage came to meet the prince in a very ancient frock-coat, an antique top-hat, patent leather "scarpinia" and white stockings!'

They returned to Alexandria by the Austrian ship *Bohemia*; the weather, the food and the accommodation were all excellent, and Constantine read *Adam Bede*.

In October Alexander married Thelxiopi Theodorou; her family was of Lesbian origin and had considerable property in Lower Egypt. In January 1902 Aristides died in Cairo; he was buried there, but a few years later when his bones were dug up (as is usual in Egypt) they were transferred to the family grave at Chatby. John visited Constantinople later in the year, and Paul went on to London, where he hoped to get a one-act farce of his on the stage.

There is no journal for Constantine's visit to Athens in 1903. We know that he saw Xenopoulos again, and it is likely that there he wrote most of those prose pages published by Michael Peridis as *Ars Poetica*.[7] He appears, as we have seen, to have met Alexander Mavroudis, and to have fallen in love with him – perhaps without telling his love. His departure from Athens was succeeded by a 'cr. of lib.': Peridis reads 'crapulence of libations'. Mr Savidis' 'crisis of liberation'[8] is more acceptable – but where was the liberation? The poems on which 'A.M.' is written still seem under the influence of the passion. We should do better to adopt a reading suggested by Mr Savidis himself: 'crisis of libidinousness.' *Libido* was not in that year yet employed in a Freudian sense, but *Libidinousness* had existed in English at least

6. Cavafy, *U. Prose*, pp. 36–7.
7. ibid., p. 13.
8. Savidis, *Bibliography*, p. 144 n.

since the late seventeenth century. It certainly seems to fit better with the facts, so far as we know them.

At the end of 1904 John Cavafy was transferred to the Cairo office of his firm. The flat in the Boulevard de Ramleh must have become too large for Paul and Constantine, and they moved to a ground-floor flat, Rue Rosette 17. This was the 'good house' where Constantine received the 'Child of Art' in the following year. It was during 1904 that the first collection of poems was printed: copies were sent to Xenopoulos, to Michailides of the *Panathenaea* and to Alexander Mavroudis. Polemis did not get a copy, nor did any of the young intellectuals mentioned in the diary.[9]

Constantine's hernia declared itself in the spring of 1905. John wrote with the most tender (one might say exaggerated) compassion from Cairo (26 April): 'All my sympathy goes out to you . . . it is not a dangerous thing provided the proper prophylactic measures be taken . . . my heart literally aches at the injustice that this fresh trial should be put to you . . . I have insured two lives, without any increase of premium on account of their ruptures.' Constantine lived for another twenty-eight years with his.

His journey to Athens in 1905 was tragic. Alexander was seriously ill there (it appears that he had gone there for his wife's confinement).[10] Constantine has again left notes for a rough journal of his brother's last illness, this time full of medical details. Doctors differed, and Constantine as the one responsible person on the spot had to take authority. Was he to trust Christomanos or Vlavianos? And he could not allow the two doctors to meet. 'The idea that – if both were maintained – he would have to pay about £1 doctors' fees per day, and perhaps more would made him *griniazei* [complain] awfully, and would *synchysein* [upset] him much. It was an intricate position; and decisions had to be made on the spot, and I did for the best. 9.9.'05.'

Constantine arrived on Friday, 11 August, too exhausted to go down at once to his brother at Old Phaleron. He went next day. 'They kill me with kindness,' Alexander said of the women around him, and he wanted to move to Athens. Christomanos said that the move could not hurt him; it was desirable that he

9. ibid., pp. 217–18.
10. ex inf. Mrs Alcmena Malanos.

should be nearer medical attention. He was given the choice between hospital and a hotel, but chose hospital, 'for peace and
quiet'. Typhoid was finally diagnosed, and Alexander died on
21 August. As in the cases of Mikès and of his mother, Constantine leaves the end in silence.

Thelxiopi Cavafy with her infant daughter Helen went back
to her family at Menouf. Her mother reproached her for not
weeping enough: 'Have you forgotten Alexander?' Thelxiopi
seems to have been rather a favourite with her brothers-in-law;
a good-natured woman with a fat laugh which she often gave for
no reason at all. 'Like an idiot', her husband used to say. They
did not care for her family at all. There were parties for tombola
in the house of her mother, Mme Theodorou, who looked on
jealously, fearing to see an attachment growing up to one of her
other two well-dowered daughters on the part of Alexander's
brothers. No wonder Constantine seldom went. Paul speaks of
other of her relations with intense dislike: 'that Maximina
"Ashantee".' Thelxiopi, thought to be a *malade imaginaire*,
surprised them (and grieved them) by dying of tuberculosis at
Vévey in the summer of 1911. She had had *une originalité à
elle*.

Constantine continued to live with Paul; they shared a
'phaethon' in which they drove about. Mention is made of their
rings and ties; one is afraid they may have been rather 'flashy',
trying to prolong youth into middle age. In the evenings they
often went out together, drank port with their friends in cafés,
and played cards or backgammon.

In 1907 they moved to the Rue Lepsius, which later became
extremely dingy and ill-famed. We do not know the reason for
this move.

In the following years something must have gone gravely
wrong: the evidence is vague. Paul bitterly reproaches himself,
but without saying what he has done (which was of course well
known to his brothers). He had lived a life of prodigality, drink
and debt, and perhaps this was enough. It is possible that he
had been involved in unwise speculations, like two if not three
of his elder brothers. He certainly owed money. Mlle Marguerite Piot, daughter of Piot Bey, Paul's colleague at the
Municipality, is recorded to have said: 'I don't want to hear a
word about the Cavafys; my father was surety for a sum of money

for Paul, and as he defaulted, he had to pay it himself, a fact which he never forgot till his daying day.'[11]

Some kind of storm seems to have broken while Paul was absent on leave in 1908. On 6 June he writes from Orient Lodge, Buxton (the house of S. S. Brittain, who had traded in the Middle East) saying that he is in a dreadful *impasse*; he is then planning to return to Alexandria by way of London and Paris. Before leaving Buxton he fell ill, and there was talk of blood-poisoning.

In November he wrote from Paris – where like John and Constantine he stayed at the Grand Hôtel des Capucines. He got as far as Marseilles on his way home, and apparently fell ill again. Dr Karamanos, whom he saw there, told him that he needed a month's rest.

On 7 December he wrote to Constantine from Toulon. He owned that he was suffering for his own stupidity and folly. 'Instead of letting the matter grow bigger and plunging into the hands of strangers, money lenders, I ought *to make a clean breast of it*.' He pleads: 'Don't curse me, dearest, though I deserve it – even though *j'ai dévié, on peut toujours reprendre le bon chemin*.' He doesn't drink any more; '*that is quite finished*.'

Almost at once he was in acute money difficulties; the Municipality had sent him his travel allowance, but he ought to have been back at work by 5 January 1909. After consideration he decided to retire from that date (though at the early age of forty-eight), when he would be entitled to a pension, and ought to receive a 'gratification'. He had to beg for urgent help from his brothers while matters were being settled. For two days early in January he lived on nothing but his morning *café au lait*. 'I dreamed of food, that I was with you and you gave me pilaff and keftedhes.' The hotel-keeper began to look askance at him because of his unpaid bills. He said he still meant to return to Alexandria; he could work on the *Egyptian Gazette*, or as a broker or as secretary to a pasha.

In February he moved to Hyères, which was to be his base until his death, eleven years later. He still expressed a wish to return, but first wanted to pull himself together. There would be no good in his going at present. He lamented over what he had cost John and Constantine 'materially and morally and for

11. ex inf. Mrs Alcmena Malanos.

the loss of home and social position and 'I won't say the love, but the respect of my brothers'. He says: 'I wrote you why I didn't return, it's the truth and I say it again. I'm afraid . . .'

He was perhaps afraid of creditors, even of prosecution; he was certainly afraid of being looked down upon in his own city, where he had had such a success: 'I remember they said, socially or otherwise: "Paul Cavafy, he's the man you must know".' It is possible that he feared his brothers, though Constantine was never cold-hearted or unforgiving towards his family, and John was always generous. If there were anything else to fear, it has not been revealed.

In April he was afraid of 'PRISON'; he repeats the word again and again. He could not pay his hotel. He had no friends in Hyères, and even thought of applying for help to the English chaplain – on whom he could have had no sort of claim. But the season was over, and the chaplain was going away.

This crisis seems to have passed, but we find him in acute distress two months later in Paris. *'J'ai gâché ma vie . . . Quelle déchéance!'* He thinks with nostalgia of their charming *intérieur* at Alexandria. His greatest sin has been towards their mother, 'my one love in all my life'. Again he goes hungry, living on two rolls for ten centimes. When he passes a restaurant the smell of food brings on an *étourdissement*.

They are tragic letters, dreadful to have written and dreadful to have received. The heart aches for Paul, writing in his dismal hotel bedroom or (with some feeling of abuse of hospitality) in Cook's office or in the English bank, and on their writing paper. In his tiny scribble he repeats over and over again the same pleas – for the sake of their mother and of the brothers whom they have lost they can't forsake him. Constantine could not; one can imagine the ache of head and heart with which he found these envelopes with the French stamp and the heavy VAR postmark. It was probably on his return home in the afternoon, when office-work is over in Alexandria, bit vitality is at its lowest.

Luckily things went much better for Paul in 1910. He was introduced to General Horsey de Horsey, who took him on as his secretary. He seems to have served the old man, who died four years later at the age of ninety, in this capacity for the remainder of his life, sometimes living in at the villa, and sometimes coming out from Hyères. He was kindly treated by the

General: '*C'est enfin le type parfait du gentilhomme noble* . . . *his conversation is delightful.* He had known Grisi, Théophile Gautier and Bulwer Lytton and, now he was blind, Paul had to write his letters to such illustrious people as Queen Margherita of Italy and Kitchener. The old man had only one hand, but he played the piano charmingly with that.

Encouraged by an increase in prosperity, Paul seems to have begun to make for himself some kind of a social life, a dim reflection of that in Alexandria. He did a little journalism, contributing a column called 'Letters to Jack' to the *Riviera News*. He was insensitive enough to send a sample to Constantine: there are pleasant remarks about Hook, the manager of the English Bank, who had been very kind to him; honourable mention is also given to Miss Fowler and her scones at the English tearoom. There are observations on the prettiness of many door-knockers in the place, for Paul had a far keener eye than Constantine. The writing, however, is distressingly vulgar: 'I have been jabbering away to a fearful extent, and yet I have tons and tons of things to write about.' The signature is 'Prince Paul'. In his letters, he never says a word about his brother's poems, and there is no record that they were ever sent to him.

This and other journalistic activities – he later wrote a guidebook to Hyères – brought him in little money, but gave him free entry to the Casino, a stall at the theatre and other advantages. He was able to say he was *quite convalescent*, that he was unlikely to be in want of money, that he had *found peace*. Constantine was now writing long letters, and it was *a treat to read them* – it is a pity that we cannot share that treat. Perhaps they were returned to Constantine, and destroyed by him, on his brother's death.

In 1911 there was bad news from Egypt, and Egyptian news always looks worse in foreign newspapers. Martial law had been proclaimed, and Paul was anxious; but he knew his brother's caution: *you would not risk yourself in a rowdy crowd out of curiosity.*

It was consoling to hear of the downfall of old enemies. The Zervudachis who, in the younger generation, had dared *to cut a grande dame* like Haricleia, were ruined. (In fact their bank was ruined, and they had ruined other people.) One ought to be sorry at the blow to the Greek community, but it was impossible to feel personal sympathy. 'That bad man George Zervudachi got off lightly with two years' prison only.' That family had *une morgue of low breeding and birth*, men and women alike : *they could see you starring and not help, exulting in the sight*. They had had to *digest* Paul, because he had greater popularity than they with all classes. He remembered Manoly Zervudachi saying : *'Cavafy, je ne sais pas comment il fait – tout le monde l'aime – il trône.'* While as for Haricleia, *combien elle personnifiait* the lady of the highest society !

There were scandals at the Municipality too : 'that thief Chataway', who had done everything to make Paul leave the office, was in disgrace, and so was Palmer 'his doll'. George Zervudachi's suicide caused no grief, but there were other deaths, and a breakup of *ce petit noyau chic* where 'we' had been leaders of society.

It is probably the case that Paul was a good deal exaggerating the social importance of himself and his family at the turn of the century, but even if allowance is made for his nostalgia it does at least appear that the Cavafy family was keeping up its position far better than the remarks of Mme Coletti would make us believe, and it is unlikely that Constantine spent much time in those years in lamenting its come-down in the world.

In the spring of 1912 Paul travelled as a sort of interpreter with an English family, the Warde Aldams of Frickley Hall, Yorkshire. As *voyageurs en prince, regardless of expense*, they visited San Remo, Genoa, Pisa and Milan, and made a few days' stay at Bellagio. They went to Lugano, then through the St Gotthard and to Basel, then back to Bellagio, which Paul particularly enjoyed. There he breakfasted 'à la Cavafina' in his room off coffee, croissants and honey, while the English family went to the breakfast room. The family consisted of a rich man, his wife, and an agreeable son of nineteen. Next year Paul travelled through France with the father alone.

Then came the war years, and they were sad. More than once Paul thought of returning to Egypt. John had told him that he could live *decently* on his pension (and that this was *insaissisable* by his creditors), but the come-down would be too painful. Almost he would prefer to live in Port Said or Mansourah than in Alexandria. The old General died (but not before he had become a considerable bore). Life was more expensive and emptier, and *les heures pénibles* between four and seven in the evening were even sadder. Paul, living in a hotel, thought with regret of their house : the green entrance, red salon, Arabian salon, and mauve dining-room. His health was breaking; he suffered from asthma as well as tuberculosis. Probably letters went astray in war-time, for he was months without news of Constantine. By now it would perhaps have cost him too great an effort to return to Egypt. But Paul was not without his share of the family power of endurance. He had pulled himself together, he did not degenerate into a drunken Riviera scrounger; his life, though shabby-genteel, was not ugly but pitiful. To the last he sighed for the great days in Alexandria : a war later there were people in Alexandria who sighed for their great days on the Riviera. Constantine never mentioned him to his younger literary friends.

In a pathetic letter (in English) to John (3 October 1919) he thanks him for help; he seems to have used the money to buy warm underclothes. 'My cough still troubles me a good deal but my lungs do not give me pain. At my age, of course, I cannot hope a radical cure . . . I think of old days, when we were so happy together. Fool, fool, that I have been – I shall never, not till my dying day, forgive myself.'

He died at Hyères early in 1920.

VII   Reading and Working Life

Northern people who find themselves (for example) in Athens
or Alexandria on a weekday morning are often much surprised
and somewhat shocked at the sight of a number of men bustling
along the streets with briefcases under their arms, or sitting in
cafés. 'Does no one here do any work?' asks the Northerner,
thinking they ought, at this hour, to be behind their desks. And
yet these people are about their business: their employers have
probably sent them to see somebody about something – which
may entail a good deal of waiting – and their job is often 'to
do one thing and then another' like the traditional English lady.

Among such a crowd we may reasonably imagine Cavafy, in
the early years after his return from Constantinople. He had been
at the Daira perhaps (we do not know how much it occupied
his time). He probably looked in at the Irrigation Office every
day to see if they had anything for him to do, or possibly to hand
in a translation, supposing he had taken it away to do at home.
Though as yet he held no salaried post with them, there is no
reason to suppose that they never paid him for piecework; he
was certainly paid for odd jobs that Peter, Alexander and John
put in his way. At the end of the morning he might look into a
café to glance at the newspapers, and then the 'Fat One' would
receive him home with open arms.

After the siesta there might be a repetition of some of the
morning's activities. The Irrigation Office was closed, but
Aristides would want his help at the Exchange: the journal
about Mikès Ralli mentions an afternoon visit there. If Constantine were free, his mother frequently claimed his company,
if she drove out or went to San Stefano or to the Sporting Club.
There must have been some social obligations to fulfil, if there
were anything at all in Paul's contention that they were 'leaders
of society'. Certainly there were hours of that café life, which to
a Northerner would be insufferably boring: these were en-

livened by a little mild gambling; an interest that some of his fictitious characters were later to share.

His notes of gains and losses begin in 1887; after the end of the century he seems hardly to have betted at all, and the entry for many months is 'nothing'. He played cards (Lansquenet, bézique, whist) also baccarat and roulette; and he betted on lawn tennis, horses and bicycle races. He was a cautious gambler, and one is never surprised to find him ending a year fairly level. His character as a card-player is very much what one would expect. 'Resolution', he wrote in English: 'Never play when I have an *ennui* on my mind. I do not bestow enough attention and I lose invariably. This thing happened to me already . . . in June '98 when I played *pour divertir ma pensée* after the incident of Bur. and I lost £2.' 'Play should be conducted with much will and strength of character or it may prove a source of invariable loss . . . After a *déboire* . . . I played with Cos[ti] Ralli and lost 10 fr. Happily he was in a hurry to get the middle trick, or else through inattentiveness I would have lost more.'

The Cavafy family dined at home at half-past seven, and Haricleia liked to have Constantine beside her until after ten o'clock, when she began to retire for the night. Afterwards he might perhaps spend an hour of two with a friend, such as Pericles Anastassiades; and sometimes he slipped off at a late hour to the house in the Attarine quarter, or to a low café near the Custom House. The next day would suffer for this, if it began with a hangover, or mental perturbation, or a 'stomach derangement'.

Such a programme (an imaginary construction, but firmly based on documentary evidence) is hardly compatible with a life of 'study and contemplation'.

However, a man who is fond of reading will always find time for it, and we cannot imagine that Constantine was an exception. Every day could not have been so completely filled as that which we have outlined; there must have been free afternoons or evenings, or missed siestas. But it is unlikely that he ever read really hard after he left Constantinople, even that he put in the six or seven hours a day that a university man does, or should do. Though he had a wide culture and a great deal of miscellaneous information, there is no reason to exaggerate or to call him or his poetry 'learned'. He was, as Marguerite Yourcenar justly says, 'un lettré plutôt qu'un érudit'.[1]

Some notes of his reading survive, and are of considerable interest. His *scholia* on Ruskin are in Greek. They comment on *Selections from the Writings of John Ruskin*, first series, 1843–1860 (London, 1893) published by George Allen and Unwin. These notes were the property of the poet's friend, Pericles Anastassiades, whose sister Clio owned the copy of the book that seems to have been used. The notes were probably written during the three years that followed her acquisition of the volume (23 September 1893), for Cavafy uses the middle initial 'Φ.' Each note is preceded by the number of the extract from Ruskin on which it comments.

47. 'It is not by the mode of representing and saying, but by what is represented and said, that the greatness either of the painter or the writer is to be finally determined.' Ruskin, *Modern Painters* I. 1.*i*.2 §§ 1–4.

'Many works of the highest art have been achieved by the mode of representing and saying.' Cavafy.

48. 'Poetry is "the suggestion, by the imagination, of noble grounds for the noble emotions" . . . These passions in their various combinations constitute what is called "poetical feeling", when they are felt on noble grounds, that is, on great and true grounds. Indignation, for instance, is a poetical feeling, if excited by a serious injury; but it is not a poetical feeling, if entertained on being cheated out of a small sum of money' . . . Ruskin, *ibid.* III–IV, 1. §§ 13–14.

'This restriction of Poetry within the bonds of "noble grounds" is an error. The example of indignation "on being cheated out of a small sum of money" has been chosen with such craft – with such bad faith – that one agrees willy-nilly. But that is not the case with the second example: "In like manner energetic admiration may be excited in certain minds by a display of fire-works, or a street of handsome shops, but the feeling is not poetical, because the grounds of it are false" – why false? – "and therefore ignoble. There is in reality nothing to deserve admiration either in the firing of gunpowder,

1. Yourcenar, p. 18, n. 2.

or in the display of the stocks of warehouses." These words demand an energetic protest. Wonderful works can be created in the framework of the "street of handsome shops", not out of the nobility or not – empty words – of the "street" etc., but out of the feeling or sentiment in relation to the street, that surround it all like a circle.' Cavafy.

57. 'The artist who *represents brutalities and vices*, and not for rebuke of them is absolutely condemned (by Ruskin, *ibid.* III. iv. 3, §§ 5, 6, 9). Precisely the first characteristic of the artist is disregarded – calm of spirit and complete pardon in the face of things which rouse the indignation and *rebukes* of the vulgar. The true artist writes in serenity of soul.

> *N'as tu pas fouillant en les recoins de ton âme*
> *Un beau vice à tirer comme un sabre au soleil?*[2]

The true artist does not have, like the hero of a myth, to choose between virtue and vice; but both will serve him and he will love both equally.' Cavafy.

In general Cavafy shows himself hostile to Ruskin's priggishness and dogmatism. Ruskin (123) asks of Murillo's beggars: 'Do you feel moved with any charity towards children as you look at them? Are we the least more likely to take an interest in ragged schools, or to help the next pauper child that comes in our way, because the painter has shown us a cunning beggar feeding greedily?' (*Stones of Venice*, II. vi.§ 60).

'What is the meaning of these questions? What have they to do with Art? Is it the task of Art to answer such questions?' Cavafy.

He notes (on 151, *Stones of Venice*, I. xx §§ 15–17) 'The absolute condemnation (by Ruskin) of that kind of architectural ornament which "takes for its subject human work" is absurd and unjustified.'

This is the only passage purely concerned with the plastic arts on which Cavafy has commented; his lack of visual sensitiveness confined him otherwise to passages that bore upon literature and a few ethical or diadactic pages.

When (181) Ruskin writes (*Modern Painters,* v. ix §§ 16–23) of

2. Verlaine, *Sagesse*, I.iii, 11, 41–2.

a 'vulgar regard for appearances', Cavafy replies: 'What is important for our happiness is not how others judge us but how we think they judge us. In our fancy, not in reality, consists the basis of our life.'

Ruskin (187) praises extravagant reverence for a superior, such as that of 'that old mountain servant, who, 200 years ago, at Inverkeithing, gave up his own life and the lives of his sons for his chief – as each fell, calling forth his brothers to the death. "Another for Hector!"' (*Stones of Venice*, II. vi. §§ 13–17).

'The "old mountain servant" is worthy of pity and revulsion. The praise of submission which precedes and is developed again a few pages later, is immoral.' Cavafy.

201. 'You talk of the scythe of Time and the tooth of Time. I tell you, Time is scytheless and toothless; it is we who gnaw like the worm – we who smite like the scythe. It is ourselves who abolish – ourselves who consume . . .' Ruskin, *A Joy for Ever*, §§ 73–5.

'When we say "Time" we mean ourselves. Most abstractions are simply our pseudonyms. It is superfluous to say "Time is scytheless and toothless". We know it. We are time.' Cavafy.

'This speed and the many and wonderful inventions are not useless. Rushkin (202. *Modern Painters*, III. iv. 17 §§ 35–8) makes the mistake of considering them as an end, when they are merely means. They are of service to his Utopia. The "cloud pace" that shortens distances and extends the interdependence of mankind hastens the coming of the kingdom – *Kingdom of Peace* – that the poets of bygone ages prophesied and the poets of the day await full of hope with their eyes fixed on the horizon where one morning will appear the walls and towers of gold.' Cavafy.

This romantic idealism is notably absent from the poems of maturity: Cavafy lived long enough to foresee the dangers of 'cloud pace'.

On 204 (*Modern Painters*, II, iii, 1. 2. §§ 8–10) he comments: 'For the vision of the Beautiful "purity of heart" is not indispensable. Beauty is infinite compassion which ignores the small distinctions of just and unjust. In writing this I am speaking of the narrow "purity of heart" which the author's tone indicates, not the broad conception of the two words, which forgives, justifies and includes everything, because it understands.'

Another set of notes, of considerable interest, was given by Cavafy to Pericles Anastassiades : the notes are in English, and comment on a critical article (as yet unidentified) on Hardy's *Jude the Obscure.* Cavafy had evidently read the book with attention, and Mr Tsirkas makes the interesting suggestion that *Walls* (15) owes something to the following passage.[3]

'It was not till now, when he found himself actually on the spot of his enthusiasm, that Jude perceived how far away from the object of his enthusiasm he really was. Only a wall divided him from those happy young contemporaries of his with whom he shared a common mental life; men who had nothing to do from morning till night but to read, mark, learn, and inwardly digest. Only a wall – but what a wall !' (Part II. ii).

As against this identification of a 'source' (which may have some truth in it), it may be objected that many readers[4] see in the Cavafian walls more a symbol of *claustrophobia* than an obstacle – we are more conscious of them as shutting in than as shutting out. Moreover they seem to have grown up insensibly, unlike Jude's barrier. But the wall is so common a symbol in literature, that no example of it is specially worth comment. And if Mr Tsirkas' theory could be followed (as we see it cannot) Cavafy would have had 'nothing to do from morning to night but to read, mark, learn and inwardly digest' until the age of twenty-nine. Few of Jude's happy young contemporaries were so privileged.

At about the same time Cavafy wrote a number of notes on Gibbon : these are in English, and attached to the text by paper-clips. Some of them are worth quoting.

On the suppression of books of alchymy by Diocletian (Gibbon, II. xiii) he wrote : 'It may not be "the effect of *jealous* tyranny" but it certainly is an act of tyranny, and it is by no means "to be applauded as an act of prudence and humanity". Any interference of the State with the literary or scientific pursuits of the people [*sic*] is tyrannical in its origin, its essence and its effects.'

---

3. Tsirkas, *Epoch,* pp. 264 ff.
4. It is temerarious to differ from so great an authority as Mr Malanos but honesty compels me to admit that I cannot accept his reading of *Walls* (see p. 62), though this may be a confession of invincible ignorance.

His observations upon the Christians should also be noted, because there is some controversy over the poems about Julian the Apostate. On one hand it is argued that Cavafy could not have been on the side of the barbarous, superstitious Christians, on the other that he must have been against the priggish, Puritan Julian.

It is most unlikely that he felt any religious or anti-religious bias. He never renounced Orthodoxy, and died with its last sacraments – whether from conviction or as a formality – though in life he had been far from *pratiquant*. On the other hand, he can have had no more than an aesthetic feeling for Julian's ancient gods, a feeling never so strong (for example) as Swinburne's. He was, of course, highly critical both of Julian and of the Christians; he was on neither side, and treated both sides with irony, while he regarded them both as integral parts of the Greek past.

When Gibbon (iv. xxiii) says that Julian's edict 'may be compared with the loose invectives of Gregory', Cavafy, an admiring reader of St Gregory of Nazianzus, replies that 'some of these "loose invectives" are very noble and lofty' and that 'no artist – the word is not misplaced here – had spoken so boldly before.'

Another passage about the Christians shows Cavafy's reference to the sources. 'Eunapius accuses (*Vit. Max.*) the monks or Christian priests as having been privy to the treacherous surrender of Greece; and it is a matter for considerable surprise that Gibbon did not quote the curious passage . . . It is true that the words of Eunapius do not carry any extraordinary weight. Certain doubtful remarks of Zosimus about the respectable (pagan?) Antiochus, his two good (pagan?) sons Musonius and Axiochus, and his bad (Christian?) son Antiochus, and the fact that the great majority of the inhabitants of Greece proper were pagans, is all the extraneous evidence that comes to corroborate Eunapius' accusation. But it is insufficient, and the accusation can be disregarded.

Still we are not used to so much favour – or justice – to the Christian cause from the pen of Gibbon.'

Perhaps the most personal note is that on Attalus. 'The degraded emperor,' says Gibbon (v. xxxi) 'might aspire to the praise of a skilful musician.'

Cavafy wrote : 'The subject for a beautiful sonnet, a sonnet full of sadness such as Verlaine would write –

"Je suis l'empire à la fin de la décadence."[5] Lost in the Gothic tumult and utterly bewildered, a melancholy emperor playing on the flute. An absurd emperor bustled in the crowd. Much applauded and much laughed at. And perhaps at times singing a touching song – some reminiscence of Ionia and of the days when the gods were not yet dead.'

Michael Peridis gives us an account of Cavafy's library : he visited it in 1941–2 and gained the impression that it was no longer intact.[6] This was so strongly my own impression when Alexander Singopoulos showed it to me two or three years later, that I abandoned my intention of making a catalogue. Nothing can fairly be deduced from gaps : books may have been lost or sold, and we know in any case that Cavafy's reading was much more extensive than his library. He borrowed books from his brother John or from Pericles Anastassiades or other friends, also from the library of the Patriarchate and later, after its foundation, from that of the Municipality. Etienne Combe, the last European director, told Peridis that Cavafy used to borrow collections of inscriptions, and Mr Malanos learned from the same source that he was continually asking for the historical works of Bouché-Leclerq.

His own books, mostly acquired between 1890 and 1903, have not very much to tell us. The fifty ancient Greek volumes include more than one edition of the *Iliad* and of Philostratus, also Mackail's selections from the Greek Anthology, and Headlam's edition of Theocritus, Bion and Moschus. There is no copy of Callimachus.

The only Latin authors (mostly in French or English translations) were Suetonius, Sallust, Catullus, Propertius and Marcus Aurelius.

Most of the original sources for Ancient and Byzantine history are lacking, though Cavafy's acquaintance with them is sufficiently demonstrated by the poems. He had, however, Gibbon, Mommsen (in English), Grote, Mahaffy's *History of Egypt under the Ptolemaic Dynasty*, and Bevan's *House*

5. Verlaine, *Langueur* (ed. Pléiade, p. 370).
6. Peridis, pp. 65 ff. But Cavafy's books seem always to have been few and haphazard (Sareyannis, p. 35).

of Seleucus. He had also some historical works dealing with subjects outside his field, such as Macaulay's *History,* Andrew Lang's
Historical Mysteries and Southey's *Life of Nelson.*

In the category of *belles lettres* we may note Matthew Arnold's
lectures on the translations of Homer, and Gilbert Murray's
history of ancient Greek literature. He also had *Sartor Resartus*
and Walter Pater.

Of his modern Greek books in prose, Psycharis' *Journey* and
Röidis' *Idols* show signs of careful reading.

Goethe's *Faust,* Schiller, Dante (in English) and Tasso's
Gerusalemme Liberata (in the original) were the only representatives of German and Italian literature. Victor Hugo was there,
in many volumes and several editions, and almost alone as a nineteenth-century French poet, apart from Théophile Gautier,
Leconte de Lille and one or two others. But for the grand siècle
there were collected editions of the greater poets, and he also had
works of Rabelais, Montaigne, Voltaire, Fénelon and Rousseau.

He had the complete works of Shakespeare and Milton and of
many English poets of the eighteenth and nineteenth centuries;
also Longfellow and Poe. Shelley and Keats were absent, though
he translated Keats' *Lamia* and Shelley's poem to the Moon : *Art
thou pale for weariness.*

There was a quantity of French and English novels : Balzac,
Stendhal, Flaubert, Zola and his beloved Anatole France, Paul
Bourget and an almost completely uncut set of Pierre Loti – also
Defoe, Fielding, Jane Austen, Scott, Dickens and George Eliot,
not to speak of Ouida, Marion Crawford and a lot of detective
or adventure stories. There was a whole set (1899–1905) of the
periodical *Black and White.*

There was some modern Greek history and some of Politis'
work on folk poetry. There were two well marked editions of Solo-
mos, and some volumes of Palamas were also marked. There
were the poems of Valaoritis, also those of Paraschos, Drosinis
and other less-known poets.

After 1920, when he was better known, Cavafy began to receive inscribed copies of their works from other writers; he did
not always take the trouble to cut them. The *Nepenthe* of
Karyotakis – a poet in some ways influenced by him – remained
in a virgin state, in spite of the warmth of the inscription.

He had, by then, for some years past taken little interest in contemporary life and letters; though he kept up to date in his knowledge of modern Greek poets, always ready to defend his own first place. 'If we examine his knowledge of literature and his general information, we shall find they come to a stop round 1900,' says Mr Malanos.[7] 'After that date his interest in anything new or contemporary gradually dwindled to nothing. In the 17 years that I knew him [1916–1933] he never bought new books and any that he borrowed were historical works necessary to his poetry.' Again he writes: 'His curiosity is of a kind that refers rather to the past . . . The past is the necessity of life to his poetry, the "atmosphere" of his imagination.'

'To me,' said Cavafy, 'the immediate impression is never a starting-point for work. The impression has got to age, has got to falsify itself with time, without my having to falsify it.'

'I have two capacities: to write Poetry or to write History. I haven't written History, and it's too late now. Now, you'll say, how do I know that I could write History? I feel it. I make the experiment, and ask myself: "Cavafy, could you write fiction?" Ten voices cry "No!" I ask the question again: "Cavafy, could you write a play?" Twenty-five voices again cry "No!" Then I ask again: "Cavafy, could you write History?" A hundred and twenty-five voices tell me "You could".'[8]

What sort of history would he have written? One is tempted to imagine that if he had asked: 'Cavafy, could you write historical fiction?' a thousand voices should have answered 'Yes'.

> Partly to verify a period's descriptions,
> Last night I picked up and began to read
> A volume of Ptolemaic inscriptions. (73).

He had a passion for accuracy of detail. In the poem *Alexandrian Kings* (35) Caesarion was *Dressed in pink tinted silk*. 'I dressed him in pink silk,' he said, 'because at that time an ell of that sort of silk cost the equivalent of so-and-so many thousand drachmas.'[9] And he was of course aware that the Roman world knew Coan silk, long before the silk of the mulberry-leaf-fed worms of China was known to the West.

He was reproached by the eminent botanist Yannis Sareyannis

7. Malanos, *Cavafy*, p. 45.
8. Malanos, *Memoirs*, p. 148.
9. Malanos, *Cavafy*, p. 33.

for the unseasonable roses at Pella, on the table of Philip V of Macedon on the day when he heard of the defeat of Antiochus at Magnesia (54), a battle which took place in December. Sareyannis reminded him that important news travelled quickly at that date, for there were various kinds of telegraph, extensively described by Polybius; Philip's dinner must therefore have been in December or early January.

Cavafy replied :[10] 'It's a historical possibility. It's the case of a king with much wealth at his disposal, for whom the means of having these flowers in winter was easy. Apart from this, there was a winter export of these flowers from Egypt. We know Egypt exported roses to Italy in the winter. In the first century Italy became independent, through the improvement of agriculture, and had its own *rosae hibernicae.*'

Nevertheless, his accuracy was a matter of charming detail, and it is seldom that he exhibits – as, for example, in the poem on Demetrius Soter (89) – a historian's view of cause and effect. So shrewd an investor as he was must have had some grip on economics, but there is little sign in him of any interest in politics.

Though he eagerly sought for information from his friends, he was not open to correction as a true scholar must be, but clung obstinately to an idea; this might be no fault in a historical novelist. This obstinacy increased with the years, and Mr Malanos[11] relates how Cavafy would not accept defeat in an argument with Christopher Nomikos (a genuine historian) about Byzantine feudalism. Nomikos made an appointment, and brought texts to prove his point; Cavafy did not turn up, nor did he come later to glance at the texts, though they were left for his perusal. Another anecdote recorded by Mr Malanos[12] shows that even when Cavafy was right in his main contention, he could overstate his case with such force as to crush any opposition.

A friend had maintained that all historical events were explicable in terms of economics; Cavafy said that there were other causes as well; for example the religious sentiment. ' "How do you explain the fact that in 600 A.D. in Egypt half the population went into monasteries, a remarkable fact – don't interrupt

10. Sareyannis, pp. 36–7.
11. Malanos, *Memoirs*, p. 186.
12. ibid., p. 205.

me!" (No one had interrupted so far.) "And it wasn't only the poor who went, but people from all classes of society." ' He was able to impose belief in his date and his figures, just as some people manage to convince us of the truth of their statistics, if they state them with sufficient force.

We shall find that his best historical poems are generally the re-creation of an atmosphere, or the poetical expansion of a character from a line or two of an ancient text, or a deduction from a face on a coin. Many of the people through whom he reveals his vision of the ancient world are his own inventions, and they are by no means his least successful characters: in his way he wrote historical fiction.

As we saw, Cavafy entered the Third Circle of Irrigation as an unpaid clerk in 1889, apparently towards the end of that year, and that he obtained a salaried position in the spring of 1892. Mr Tsirkas (who had not seen the other documents, which were perhaps not then available) was inclined to discount a letter of 19 April 1894, copied in Cavafy's hand, in which his superior asked for an increase of pay for him, and said that he had worked in the office for four and a half years, two and a half without pay. Mr Tsirkas supposes this to be something of a pious fraud, contrived to serve the poet: 'Who could ever believe that Cavafy worked as an *unpaid* clerk for two and a half years?'[13] But if no one could have believed this statement, there could be no point in making it, and we have seen that it is fully corroborated.

A letter (signed Gail W. Foster) of 1 May 1894 repeats the request, adding: 'Being a Greek he can never expect to get into the permanent staff.' We do not know if he had abandoned his British nationality (which seems improbable at that date – on 11 December 1890 we found him described as 'Greek by birth but an English subject') or if this is merely a reference to his 'Greek birth'.

Mr Tsirkas shows us that Cavafy's life as a clerk in the Irrigation Office, which was shut in the afternoon, was perfectly compatible with his work as a broker,[14] for the Exchange was busiest in the afternoon, and it was hardly more than a stone's throw from the house in the Boulevard de Ramleh. It may be

13. Tsirkas, *Epoch*, pp. 228–9.
14. ibid., p. 230.

that Cavafy preferred to think of himself as a broker than as a minor government official, a being lower in the social scale; and no doubt he wished to add to his salary by other work. It is, after all, a common experience in Greece and Egypt to find people, whose official work ends at one or two o'clock, adding very considerably to their earnings in the later part of the day.

It is however a mistaken (though an ingenious) conjecture[15] that he entered the Exchange in 1895 with his friend Pericles Anastassiades: we have seen that he worked there with his brother Aristides at least from 1888. We do not know at what date he left off work there: as early as 1898 his brother Alexander – who had a great gift for upsetting his family, although they were so fond of him – tried to get Constantine to give up his work as a broker, but he certainly continued after that year. We may doubt if his poetry really gained anything from the 'feverish atmosphere of the Exchange with its decline, panic, disappointments and lightning catastrophes',[16] but he told Nanis Panayatopoulos that he had picked up the phraseology of the people and the petite bourgeoisie as an eavesdropper in the cafés or on the Exchange.[17]

Cavafy started at the Irrigation Office with a salary of seven pounds (Egyptian) a month: a sum not so contemptible as it sounds, for it must be multiplied many times to represent its value in money of today, and life in Egypt was cheap in those years. Mr Tsirkas has made a careful survey of the outward circumstances of Cavafy's office life,[18] and provides a complete table of his salary with the periodical and irregular raises that he received. By July 1912, when he signed a five-year contract, he was receiving £E22. In 1917 he renewed his contract for another five years and was sub-director of a section. With an augmentation in 1919 his salary reached £E33.6, and in April 1922 he retired. His leave is also recorded: six weeks at first, later two months, and finally something between ten and twelve weeks a year. Apart from making the journeys already mentioned, he always passed his leave in Egypt.

On his 'Character Roll' his superiors testify to his capacity;

15. Tsirkas, *Epoch*, pp. 231 ff.
16. Seferis, *Essays*, p. 246.
17. Tsirkas, *Epoch*, pp. 224 ff.
18. Halvatzakis, *passim*.

but 'a trifle over-deliberate' was the verdict in 1913. The last report (recommending him for head of section) mentions his usefulness in teaching English to junior members of the staff.

A personal account of the last years of his office life has been provided by Mr Manolis Halvatzakis, who was able to interview Cavafy's former colleague, Ibrahim el Kayar.

'I worked eight years with him, under his orders, and when he retired in 1922 I took his place.

'Did I see him after his retirement? I once visited him at his house in Rue Lepsius to ask for some information. He received me very politely but didn't ask me to come in. I had gathered that he had a visitor. I left the Irrigation in 1925 to work in Cairo.

'Where were the offices of the Third Circle of Irrigation? At Ramleh station, over what is now the pâtisserie "Grand Trianon", once "Athinaios".

'Cavafy had undertaken the control of correspondence in the European office (there was an Arabic office too). If I'm not mistaken, I've heard he owed the place to Zananiri Pasha. Our chief accountant, Michael Zananiri, who had considerable influence, belonged to the Zananiri family; so did Gaston Zananiri, later a friend of the poet's.

'Cavafy began his life in the office as a "copyist", copying letters, as at that period, twenty-two years before my time, they hadn't got typewriters. He knew English very well, and was acting chief of section, when I knew him first, he looked after the composition of answers to correspondence. Once his English superior found a mistake in a report of his on a messenger: "A tall man, Mr Cavafy, not a long man."

'Don't imagine that our office was large. Under Cavafy's immediate orders were only two people: two typists, Constantin Naggar, a man of Syrian extraction, and myself. But Cavafy corrected not only our letters but those of other offices. He would correct the same letter many times and insist pedantically on marks of punctuation. He had a separate room of his own. When a letter was brought him to see if it were properly written he didn't correct it by hand, nor call for the man who wrote it. He sent little notes from his own to the neighbouring offices: "Please see me. Please telephone me." The clerk came and he showed him that a comma was missing. He gave him the letter back and

sent him to another room to fill it in, and to come back and hand
it over with the added comma. Often he tormented us. My
former colleague Constantin Naggar won't hear Cavafy spoken
of . . .[19] I got on very well with him, though he thoroughly
flustered me : "Mr Kayar, Mr Kayar" . . . Once I lost my temper
and said : "Mr Cavafy, you penelopise my work." This verb
delighted him.

'Generally the correspondence was late. Cavafy let the time
go by, and then was in a hurry when it was near closing time.'

'Was Cavafy deliberately late with his work in order to sabo-
tage the English ?'

The Ustaz Kayar smiled.

'Cavafy was very cunning. He covered his desk with folders,
opened them and scattered them about to give the impression
that he was overwhelmed with work and, when the time came
for us to go off, he collected them and put them back in their
place. "I am very busy," he constantly replied on the telephone.
On very rare occasions he locked himself into his room. Sometimes my colleague and I looked through the keyhole. We saw
him lift up his hands like an actor, and put on a strange expression as if in ecstasy, then he would bend down to write something. It was the moment of inspiration. Naturally we found it
funny and we giggled. How were we to imagine that one day
Mr Cavafy would be famous !

'He didn't trust us, his assistants. He shut up the file with the
documents in a safe, fixed on the wall, and took the key with
him. But in the morning, as he was late and we were left without anything to do, he had to send us the key by his servant,
Mirgani.

'Our hours were from eight to half-past one, five and a half
hours in all. But Cavafy never arrived at work before half-past
nine, and managed to hide his unpunctuality from the English
directors, who were themselves late. Though his house was very
near, he took a cab and paid three *grosia*. He never used the lift,
so as not to be scolded for being late. He climbed the stairs
thoughtfully, ready to give some sort of justification if he were
seen. What bothered him was his hat . . . sometimes he tried to
get rid of it, or to use it as an alibi. If he happened to meet one of

19. Perhaps Naggar was the author of the anonymous letter (Peridis,
pp. 60–1) denouncing Cavafy for laziness.

the messengers when he arrived, he gave him his hat to hang up in his office before he himself came. He had us well trained to cover up for him. "If the Englishman comes before me and asks where Mr Cavafy is, you'll say he was here, and has just gone down about something urgent. If he asks after ten minutes, subtract them from the half hour and say Mr Cavafy will be back in twenty minutes." He said "the Englishman", and he meant any of the English that we had in the Irrigation, six or seven in the senior posts . . .

'His servant Mirgani often came, nearly every day, sometimes with the key I have mentioned, and sometimes about shopping. Before he bought a chicken he took it to show his master and get his approval, and the office was full of cackling. Cavafy carefully examined the wings and perhaps took a sample so that he could see afterwards if his chicken had been changed. He was very close-fisted. Sometimes we got up some small charitable collection among us. He never contributed even a millième : "I have too many calls ! I have too many calls !"

'He cut his cigarettes in two. Not because he suffered from the throat, who told you that? At the time I knew him he was not yet ill. He always smoked half cigarettes, perhaps as a health precaution, perhaps from stinginess.

'Was he alcoholic? No, we never formed the impression that he drank . . . What were his relations with us? Strictly official. He was rather talkative and meticulous about anything to do with our work . . . about other things he was taciturn. He showed great reserve, above all to us his Egyptian colleagues, and usually had no conversation with us, perhaps out of disdain. I only remember that once we talked about the religious question, and he told us the religions were "cooked". Not a word about politics : he seemed neutral or rather indifferent . . .

'In what language did we talk?

'English, of course. Did he know Arabic? Classical Arabic not at all. He couldn't read or write. Colloquial Arabic? Nor that either. Is it mentioned in his file and on his identity card that he knew Arabic? But it's not true. I assure you he knew very little Arabic, just enough to talk with his servant Mirgani about the chicken. He hardly ever made use of his sketchy Arabic; besides, he liked to appear a foreigner.

'What do you say? That Cavafy heard an Arabic song in a

house of ill-fame and was influenced by it in a poem? But since he didn't know Arabic...

'Was Cavafy interested in Arab men of letters? He certainly wished them to know him. I know he met the poet Sháouki at "Athinaios". A mechanic at the Irrigation brought them into contact, the technical sub-director, Mahmoud Sami. They were half an hour together and talked French. Not about Arabic poetry or their own work, as one might expect, but about Molière, whom Sháouki much admired, as Cavafy himself told me.

'Had Cavafy an Egyptian wet-nurse as a baby? Did he suck Arab milk? But who knows this for sure? Someone wrote it lately?[20] Where did he get the information and what is his motive for bringing it up? To explain how Cavafy remained faithful to Egypt and its people and "repaid his nursing"?'

Here Mr Kayar raised his arms and cast up his eyes.

'Mon Dieu! Nonsense! So Cavafy is being made out an enemy to British imperialism?'

Mr Kayar raised his arms again.

'*Mon Dieu! Ce n'est pas raisonnable! Impossible!*'

And he continued: 'If Cavafy really hated British imperialism, he should have been cold and formal with the Englishmen in Irrigation, he wouldn't have had much talk with them. But he was as talkative and agreeable with the English, of whom he was very fond and they were fond of him, as he was laconic with us about anything outside our work. They made a difference between him and the rest of us and treated him with great respect. He must have fascinated them, for they often called him into their offices, and got him to talk about historical matters. They listened to him going on and on about the Ancients... The English were delighted with him. Only the Inspector General did not encourage him and kept him at a distance. Once I happened to hear the Inspector General making a severe remark to him in the passage: "Mr Cavafy, you are not giving satisfaction." And Cavafy, thoroughly upset, replied without a touch of irony: "I shall try to give you satisfaction. I shall try to give you satisfaction."

Mr Halvatzakis remarks that this visit to Ibrahim el Kayar,

---

20. i.e. Mr Tsirkas.

at his flat in Anfouchy, overlooking the eastern harbour, was only the second visit in his life to an Egyptian house : 'This shows how far some of us are, for all our good feeling, from the life of the Egyptian people.' He wrote this in 1967 : it is probable that Cavafy never entered an Egyptian house at any time. Mr Halvatzakis continues : 'We Greeks of Alexandria for the most part – if we except the younger generation, and those who have lived in Cairo or the villages, don't know Arabic well. Some don't know it at all.' He spoke in French or English with Mr el Kayar, helped out by Arabic-speaking friends.

Mr Malanos added a confirmatory note : 'From the way he spoke to his servant Mirgani, at the time when I used to visit him, Cavafy only knew the few indispensable Arabic phrases in common use employed by most European Alexandrians . . . for communicating with their servants.' In an autobiographical note contributed by the poet to *Nea Techne* in 1924, he wrote : 'I know English, French and a little Italian' – his rudimentary Arabic was not worth mention.

VIII   The Poems before 1911

As Cavafy himself caused a line to be drawn dividing his poems written before 1911 from those written after that date, it seems natural to make use of it, though it need not be given undue significance; there were several dates in his literary development.

It will be best to set out briefly and clearly the facts about the early poems: considered as publications, they fall into three groups:

(1) Poems published in periodicals – in Leipzig, Alexandria and Athens.

(2) Six poems issued on broadsheets by the poet between 1891 and 1904.

(3) Two pamphlets printed for private distribution: that of 1904 contains fourteen poems, and that of 1910 increases the number to twenty-one.

A poem may, of course, belong to one or two or all three of these groups, one method of publication not excluding another. In 1910 Cavafy invented a new and original system for the dissemination of his subsequent work, which must be discussed in its place.

Another cross-section of poems must be made, in accordance with their later fate.

(A) The 'canon', i.e. poems included in the posthumous edition of 1935. Here twenty-four poems 'before 1911' appear, and their retention was sanctioned by the poet. They include the twenty-one poems of the 1910 pamphlet, together with two poems written in that year, *The town* (23), and *Satrapy* (24), also *Walls* (15), which had been issued a year after its composition as a broadsheet in 1897, but had been left out of the pamphlets.

(B) 'Rejected poems' – these are the three poems printed on broadsheets that the poet did not allow to reappear, and twenty others that had been printed in periodicals.

(C) Unpublished poems – these poems, 75 in number (62 belonging to the period before 1911) remained in manuscript, and were not included by Alexander Singopoulos in his collected edition because they lacked the poet's sanction, although he included *On the outskirts of Antioch* (154) which was not printed till after Cavafy's death.

They are certainly not all the poems that Cavafy wrote and omitted to publish : between 1891 and 1925 he kept a register,[1] which contains many titles to which no extant poem corresponds. The preservation of several has been deliberate. Some are marked : 'Not for publication, but may remain here.' The poem on Nichóri may remain 'as autobiographical'. Others perhaps survive because Cavafy found them too good to throw away, if not good enough to print. On one poem he writes : 'It does not deserve to be suppressed.'[2] Some of them may have been kept for further revision, or because they contained a line or phrase worth keeping : we know something about the slow gestation and frequent revision of many pieces in the canon. A few may have been held back as being too outspoken, and some because they do not fit in with the pattern which his work was gradually assuming. Some of the unpublished poems are as worthless as those 'rejected', some are worthy of a place in the canon; and as a class they have not been repudiated by their author.

Though a slow developer, Cavafy was by no means a late beginner. He had been writing since 1882, as an English note of 1906 proves :

'By postponing and repostponing to publish, what a gain I have had!

'Think of . . . trash (at the age of 25, 26, 27 and 28) of Byzantine poems and ma[n]y others which would disgrace me now.

'What a gain!

1. Cavafy, *UP*, p.ia'.
2. ibid., notes *passim*.

'And all those poems written between 19 and 22. What wret[ch]ed trash!'[3]

In this note, which is harsh but by no means unjust, he seems to date the beginning of his poetical career in 1891; he draws the first line there, repudiating all that had gone before. There seems to have been a brief pause in 1886-7, at the age of 23 and 24, when he was getting back into Alexandrian life. But he must have been writing continuously between 1887 and 1891. As we have no poems dated between 1888 and 1890, we may suppose that some of them have come to us in a later version and the others have been destroyed.

In 1886, the year following his return to Alexandria, Cavafy had a burst of publication. In January and April he published prose articles in a Constantinopolitan paper; the first was on coral in mythology, the second on 'the inhumane friends of animals', that is, on their inhumanity to man.

Meanwhile, between March and August, he published three poems in the Greek paper *Hesperos* of Leipzig. They were *Bacchic*,[4] *Vain, vain love*[5] – a free version of Lady Anne Barnard's *Auld Robin Gray* – in Greek decapentesyllabics and with a Greek setting for the story; also *The Poet and the Muse*.[6] Most if not all of this work had probably been written at Yeniköy.

To these 'rejected' poems we may add six that were never published in his lifetime. There are two translations, one of a French song (as yet unidentified), another of *Sigh no more, ladies* from his projected version of *Much Ado about Nothing*. Two poems about Constantinopolitan life have a faint interest. Reference has already been made to *Dünya Guzeli*. *The veïzades to his love*[7] is another dramatic monologue. The young Phanariot aristocrat (*veïzades*) regrets that class separated him from the fisherman's daughter. It is straining these poor little poems (and the lyric *Friends, when I loved*) to cite them as evidence of Cavafy's bisexuality at that time (though it may well have exist-

3. Savidis, *Bibliography*, p. 107. The notes to this chapter, already profuse, would be intolerably increased were I to acknowledge individually every debt to Mr Savidis' *Bibliography*.
4. Dalven, p. 177.
5. ibid., pp. 178-80 (there entitled *A love*).
6. ibid., p. 181.
7. Cavafy, *UP*, p. 5.

ed). There is a gentle, trivial little poem *Nichóri* – surprisingly affectionate when we remember how unhappy his family was at 'cette affreuse Yenikeui'.

A more reasonable deduction from these poems (and from the note on the destroyed 'Byzantine poems') is that Cavafy's earliest source of inspiration was Constantinople. His return to his birthplace must have shown him that Alexandria was the centre of his world, the Hellenistic world, which had roots in Hellas and offshoots in Byzantium. This he gradually discovered in the years before 1911. Afterwards he was no more to write about themes beyond his range, such as *Shem el Nessim*[8] and *The daughter of Menkera*[9] (1892) and the other 'Egyptian' poem, *27 June 1906, 2 p.m.*;[10] or the two Lohengrin poems[11] (1898), or the poem of the clock at Bruges *Vulnerant omnes ultima necat*[12] (1893) or that about Hamlet, *King Claudius*[13] (1899) and others.

The year 1891 was marked by renewed journalistic activity and also by the beginning of his chronological register, in which he records the revision of various poems during that summer. His most interesting composition in the year is the sonnet, *Builders*.[14] This has been called the first 'Cavafian' poem, for here for the first time is found that strange ironical compound of stoicism, pessimism and cynicism that underlies so much of his work. The builders begin in good spirits, everyone contributes what he can; then the storm comes, the work is left to collapse and – anyway – it was destined for a happy future generation that will never exist.

Seferis remarks on various features characteristic of Cavafy that here appear in a rudimentary form: the use of myth or parable, the *rime calembour* and *enjambement*.[15] The two last, of

8. Dalven, pp. 184–5.
9. Cavafy, *UP*, p. 23.
10. ibid., p. 149.
11. ibid., pp. 103–7.
12. Dalven, p. 187.
13. Cavafy, *UP*, p. 113; Savidis and Keeley, pp. 6–13.
14. Dalven, p. 182.
15. Seferis, pp. 294–5. As an example of *rime calembour* (ibid. p. 231) he quotes Derême:

> et pas plus tard que
> Demain je te lirai les œuvres de Plutarque.

course, cannot be illustrated without the Greek text; they were displeasing to the editors of the *Attikon Mouseion* who, nevertheless, recognised an interesting new voice, and were glad to print the sonnet.

Cavafy also issued it as a broadsheet for private distribution, perhaps to mark his emergence as a poet : at last he had produced a poem which was not contemptible, and which had the cachet of publication in Athens. Probably this was his first publication of the kind, and there was nothing singular about the method. Mr Savidis[16] cites many contemporary instances of poems issued in this way, and it has not yet fallen completely into desuetude.

In the decade 1891–1900 we know that he composed 148 poems in all; he published 32 poems (four on broadsheets), and forty of the surviving unpublished poems are of this time. Only seven out of the 148 reached the 'canon'.

Walls (5), probably printed in 1897, was his next broadsheet; it is issued with John Cavafy's version and perhaps marks the beginning of a collaboration between the two brothers, which was continued on John's side until 1917 or even later, though no other of his versions was printed : they are not very good.

Constantine wrote to John, with questionable sincerity, on 21 September 1898 about his version of the 'rejected' poem *Addition*,[17] which he found 'a true gem' – but the gem had a bad flaw. 'On all accounts the *smallest care* must come out. It's a thing I didn't say in my poem, a thing I had no intention of saying and that I don't believe I shall ever write. It's a dangerous *statement* that, so to speak, *commits* the *recueil*, and is opposed to the spirit of previous poems already translated (*Walls*, *The windows*, *Lohengrin*, *The suspicion*, which are a complaint against unhappiness), and it will perhaps be opposed to the spirit of other poems that will be translated. Finally, it's a *profession* which I in no way want to make.

'What I wrote is that "I don't examine" whether I'm happy or unhappy. That is, for the moment, the moment of writing, I describe the idea that gives me pleasure, that I'm not a number in the *Addition* [he seems to mean the sum of conventional

16. Savidis, *Bibliography*, p. 119.
17. Cavafy, *Prose*, p. 239. The text is in Greek, the words italicised are as quoted. Dalven, p. 200.

bourgeois people], and doing this, I don't examine if I am happy or unhappy. I don't examine, not I don't care.

'The substitution of other words for *smallest care* will, I know, be very difficult, but it must be done. I wonder if the rhyme *share* could be used? *Whether I have or I have not a share of happiness* or *Even if I have not a share of happiness.* But these phrases are bosh.'

The next privately printed poem, *Prayer* (3), issued as a broadsheet on 23 October 1898, exhibits the typical Cavafian theme of the *mater dolorosa*. Seferis[18] sees in it the trickery of the immortals, but it is better to see (with Mr Savidis) the double incapacity of mortals to be helped and of immortals to help. The Virgin is sorry that the sailor's mother comes too late to pray to her, when he is already drowned. So in *Interruption* (10) the beneficent actions of Demeter and Thetis are misunderstood and thwarted by Metaneira and Peleus, who snatch their babies from the fires in which the goddesses were attempting to give them immortality. Thus in *The funeral of Sarpedon* (18) Zeus could not prevent Patroclus from killing his son Sarpedon; the best he could do was to arrange that Phoebus should look after his body and bury it in 'rich Lycia'. And when Patroclus in his turn was killed, Zeus was sorry for *The horses of Achilles* (20) who wept over him, and he regretted that he had exposed these immortal creatures to mortal griefs.

A broadsheet published in 1898 and entitled *Ancient Days* contained two poems later rejected: *The tears of the sisters of Phäethon*[19] and *The death of the Emperor Tacitus.*[20] The former had been written in 1892, the latter four years later: we can observe a great progress towards bareness of style achieved during those years, but apart from this the second poem is only remarkable for its failure to come to life. Cavafian themes are there: age, death and nostalgia – but it is not animated by a breath of inspiration. This is the summit of Cavafy's Parnassianism (already responsible for a number of lifeless sonnets). If Mr Malanos had chosen this as an example of his prosaic history no one could have quarrelled with him – least of all the poet, who vainly tried to revise it in 1906.

18. Cavafy, *Prose*, p. 301.
19. Dalven, pp. 202–3.
20. ibid., p. 201.

It has to be owned that the output of Cavafy's first decade as an adult poet was not extremely distinguished. The 'rejected' poems well deserve their rejection. It is disturbing to find the very worst of these, *Ancient tragedy*[21] written in 1897, the year after *Walls*. No one is likely to blame Messrs Keeley and Savidis for their choice of only three of the unpublished poems of this period for inclusion in their translation.

Julian at the Mysteries[22] (1896) is an interesting poem, that may be considered with the later poems on this subject. The other two are cynical, amusing, untragical commentaries upon tragic themes. In *When the watchman saw the light*[23] (1900) we have an ironic reaction to the prologue of the *Agamemnon*: the bourgeois of Argos are glad the waiting is over, but do not expect too much of the king's homecoming: no one is indispensable. *King Claudius*[24] (1899) is a similar poem about *Hamlet*: the comments of the world of Elsinore after the fact, when Fortinbras is firmly established on the throne with Horatio's collaboration (Cavafy anticipates Professor J. I. M. Stewart). This is a long-winded poem, and was perhaps chosen by the translators for the amusement of the English reader rather than for its intrinsic merit.

> In all the houses of the poorer folk
> Secretly (they were afraid of Fortinbras)
> They wept for him. For he was mild and gentle,
> A peace-maker (the country had much suffered
> From all the battles of his predecessor).

Hamlet, of course, had been the victim of an hallucination.

> The Prince was always a complete neurotic.
> And when he was at Wittenberg
> Most of his fellow-students thought him mad.

At the end Horatio is reported as making a feeble apology for Hamlet, in which the ghost is dragged in as evidence. No one believes a word of it.

21. Dalven., pp. 204–5.
22. Keeley and Savidis, pp. 2–5.
23. ibid., pp. 14–15.
24. ibid., pp. 6–13.

So therefore, while they listened to him speak,
The great majority of them in their hearts
Were sorry for the good king . . .
But Fortinbras, who profited by it all
And easily won the power and the throne,
Gave great attention and authority
To all the sayings of Horatio.

'*Candles* is one of the best things I ever wrote,' said Cavafy in a
letter to his friend Pericles Anastassiades,[25] some time between
1895 and 1897, and it is as the author of *Candles* (6) that he
has been esteemed by many people who otherwise did not care for
his work.

The days of the future stand before us
Like a row of little lighted candles –
Gold and warm and lively little candles.
The days past remain behind,
A sad line of snuffed out candles;
The nearest are still smoking,
Cold candles, bent and melted.
I don't want to see them, the sight of them hurts me,
And it hurts me to remember their first light.
I look in front at my lighted candles.
I don't want to turn round and see and tremble
At how fast the dark line is growing,
How fast the snuffed out candles are multiplying.

It would appear that a second line – rather a wavy line – is to
be drawn between the years 1899 and 1901 or later. Produc-
tion is very much slowed up. He had seen Xenopoulos in 1901
and had received judicious praise. He had visited Athens, which
was to him his intellectual capital. His artistic conscience was being further refined, and there were to be no more 'rejected'
poems; the register records more rewriting at this time.

It is unnecessary to search in his biography for causes, and to
argue *post hoc propter hoc*. His family bereavements between
1899 and 1902 may have been unconnected with his poetic
development. The emotional crisis through which he went in the

25. Savidis, *Bibliography*, p. 123.

autumn of 1903 may have been an effect rather than a cause : the excitement of finding new powers of expression may have upset his equilibrium more profoundly than the meeting with the young man of the sheep's eyes and the green great-coat.

Between August and 25 November 1903 Cavafy wrote (in English) that document printed with the misleading title of *Ars Poetica*[26] – beginning it in Athens, and finishing it after his return to Alexandria.

'After the already settled Emendatory Work, a philosophical scrutiny of my poems should be made.

'Flagrant inconsistencies, illogical possibilities, ridiculous exaggeration should certainly be corrected in the poems, and where the corrections cannot be made the poems should be sacrificed, retaining only any verses of such sacrificed poems as might prove useful later on in the making of new work.

'Still the spirit in which the Scrutiny is to be conducted should not be too fanatical . . .

'Also care should be taken not to lose from sight that a state of feeling is true and false, possible and impossible at the same time, or rather by turns. And the poet – who even when he works most philosophically, remains an artist – gives one side, which does not mean that he denies the other, or even – though perhaps this is stretching the point – that he wishes to imply that the side he treats is the truest, or the one oftener true. He merely describes a possible and an occurring state of feeling – sometimes very transient, sometimes of some duration.

'Very often the poet's work has but a vague meaning : it is a suggestion : the thoughts are to be enlarged by future generations or his immediate readers : Plato said that poets utter great meanings without realising them themselves . . .

'My method of procedure for this Philosophical Scrutiny may be either by taking the poems one by one and settling them at once – following the lists and ticking each on the list as it is finished, or effacing it if vowed to destruction : or by considering them first attentively, reporting on them, making a batch of the reports, and afterwards working on them on the basis and in the sequence of the batch : that is the method of procedure of the Emendatory Work . . .

'If a thought has been really true for a day, its becoming false

26. Cavafy, *U. Prose*, pp. 36–69.

the next day does not deprive it of its claim to verity. It may
have been only a passing or a short lived truth, but if intense
and serious it is worthy to be received, both artistically and
philosophically...'

On 23 February 1902 Xenopoulos[27] had written to thank him
for a collection of his 'marvellous poems'. This was in manuscript, in red and black ink. It was apparently in some sort of
loose-leaf folder, for Cavafy asked (as Xenopoulos says in his
article of 30 November 1903) 'to take back an old poem, which
he thought was not "worthy of the honour to be in my hands".'[28]
'I was very sorry, but as I respect the idiosyncrasies of poets,
I sent it back to him.' It was *The Tarentinians carouse*.[29]

Xenopoulos' article of 1903 appeared in the *Panathenaia* at
the time when Cavafy had just finished or was finishing the *Ars
Poetica*. Xenopoulos had received twelve poems (thirteen, including *The Tarentinians*). This he must have returned with
special regret, for it had been (if he remembered rightly) the first
poem to call his attention to the unknown name of Cavafy and
make him look with interest at all subsequent poems with his
signature. He remarks on the 'danger' of coming to admire a poet
whose verses only appear from time to time in periodicals, and he
presents eight for the admiration of his readers – he says justly
that 'with his microscope' the poet shows us things that we never
imagined; the thoughts are (as Cavafy said) to be 'enlarged' by
the readers.

Until the first pamphlet of 1904 appeared, Cavafy sometimes distributed his poems thus, in manuscript or in cyclostyled
copies. He had cultivated an elegant and easily legible calli-
graphy, to which his superiors in the Irrigation bear witness, but
it had very likely been developed for literary purposes.[30] It was
not a family characteristic, for among the Cavafys only John –
also a poet – wrote a good hand; and the letters of the three
school-friends show that it was not learned in Papazis' Academy.
When he gave away offprints of published poems or broadsheets,
it would appear that they had generally undergone correction.
He feared the finality of print for his work, which he was

27. Savidis, *Bibliography*, p. 99.
28. *NE* 1963, p. 1444.
29. Dalven, p. 206.
30. Savidis, *Bibliography*, pp. 150–1.

continually rewriting, revising and suppressing; he would never consider any poem as having reached its final form, and even when it had been printed he treated the printed version as a manuscript, and continued to work on it.[31]

At the end of 1904 he gave fourteen poems to be printed: the result, no doubt, of his 'Emendatory Work'. On 7 May 1905 he wrote to Xenopoulos:[32] 'Last year I printed 14 poems in one pamphlet. The reason was that I am often asked for copies of my verses, and in this way it is easier for me to give samples of my poetry. I didn't send you the pamphlet sooner, because this year I intended to print another fuller one – of about 25 poems – and to send you that. But for various reasons the plan was put off till next year, or perhaps 1907.

'Therefore I send you the 14 poems, of which you already have the majority.

'The pamphlet has not been sent to a newspaper or periodical.'

The same day he wrote to Michaelides of the *Panathenaia*:[33] 'I have a poem – *Waiting for the Barbarians* – that I should like to be published in the *Panathenaia*.

'It has not been printed in any paper or periodical. I printed it in a pamphlet last year – with a few other poems of mine – simply for distribution to those who sometimes ask me for my verses. The pamphlet has not been sent to any paper or periodical. The two copies I send you are – one, for you to take out *Waiting for the Barbarians* for printing (if you like), and the other *personally* for yourself, *not* for communication to the *Panathenaia*.'

In fact Xenopoulos and Michaelides come sixth and seventh on Cavafy's list of recipients, immediately following his family and Pericles Anastassiades, when the pamphlet was to be sent out in April 1905[34] – it bore the date 1904 but was probably not ready that year.

It appears, then, that this pamphlet is for private circulation, to take the place of manuscript copies etc., that it contains a choice out of a larger body of work, and that a second and fuller

---

31. Savidis, *Bibliography.*, p. 152 n.
32. ibid., p. 40.
33. ibid., p. 41.
34. ibid., p. 217.

edition is on the way. This, however, was delayed. Mr Savidis enumerates the possible reasons. Perhaps Cavafy could ill afford to pay for the publication – though this was by no means expensive. Secondly, his health might be an impediment: he was much worried by the hernia that declared itself in April 1905. The 'confessions' reveal that he still had psychosomatic 'de-rangements' and it is not impossible that he drank too much. But the main reason must have been artistic; he found (and his regis-ter proves it) that he wanted to do a great deal of re-writing.

Cavafy still had no thoughts but of private distribution, and a passage written by him in 1907, entitled *Independence*, is very much on the point. There had been a discussion in the *Panathenaia* about the general indifference to literature in the modern Greek world, and the difficulties of the writer.[35]

'But side by side with all that is disagreeable and harmful in the situation, which becomes felt every day, let me note – as a piece of comfort in our woes – an advantage. The advantage is the intellectual independence which it grants.

'When the writer knows pretty well that only very few volumes of his edition will be bought . . . he obtains a great freedom in his creative work.

'The writer who has in view the certainty, or at least the probability of selling all his edition, and perhaps subsequent editions, is sometimes influenced by their future sale . . . almost without meaning to, almost without realising – there will be moments when, knowing how the public thinks and what it likes and what it will buy, he will make some little sacrifices – he will phrase this bit differently, and leave out that. And there is noth-ing more destructive for Art (I tremble at the mere thought of it) than that this bit should be differently phrased or that bit omitted.'

This passion for verity already appeared in the *Ars Poetica*. As Seferis[36] well said: 'Strange lesson: the poet who has been accused above all other of insincerity, gives us a lesson in sin-cerity. It may be the case that, as a man, he had little tendency towards confessions; but as a poet he seems condemned to the truth, to his truth, on pain of death.'

Sincerity being a literary as well as a moral virtue, it is not to be

35. ibid., pp. 164–5.
36. Seferis, *Essays*, p. 348.

achieved until we have learned exactly how to express our thoughts and feelings – and parents and educationists too often forget that no child, however honest, can be sincere about any complicated thought or feeling – it is a thing to be worked for. That must be the main reason for Cavafy's frequent revisions, and he was bringing his language nearer to demotic speech.

The arrangement of the 1904 poems was not chronological, but subjective (that is, in the order in which it pleased the poet to present them); the pamphlet of 1910 was a second edition in which seven other poems were inserted, some between poems already printed, and four new poems at the end. The first pamphlet was issued in an edition of a hundred copies of which about sixty were given away; they seem to have been sent out on five occasions, mostly to relations, or to friends or acquaintances in Alexandria. After a third distribution he notes : '7 are to be kept as useful – for examples – for the new edition'; and during the fourth distribution : '9 are to be kept so that I can have them to give away while the new edition is being made, then they may be destroyed or remain as documents of chronology and that sort of thing.' Two hundred of the second pamphlet were printed; the distribution began in April 1910 and in that year fifty-five copies were given away, and others in the years that followed, the last going to Alexander Singopoulos in 1915 – this is the first appearance of the name of his friend and future heir.

It is, however, the case that Cavafy might have found it difficult to issue his poems in a saleable edition had he wished to do so. He would, of course, have had to pay for their publication (a very much larger outlay than for the economical pamphlets), and it would have meant an almost certain loss. In his Athens journal on 23 June 1907 he wrote : 'Tsocopoulo[37] says that it is considered quite an achievement to have been able to publish a volume and realise not profit but no loss from it.' There was no literary agent to find him a publisher in Athens, and Stephen Pargas of *Grammata* in Alexandria did not start publishing until 1914.

After the Asia Minor disaster in 1922 he remarked to Mr Basil Athanassopoulos[38] (and, as the latter tells me, in all seriousness) that this meant the loss of centres where Greek men of letters

37. Cavafy, *Prose*, p. 268.
38. *JHS*, 1933.

8. Cavafy, 1932. Athens

9. The salon, Rue Lepsius

10. 'The poet's corner', Rue Lepsius

could dispose of their books. In the same way he said to Mr Malanos (who tells me that Professor Dawkins was utterly mistaken in believing this to be a joke):[39] 'As a good merchant advertises his wares for sale, so a poet must advertise the line that he is offering.' Again he said: 'People are busy, very busy, so that there's no time to take an interest in one's neighbour. So it's our duty to talk about ourselves and our works, till we have made people stop, and leave their work and attend to us . . .' He added: 'I think I've read that somewhere' – but it sounds like his invention.[40]

It is unlikely that he ever thought of publicly advertising his work for sale, or ever pictured it in the bookshops of Smyrna; he probably wished to retain the amateur status preferred by persons in good Alexandrian society when they practised the arts. He was certainly too businesslike and probably too stingy to throw his money away on a certain failure. Moreover, while his reputation was forming, he wished to choose his readers, and it is not likely that he would have cared for the idea of unbought copies of his poems gathering dust in bookshops or being fingered contemptuously by his enemies.

Between the two pamphlets Cavafy was beginning to become known, even in his own city, for the Alexandrians were finding out that they had a poet. In July 1907[41] a young doctor who was also an intellectual, Paul Petridis, called on him. Petridis belonged to a circle consisting of the young, *Nea Zoë* (*New Life*): their age-limit was thirty, so Cavafy could not become a member. He was no doubt pleased to be sought by the young, and perhaps not displeased to enjoy the position of an independent and honoured guest rather than that of a full member of the association. He often attended their meetings.

On 23 April 1909 Petridis lectured on him at their centre to a limited audience. He commented (among other poems) on *Windows*, *Walls* and *Waiting for the Barbarians*, strongly emphasising Cavafy's pessimism. It is supposed that the lecture was largely inspired by the poet himself, or at least that it had his *imprimatur*. It was subsequently published in the journal of this group.

39. Malanos, *Cavafy*, p. 33.
40. Tsirkas, *Chronology*.
41. Peridis, p. 92 n.

We cannot see, with Mr Tsirkas,[42] any irony or revenge in the
fact that poems such as these, and *Thermopylae* and *Treachery*,
were read for the admiration of an Alexandrian audience by a
'deuteroclassatos' and the son of a notable 'deuteroclassatos' for
we have seen that there was nothing in them to offend their
sensibilities. Nor were there any 'shocking' poems: Cavafy had
not yet published anything that could be called erotic; nor do we
know that he had written anything, apart from the five unpublished poems of 1904. If anyone was annoyed, it was because a
'demotic' writer was being commended. There is a pleasant tale
that Petridis' father was somewhat disturbed, because he thought
that his son meant to speak not about Constantine Cavafy but
the scandalous Paul – poor Paul, however, was now in exile,
and it was not love but money that had been his ruin.

At this time there was another turning point in his poetical
career. His friend Sareyannis[43] wrote: 'Cavafy was not born a
poet, he became one with the years. He found his final form in
1911. Afterwards he felt that only from that date had he become
"Cavafy". In the first period of his life, which can be called "pre-
Cavafic", he experimented and tried to write poems, but he was
not yet master of his Art. Of these attempts he considered some
genuinely successful and printed them in the first pamphlets that
he published later: to this category belong: *The town, Satrapy,
Monotony, There he is!, The footsteps, Bacchus and his crew.*
Others he judged to be absolute failures and denied that they had
been written by him. And there were others – at least so it seems
to me – over whose acknowledgment he hesitated for many years.
To this last category belong most of the poems "before 1911".
There was something in them that did not satisfy him. He
systematically avoided speaking of them or letting people speak
of them to him. He was continually trying to correct them. He
caused the pamphlets of 1904 and 1910 to disappear very
quickly, and not only did he refrain from giving them, but he
looked out to see if it were possible to take back those that were in
circulation. I do not know of which of the two pamphlets he was
speaking of when he said that 12 or 15 copies were circulating on
which he had his eye and knew where they were to be found.

42. Tsirkas, *Epoch*, p. 277.
43. Sareyannis, pp. 128–9.

It was precisely because he regretted the publication of his first
collection in 1904 and 1910 – so it seems to me – that Cavafy
adopted the system of F[euilles] V[olantes]. By this new method
he was able to make all the changes he wished and to reprint a
poem or – if need be – to take one out of one of his collections
without rendering useless the other poems that had been bound
up with it. It was only after many years had passed and he
thought that a whole series of his poems had been stabilised and
did not admit of further change, only then did he decide to bind
them together in collections.'

The information given by Sareyannis is not entirely accurate.
He might have added several poems to those which he mentions; it was not only the pre-1911 poems that Cavafy continued to correct, but also poems written after that date; he did
indeed smuggle away extra copies of the 1904 pamphlet, but he
distributed nearly all of that of 1910. Nor was he unwilling to
answer questions (and sometimes by letter) about the early
poems from people interested in them; of whom Sareyannis was
not one. He was interested in the historical poems, and bored
with *Candles* and other early works. Nevertheless his general
contention is true; Cavafy initiated a new method of issuing his
work at this time, and his register records the re-writing of poems.
But above all it is the new maturity and unity of his subsequent
work that must strike us.

Of the early historical poems, some fail to hit their mark (such
as *The death of the Emperor Tacitus*); in the erotic poems there
is a touch of sentimentality, perhaps because they seem to be
near in time of composition to the actual experience that inspired
them – and the Denshawi poem may also be called sentimental.
If the 'suggestion' in *Thermopylae* or *Che fece . . . il gran rifiuto*
is to be 'enlarged by future generations', rather too much work
has been left to those future generations. Dare we say that the
poet may have hoped that he was writing a 'great meaning'
without realising it himself? Some of the better poems (*Windows*,
Monotony, even *The town*) might have been written by some
other poet influenced by Baudelaire and Verlaine, if he were a
poet good enough; they lack Cavafy's personal voice. This voice,
however, is unmistakably heard on several occasions, in the last
lines of *Waiting for the Barbarians*, for example, or in the
Trojans:

> Achilles comes out into the trench before us
> And frightens us with his loud shouts.

It would seem that the truth lies between the two schools of Cavafian interpretation, or rather that (with a little moderation of language) they can be reconciled. Critics as authoritative as George Seferis and Mr Dimaras see a real cleavage about the year 1911. On the other hand Mr Malanos says that in Cavafy's work from first to last there is a unity of mood, of mental climate and of *Weltanschauung*[44] – and it would be hard to deny this. On this view, the heading 'before 1911' was simply adopted as a convenience; after that year the poems appeared on *feuilles volantes* each automatically dated by the year of publication. The earlier poems could not so be arranged – and there might be legitimate difference of opinion as to how they should be dated – they were therefore lumped together in this way, and the fact has no other significance.

He may be quite right, and it may only be coincidental that it should happen in this year. What is undoubtedly true and significant is that Cavafy at about the age of forty-eight had yet another literary coming-of-age. Such a thing had happened in 1891, and again between 1900 and 1903. But since 1891, when he wrote *Builders*, he had recognisably (though not invariably) been the poet he was to be.

The consensus of good critical opinion is that he grew better and better as a poet, and that his latest work was his best. Critics who have based their interpretation of him on an over-valuation of his earlier work are not unnaturally led into eccentricity of one sort or another.

Professor Baud-Bovy praised the earlier work, in which he thought a need for reticence made the poet express his abnormality and his consequent *malaise* in terms of appealing imagery : he regretted that the inter-war years, with their relaxation of tabus, should have encouraged him to admit into his later poems a *louche* and boring company of workmen or shop-assistants in pink or mauve shirts. Here is an over-development of the 'Cavafy of the Letter T', *ante litteram*.

Mr Tsirkas' theory of the 'political Cavafy' leads him into

44. Malanos, *T.*, pp. 19–20. Of course he cannot mean to include the 'trash' before 1891.

equally strange statements..[45] 'In 1911 – both in his preceding life and in his work – Cavafy drew a line, dug a trench . . . His ideals and ambitions take another direction. His *Weltanschauung* is altered. Above all he ceases to be "worldly" (κοσμικός), both in the literal and metaphorical senses of the word. He stops worrying about social matters. He makes a truce with "the bad men". Gradually he adopts their way of seeing things. He jeers at and makes fun of ideals for which he once suffered . . . At one time his symbols were those of heroic struggle, personages from Mythology, from the Trojan and Persian wars, and the Roman and Byzantine empires. Now they become aesthetes. Hellenistic Antioch began to beckon him in 1896 [*Julian at the Mysteries*]. Decadent Alexandria had surrounded him from childhood. He has resisted them long enough. He'll "go" – with all his outfit and all his armour!'

This is not quite an accurate account of the work. It is true that mythology has more or less disappeared from the 130 later poems of the canon; but the three poems inspired by Greek history: *Who fought for the Achaean League* (105), *In Sparta* (139) and *Come, O King of the Lacedaemonians* (146) – are nobly stoical. Moreover there are, proportionately, more poems on Roman and Byzantine themes than there were among the twenty-four poems before 1911. However it is indeed the case that Cavafy has profited by the discovery that the outer Greek world is his true country, and all who love his work must rejoice at this.

Mr Tsirkas' word κοσμικός cannot (as he uses it) be adequately translated by a single word for both its 'literal and metaphorical senses', in the 'metaphorical' sense (and in common parlance) it is the equivalent of *mondain*. It is true that Cavafy went out less in later life, but he never ceased to be interested in society and its doings, and was far from cutting himself off from it. The death of his mother in 1899 of course put an end to the receptions in the Boulevard de Ramleh on the second and last Fridays in the month. Family mourning for her death, and for the deaths of his brothers George (1900) and Aristides (1902), must have disrupted his social life; and when Alexander died (1905) the part of his social activities revolving round that household came to an end. Then in 1908 followed the disgrace

45. Tsirkas, *Epoch*, pp. 16–17.

and exile of Paul, who may have been his chief link with the world – for Paul had great social success. He repented of having harmed John and Constantine 'materially and morally' – which may include 'socially'. The story of Piot Bey suggests that the Cavafys lost caste after his débâcle. After his departure Constantine lived alone, and a man in his late forties who is without family and does not greatly care for female society is likely by degrees to become 'the world forgetting by the world forgot'. Not that Cavafy wished to be much forgotten.

The other meaning of the word κοσμικός may perhaps be rendered (more or less) as 'socially conscious', in the sense in which left-wing intellectuals use (or used) those words. There is, however, as we have seen, no reason to believe that Cavafy was in any way opposed to the establishment before 1911 : after that time his complete collaboration with it is attested by abundant evidence and living witnesses. It is to be doubted if he ever jeered at ideals – Mr Basil Athanassopoulos tells me how respectful and tender he was of the enthusiasms of the young, even when they were for men and causes not his own. There is no suggestion that he himself ever suffered for other than literary ideals, or ever cherished them.

IX Alexandrian Literary Life

During 1910 Cavafy made a change in his method of issuing his work. The pamphlet form seems to have dissatisfied him as too permanent; it was harder to correct poems thus printed, and harder still to suppress any should he wish to do so. He therefore combined, as it were, his earlier broadsheet practice with that of the pamphlet: 'Whenever a poem appeared in a periodical the poet would order a set of offprints primarily for distribution to the select few whom he considered his serious audience, or he would distribute broadsheets in advance of publication, and then he would gather the remnants of these "printings" into folders, with each new offprint or broadsheet clipped to the last and the title of the latest poem added by hand to a list of the contents.'[1] Cavafy continued to give away individual broadsheets to those who wished to complete their collections, but more often he distributed his work in these folders, which he always kept up to date.

'By 1917 when the single clip in each folder could no longer bear the load of further broadsheets, Cavafy withdrew some of the earliest poems and had them sewn into booklets that were intended to accompany the ever-expanding folders, now given new life.'[2] He repeated this process, and at the end of his life there were two sewn booklets, one containing 68 poems arranged thematically, and another 69 more recent poems in chronological order. 'Chronological order', as applied to his poems, is only a relative term, as Sareyannis has written: 'Cavafy himself told me he never managed to write a poem from beginning to end. He worked on them all for years, or often let them lie for whole years and later took them up again. His dates therefore only

1. Keeley and Savidis, p. x. A more detailed account is to be found in Mr Savidis' *Bibliography*. Mr Malanos notes that very few poems were first issued as offprints.
2. ibid.

represent the year when he judged that one of his poems more or less satisfied him.'[3]

Cavafy kept piles of broadsheets, offprints etc. in a room at the back of his flat, which he called the 'bindery'. It had very probably been Paul's bedroom. 'It was an empty room which (says Sareyannis) 'when I saw it, had all the shutters open and the full sun on it. It was full of plain tables (or perhaps trestles with boards on them). There were his poems in various piles, and each pile represented a poem. When he decided to send a collection of his last poems, he sat down the day before and with his own hand added to the printed title of contents the titles of poems he had added in the meantime. The next day, while he collected his poems and put them into chronological order, he went back and forth each time to his desk and erased, and added the variant he then preferred.'[4]

If the poems were to be sent away, he often waited for the opportunity to send them by a trusted hand. He distrusted the post office, or rather his own power to get efficient treatment from it. He preferred to get the papers despatched by a practical man, such as the publisher Stephen Pargas. Even then he often wished that no one in Alexandria should know who the recipients were to be, and he would try to send his poems in a roundabout way, addressing them to friends or relations of those for whom they were intended, choosing persons who were themselves unknown, and not men-of-letters.

Mr Savidis observes justly that Cavafy's changes in the method of distributing his poems in each case correspond with his periods of literary advance. We may, however, doubt that they also mark off decades in his life. It is not unlikely that consciousness that he was approaching his thirtieth year made him do his best for *Builders* by issuing it as a pamphlet. It is often said that those who have not published by the age of thirty will never publish at all. It is perhaps a coincidence that the emotional disturbances of 1903 shortly followed his fortieth birthday, and the last change began less than ten years later. In 1911 he seems to take farewell of symbolism in two of his most exquisite poems, *The god abandons Antony* (26) and *Ithaca* (32). These poems, though still symbolist, are highly individual, and the voice of

3. Sareyannis, p. 33.
4. ibid.

Cavafy is unmistakably heard in each of them. In the first there is his own blend of stoicism and epicureanism; in the second a touch of cynical humour.

> When suddenly at the hour of midnight there is heard
> An invisible company going by
> With exquisite music, with voices –
> Do not uselessly lament
> Your luck that is giving way, your work that has failed,
> Your life's plans that have all ended in despair.
> Like a man long prepared, like a man of courage,
> Bid her farewell, the Alexandria that leaves you.
>
> Above all, do not deceive yourself, do not say that it was
> A dream, that your hearing was mistaken;
> To such empty hopes you must not condescend.
> Like a man long prepared, like a man of courage,
> As befits you, who were found worthy of so great a city,
> Go firmly to the window,
> And listen with emotion, but without
> The complaints and entreaties of a coward,
> As a last rapture listen to the sounds,
> To the exquisite instruments of the mysterious company,
> And bid her farewell, the Alexandria that you are losing.

The source of this poem is that passage in Plutarch which (in North's version) also inspired some lines in *Antony and Cleopatra*. 'Furthermore, the selfsame night, within little of midnight, when the city was quiet, full of fear and sorrow, thinking what would be the issue and end of this war: it is said that suddenly they heard a marvellous sweet harmony of sundry sorts of instruments of music, with a cry of a multitude of people, as they had been dancing and had sung as they use in Bacchus' feasts, with movings and turnings after the manner of Satyrs: and it seemed that this dance went through the city unto the gate that opened to the enemies, and that all the troupe that made this noise they heard, went out of the city at that gate. Now such as in reason sought the depth of the interpretation of this wonder, thought it was the god upon whom Antonius bare singular devotion to counterfeate and resemble him, that did forsake him.'

The other poem, even if it should owe a suggestion to Petronius' *Exhortatio ad Ulyssem*, is splendidly imaginative.

As you go on the journey to Ithaca,
Pray that your way may be a long one,
Full of adventures, full of knowledge,
Do not be afraid of Poseidon's anger,
The Cyclops or the Laestrygonians,
You will never find such things upon your journey
If your thoughts remain lofty, and if a fine
Feeling has touched your body and your soul.
You will not meet the fierce Poseidon,
The Cyclops or the Laestrygonians
If you have not brought them with you, in your spirit,
If your spirit does not set them before you.

Pray that your way may be a long one.
Many let them be, the summer mornings
When with what pleasure, with what joy
You enter harbours never seen before;
You stop at Phoenician trading-stations,
And buy their lovely things;
Mother-of-pearl and coral, amber and ebony,
And delicious perfumes of every kind,
As plentiful as you like, delicious perfumes.
You go to a number of Egyptian cities,
You learn and learn from the men of science.

Always have Ithaca at the back of your mind.
The arrival there is your objective.
But do not be in any hurry on your journey.
Better to let it last for years.
In old age you will anchor at the island,
Rich with all you have gained upon the way,
Not expecting Ithaca to give you riches.

Ithaca gave you the lovely journey.
Without her you would not have started –
But she has nothing more to give you.

And if you find her poor, Ithaca has not deceived you.
With so much experience you have become so wise
That you knew already the meaning of our Ithacas.

One poem of 1911, *What things are dangerous* (30) is the first of Cavafy's poems to be 'outspoken'. Myrtías, a fourth-century Syrian student in Alexandria, part pagan part Christian, is so much 'strengthened by contemplation and study' that he will venture to give way to bodily passions, being sure of his power to regain self-mastery. Thenceforward the poems become more revealing, and it is well to examine the erotic poems of the next few years in chronological order of publication: this is the history of his gradual self-revelation.

His age was probably one of the reasons why Cavafy became more outspoken in his poetry. Michael Peridis wrote: 'After 1912 his eroticism calmed down, and in time nothing remained but the memory of its manifestations and a dominating need that made him continue to walk in the streets and places which he used to frequent, to satisfy the thirst no longer of his body, but of his eyes and brain.'[5]

Mr Malanos (who calls Peridis a 'hagiographer') disputes this – and indeed (as it will be seen) gives proof of Cavafy's sexual activities at a much later date.

Peridis, however, continues: 'I don't say that every sort of erotic manifestation stopped after 1912. I only say the form of manifestations that provoked bodily and spiritual pain and struggle and resistance were not to continue. How otherwise can one explain the change from anguish to exaltation and glorification? Why, while the struggle was going on did he transpose no erotic experience into poetry?' (Peridis did not know the unpublished poems of 1903–4.)

'Freed from the struggle, and the ill-treatment of his body and soul, he lived through his old adventures in memory. He purged them of their harshness, the pain and the dirt, and transformed them into exalted feelings in which remained the distillation of the daring, the danger, and the sharpest sensation.'[6]

Mr Malanos explains the situation a little differently: 'He began gradually as the years passed to have less fear of his sexual instinct – perhaps from greater self-confidence, perhaps from various soundings he had made, perhaps from observation that his environment was no longer so hostile.'[7] Marguerite Yourcenar

5. Peridis, p. 49.
6. ibid., p. 60.
7. Malanos, *Cavafy*, pp. 75–6.

comments: 'L'angoisse, en matière sensuelle, est presque toujours un phénomène de jeunesse; ou elle détruit un être, ou elle diminue progressivement du fait de l'expérience, d'une plus juste connaissance du monde, et plus simplement de l'habitude.'[8]

The confessions stopped in 1911. We may perhaps make a compromise between the views of his critics and say that Cavafy had now made peace with a (probably) less demanding body. His poetry now becomes more revealing, especially after 1915; and in 1918 the lecture given by Alexander Singopoulos (inspired and probably dictated by the poet himself) made it impossible to pretend that the writer's work did not come out of his own life.

We are asked to believe[9] that the moment was particularly unpropitious, as far as Alexandrian society was concerned. But though, as George Eliot has written, 'there is no private life which has not been determined by a wider public life', the determining life may not be so very wide or so very public. The politics and economics, even the war and peace of a household, may matter more to its members than any affairs of state. Individuals have led free and happy lives under the worst possible governments, and have lived as frightened slaves under the best.

Cavafy was now virtually without family: Paul was at Hyères and John in Cairo, but not in very close touch – the rest were dead. His age made it possible to give the impression that his sexual adventures were all in the past, even if this were not entirely true: and the past is easily forgiven. He was more and more courted by the literary world: literary people are not usually puritanical about private morality, and in their world he was the first, not a *déchu* 'protoclassatos' trying to keep up his position. He had not withdrawn from his own section of Alexandrian society, but here again his friends were usually intellectuals, from whom he might expect tolerance: Pericles Anastassiades, who was a painter as well as a businessman, the great collector Antony Benaki and his sister Penelope Delta, the gifted writer for children, and the historian Christopher Nomikos. Nor were the English and other foreign friends that he made during the war years likely to point a finger of scorn at him; E. M. Forster was not the only homosexual among them.

8. Yourcenar, p. 36.
9. Tsirkas, *Epoch*, p. 287.

Michael Peridis[10] notes that after 1912 Cavafy spent half as much on clothes. This is a footnote to a page where he speaks of the poet's sex-life, but it can hardly be intended to be relevant to it. Love in the Rue d'Anastasi was not what Forster might have called an enterprise that required new clothes – that is, perhaps, the best thing that can be said for it. It would be more reasonable to connect this information with his social life, and to suppose that he went out rather less. However he had probably a fully stocked wardrobe : the 'Child of Art' had found him in a well-cut suit (made, no doubt, of good English cloth), and in the last years of co-habitation with Paul he seems to have been rather over-dressed. He never put on weight, and might continue to wear the same things for years. A safer conjecture is that with this 'change of life' in his fiftieth year he ceased to care about fashion (though fashions for men changed slowly at that time), and began to save money on his clothes. There was no woman to keep him up to the mark (for Rika Singopoulos does not seem to have done so), and he appears gradually to have let himself go. Two Alexandrians who saw him in his last years have, independently, described him to me as 'a filthy old man'.

It was an Athenian writer, Costas Ouranis, who declared that it was no exaggeration to say that from 1909 to 1918 the seat of Greek letters was in Alexandria.[11] Not only was there the poet Cavafy, but also a group of prose-writers : Skliros, who wrote on social subjects, Nicolaidis who wrote tales, and the critic Zachariadis. There was a more urbane atmosphere than in Greece (and we may remember that Xenopoulos found Cavafy a little too polite). There were not quite such endless quarrels over the 'language question' between demoticists and champions of the *katharevousa*. Moreover there were two literary journals, *Nea Zoë* and *Grammata*.

Grammata was in fact founded by a number of writers who seceded from *Nea Zoë* and were more avant-garde. Cavafy had a preference for it, but he published his work in both these papers, although *Nea Zoë* was strongly inclined in favour of Palamas, and considered him the great poet of the age. In each of these papers Cavafy insisted that any poem of his own should have first place.

10. Peridis, p. 50 n.
11. Ouranis, pp. 147–8.

In 1912, however, *Grammata* published a letter denying his title to be a great poet 'though he tries for it sometimes by his method of wiping out other poets in order to exalt his own work . . .' The poet thereupon broke off his relations with *Grammata*, which, while they were still at enmity, published an article by Michael Peridis (later his admirer) in which he declared that 'the poetry of Cavafy was destined to die with him'. However *Nea Zoë* stopped publication in 1915 and was to take on a different character when it returned to life in 1922. Cavafy, having no alternative, was glad to return to *Grammata* in 1916.

Meanwhile, in his poetry, Cavafy was passing from symbolism to suggestion. History, said Mr Malanos,[12] 'provided him with a museum of safe and useful masks', and above all an atmosphere. 'We may say,' says the same critic,[13] 'that Cavafy made his perversion travel through history, though sometimes he forgot it in favour of History itself.' It might be better to say that, in surveying history (which had always been his passion) Cavafy's eyes brightened from time to time when he saw figures that appealed to him; and that when he created historical-fictitious figures it was generally, though by no means always, such as he could feel a particular sympathy for, by reason of a common passion. He had to create them, chiefly because history introduces us to so few private individuals, and tells us so little of the lives they led. He now began to allow this side of his interest in the past fuller expression. In *Herodes Atticus* (33) we can guess what sort of 'marvellous love-affairs' are discussed by the boys in Alexandria, Antioch and Beirut. We notice that in *Philhellene* (34) the king of a barbarous country orders 'some beautiful young athlete throwing the discus' for the obverse of his coins. In neither of these poems is sex important, each (in its way) is about the importance of the Greek name. But in *Alexandrian Kings* (35) Caesarion – of whom sculpture and numismatics tell us nothing – stands out in the beauty that is a lover's gift from Cavafy. He had everything to appeal to the poet: he was young, and he was to be betrayed and murdered. *Return* (37), also of this year, is a frankly personal poem, and an invocation of erotic memory, though as yet there is no indication of what 'the lips and the skin remember'.

12. Malanos, *Cavafy*, p. 77.
13. ibid., p. 78.

Of the four 1913 poems only *I went* (40) is revelatory, but in six lines it says a great deal: the poet 'let himself go', and went into 'the lit up night' to drink draughts of pleasure. It is in the past, and it is natural to connect it with the poet's late-night sorties, some of more than twenty years ago. In the next year *Far away* (43) is a timid, perhaps platonic memory of his 'first years of manhood'.

The grave of Eurion (44) is the first epitaph or elegy for a beautiful boy, and in the same year we find *The grave of the grammarian Lysias* (42). These two imaginary persons are interesting because they illustrate the extension of the Hellenistic world. Lysias is buried on the right of the entrance to the Beirut library. Eurion, an Alexandrian of Macedonian stock, was on his mother's side of a family of *alabarches* (the chief magistrates of the Alexandrian Jews) and had written the history of a region in Egypt. In making his picture of the Hellenistic world of Alexandria, Cavafy added illustrative references to other civilisations connected with it in one way or another – just as his friend Antony Benaki made his wonderful collection of Byzantine, Coptic and Arabian art, and (despite Chinese accretions) the visitor to Athens feels an organic unity in his museum. In the same way we feel, even as early as 1914, what Seferis called the 'basic unity' of Cavafy's work.

'My own view is that from a certain point onwards – and I should place this point at about 1910 – the work of Cavafy should be read and judged not as a series of separate poems, but as one and the same poem, a "work in progress" as James Joyce would have said, which is only terminated by death . . . we shall understand him more easily if we read him with the feeling of the continuous presence of his work as a whole. This unity is his grace.'[14] It is why he is great. As T. S. Eliot wrote, 'a whole work which consists of a number of short poems, even of poems which, taken individually, may appear rather slight, may, if it has a unity of underlying pattern, be the equivalent of a first-rate long poem in establishing an author's claim to be a major poet'.

We may continue the analogy with the Museum : a small, beautifully arranged museum, where everything tells, may be far more satisfying than a slipshod collection that (in fact) contains one or two superior works of art.

14. Seferis, *Greek Style*, p. 125.

How do the erotic poems fit into this synthesis? One might say that, like the relics of the Greek War of Independence or the folk-loric costumes in the Benaki Museum, they connect the past with the nineteenth and early twentieth centuries. One might add (sentimentally) that here is the heart of the poet, even as Antony Benaki (with a touch of Lysias the grammarian) had his heart immured in the wall at the entrance to the museum. Perhaps it is best to say, humbly, that they feel right here – and to record another subjective reaction, that it is extremely distasteful to find them divorced from their proper surroundings and issued as *erotica*.

Two of the 1915 poems, *At the café entrance* (49) and *One night* (53) are concerned with reactions to extremely beautiful bodies. The sex is not stated, but the reader of the corpus of Cavafy's work cannot doubt that they are male. It would be more true to say that the poet has not chosen to reveal their sex, rather than that he has concealed it. He is always sparing of adjectives (whose terminations indicate gender), and Greek, which conjugates its verbs, can do without the tell-tale pronouns that insist on 'him' and 'her'. The poet might reasonably profit by this ambiguity, and not only from fear of society. His poetry has for subject the universal passion of love, and he must have wished it to appeal also to people who did not experience this after his own fashion – we know that he did, for we have the lists of those to whom he sent it.

One night (53) is no doubt a reference to the shameful house in the Attarine quarter where over 'a disreputable tavern', and within sound of those playing cards below, he 'had the body of Love'. *He swears* (51) refers to his frequent broken resolutions not to go back there. Both poems are extremely poignant renderings of the anguish of the flesh and its pleasure wrung into a unique poetry. The passion in such poems sheds its almost lurid light over a historical poem like *Orophernes* (50). This Cappadocian prince, recreated from a coin and from a few pages in Edwyn Bevan's *House of Seleucus* (in which the coin is reproduced), had been sent to be educated in Ionia – 'O marvellous nights of Ionia' when this Asiatic prince gave himself up to 'Greek' pleasures.[15]

In the other historical poems of the year history is there for

15. Bevan, vol. 2, p. 157 and p. 206.

11. The entrance and bookcase, Rue Lepsius

12. The poet's bedroom, Rue Lepsius

its own sake, and it will be best to reserve them for treatment
with other poems on the same themes.

The year 1916 was marked by *In the street* (57) where the
sex of the young man coming away from his 'lawless pleasure'
is clearly indicated by 'his' in the Greek: of course all English
translators have been obliged to use pronouns in the previous
poems. In *Grey* (60) of 1917 we are not told to whom the grey
eyes belonged: their owner had gone away, 'I think to Smyrna',
to work. It is unlikely that Cavafy knew many working-women
other than prostitutes, so little doubt need be entertained of the
person's sex. Other poems of memory and desire were written in
this year. In *At evening* (65) the poet is disturbed by reading
an old letter, and goes out on to the balcony to see 'a little of the
much loved city'. In *So much I gazed* (69) he goes back to the
secret meetings in the nights of his youth. *Days of 1903* (70) is
the first of those poems with a similar title. It bears the date of
that year of emotional crisis.

> I never found them again – so quickly lost
> Those poetical eyes, that face
> Pale... in the darkening of the street.

The quasi-historical poems are all more or less erotic, and
examples of the use of 'masks'. *Tomb of Ignatius* (68) is hardly
an exception. It bridges the Byzantine and the Hellenistic
worlds. Cleon has put off his silks and diamonds that he used
to wear, and his fame for luxury in Alexandria – 'where it is
difficult to impress them' – and dies in minor orders as the lector
Ignatius. The lovely Remon wounded in a brawl *In a tavern of
Osroëne* (61) – i.e. Mesopotamia – is of mixed blood, Persian,
Syrian, Greek and Armenian (as perhaps his poet also was), but
he makes his friends think of Plato's Charmides. *One of their gods*
(62) comes down from the Heavenly Mansions for an evening's
debauch in the low quarter of Seleuceia. We return to Alexandria with poems on three dead boys. *Tomb of Iasis* (63) is
an exquisitely musical poem, unkindly damned by Marguerite
Yourcenar as 'un hellénisme à l'eau de rose'. Levkios, fallen
asleep *In the month Athyr* (67), is commemorated by a rather
tiresome broken inscription. Instructions are given to the poet

who is to write an epitaph *For Ammonis, who died aged 29 in 610* (66).

The tobacconist's window (71) is a third-person poem about contemporary Alexandria, where two strangers (obviously male) pick each other up. There follows the drive in the closed cab or 'gharry', so proverbial in Egypt for love-making, under the drawn-down hood.

It was among younger people that Cavafy's self-revelations had most effect, and during this decade he made a number of young friends. First, however, some mention must be made of a slightly older man, with whom he personally had little to do.

In 1912 he gave his poems to Enrico Pea, who was later to become a distinguished Italian poet, and the author of *Moscardino*, a novel much admired by Ezra Pound. Pea, a native of Seravezza, had emigrated to Egypt as a boy in 1896; there he worked successively as a labourer, a manufacturer and a marble merchant. From 1901 he was associated with 'La barocca rossa' in Rue Hamam el Zahab in Alexandria, which began as a commercial store-house. Over it was a flat (at some time Pea's) which became a meeting-place for anarchists of all nations, who there formed a 'Popular university', a rendezvous for intellectuals. There Pea met Ungaretti in 1906. In 1908 Pea returned to Italy for some months and at Viareggio fell in with the distinguished painter Lorenzo Viani; the two of them, with the poet Ceccardo Roccatagliata Ceccardi, founded a group called 'Gli Amici Apuani' or 'Il Manipolo d'Apuania' after the Apuanian alps in the background, a region where anarchism is almost traditional. After the death of Roccatagliata Ceccardi Viani became their 'general', and they were called 'I Vageri', a name compounded of *vagare* and *eroico*: the 'heroic vagabonds'. This group of anarchist artists, writers and musicians contained many talented people, and no doubt many young men of promise who never came to much.

Another recipient of Cavafy's poems in 1912, George Vrisimitsakis, went to Viareggio, where Pea introduced him to this group. He had some success with them, and was called 'Il filosofo greco'. When he returned to Alexandria he wished to be 'general' of a similar band of young men, and his followers called themselves 'Apuani'.

Vrisimitsakis is represented by Mr Malanos[16] as an eccentric but untalented person, chiefly remarkable for his envious disposition and his silly tricks *pour épater les bourgeois*; and indeed most of his published pamphlets give no higher idea of him. He was fond of making 'discoveries' and 'discovered' a small tavern in the Rue d'Anastasi frequented by prostitutes, the 'Tavern of Ciambourlini' where the Apuani enjoyed *spaghetti alle vongole* and Chianti. Perhaps it was there that Cavafy visited them, though he declared that he never tried 'their macaroni'.

Mr Basil Athanassopoulos remembers passing on his way to school as a boy by what must have been the back of the 'baracca rossa', or its successor. On the padlocked door he read the inscription SYLLOGO ATEO, which to him, at that age, smelled of brimstone. And at one time Vrisimitsakis and others used to make anti-religious demonstrations in front of the Catholic church of St Catherine.

In the spring of 1917 Mr Athanassopoulos, then a very young man, and affiliated to the movement, published a manifesto entitled 'Cavafy and Routine', claiming the poet as an enemy of humdrum routine, and therefore at one with the 'Apuani'. This was to have repercussions.

Mr Malanos vigorously attacked the manifesto; it might be thought that such a piece of youthful enthusiasm could be very well left alone, and it is hard today to understand the motive of the attack.

Mr Malanos, now the best critic of Cavafy, had first met the poet in 1915. In the following year when he tried to launch a periodical of his own, with the help of his friends Basil Athanassopoulos, Rhodope (later Rika Singopoulos) and others, Cavafy offered to contribute a poem. He was also a kind and patient critic of Mr Malanos' early verse, but unfortunately showed the physical attraction that he felt towards him. The account of the scene is graphic:

'I had stayed late in his salon. Then, for one moment, I felt, I remember, his whole soul concentrated in his glance and the touch of his hand, ready to hazard in my direction a movement as of a carnivorous plant . . .'[17]

Although Mr Malanos felt physically repelled, this attraction

16. Malanos, *Memoirs*, pp. 75 ff.
17. ibid., p. 39.

towards him on the part of a man whose work he revered seems
to have set up a strange love-hate relationship, which still goes
on. Moreover as a man of great, almost over-scrupulous
integrity, he felt impatient with Cavafy's code of 'literary good
manners', which forbade unfavourable criticism of a friend's
work. This impatience sometimes provoked him into 'incon-
venient candour'; he seems rather often to have thought it his
duty to say things that others would have left unsaid.

In answer to the manifesto he complained of 'colourless, faded,
illegitimate representations'. He said: 'If we could all lead the
negative life of Cavafy, then his verses would be what we want.'
He contrasted the ancient cult of the ephebe with that of the
poet: the ancient cult had all the elements of health, and that
of Cavafy was sick. He called for a poetry that smelt of wet
earth and of pinewoods drying in the sun, and not of the poet's
closed and scented rooms.

The answer should have been that Cavafy's ephebes were
not those of classical Greece, but those of the Hellenistic dispersion, and that though it would be a fault in taste, and perhaps in
character, to prefer the smell of an actual closed and scented
room to that of an actual pinewood, in art there is nothing to
choose between them – choice must depend on the quality of the
art. Moreover the pinewood has been done often enough, and
poetry written about it in the beginning of this century has been
exceedingly dreary.

Many Apuani joined in a second manifesto, from which the
good manners that Costas Ouranis had noted in Alexandria
were markedly absent. Their arguments were rather less cogent,
though Alexander Singopoulos did indeed write that above all
things Cavafy avoided the banal. The little note that he contributed is of importance, as it was probably dictated by the poet
himself, who had recently made a close friend of this young man
(his future heir) and was to use him as a mouthpiece on another
occasion. Singopoulos added that Mr Malanos had been a frequent visitor to Cavafy's house, and had written verse in his
manner.

One of the Apuani refused to participate. He was Panayotis
Panayotou, alias Syllas Veronios, alias Petros Alitis (the beggar),
a strange young man who gave up school and became a newspaper-seller in order to have more time for reading – and a very

amateurish newspaper-seller he was. He wrote to the Apuani:
'We cannot endure a work and an action that is radically opposed to all progress and all social usefulness' – this verdict
(stupid though it is) of a young man in 1917 may be remembered now that it has become the fashion to speak of the 'political'
Cavafy. Alitis showed promise before his early death from
tuberculosis,[18] and perhaps Cavafy thought of him now and again
when he was writing his epitaphs on dead boys, together with
Mikès Ralli and others.

Another of the early dead, Nikos Santoriniós, contributed to
this manifesto. He was a friend of Alitis, and he also sold newspapers, but out of need not eccentricity. In spite of his name,
his origins were not in Santorin but in Symi. He was a gentle
sweet-natured boy – to prove to Petros Alitis that his tuberculosis was cured (which he knew to be untrue) he seized a spoon
from his friend's hand and plunged it in his soup, to show that he
was not afraid of infection.

'Once when, in front of other people, Cavafy said to him:
"What beautiful eyes you have, Niko!" Santoriniós . . . was
obviously annoyed, and replied: "But what beauty do you find
in them Mr Cavafy, when one of them has a squint? I don't
like flattery." Then Cavafy, patting him on the shoulder, added:
"I knew, my poor Niko, you always were a character!" And yet
this time it was no flattery. Santoriniós' eyes had the colour of
damp turquoise.'[19]

At this time, that is from the beginning of the First World
War, Cavafy was also making friends among Frenchmen and
Englishmen stationed in Egypt, and perhaps for the only time in
his life was constantly associated with his intellectual equals. His
friend, Pericles Anastassiades, worked in the censorship with Robin
Furness, and introduced him to Cavafy[20] who, of course, had
much in common with the translator of Callimachus. Cavafy
found him 'a most cultivated man with first-class artistic
originality', and speaks of a conversation with him about the
Greek Anthology and 'its wonderful succinct expressions . . . our
attention was especially attracted by a quatrain of Paladas [sic]
which, in my opinion, is indicative of the grief and discourage-

18. ibid., p. 67.
19. ibid., p. 81.
20. Tsirkas, *Epoch*, p. 236.

ment of the pagans who witnessed the collapse of their religion.'[21]

Sir John Forsdyke of the British Museum was another friend with whom he could talk of the Greco-Roman world. He also met E. M. Forster, then working with the Red Cross – who was to do more for his literary reputation in the West than any other man. His charming essay gives an account of meeting the poet in the street, going reluctantly to his office, or gladly from it to his flat.

'If the latter, he may be prevailed upon to begin a sentence – an immensely complicated yet shapely sentence, full of parentheses that never get mixed and of reservations that really do reserve; a sentence that moves with logic to its foreseen end, yet to an end that is always more vivid and thrilling than one foresaw . . . It deals with the tricky behaviour of the Emperor Alexius Comnenus in 1096, or with olives, their possibilities and price, or with the fortunes of friends, or George Eliot, or the dialects of the interior of Asia Minor. It is delivered with equal ease in Greek, English or French.'[22]

Forster, at that time occupied in the preparation of his delightful guide-book to Alexandria, had much to learn from the poet. Sometimes he returned with him to the house in the Rue Lepsius, and tried to make out the poems with the aid of George Valassopoulos' translations, and his own recollections of ancient Greek. ' "You cannot *possibly* understand my poems, my dear Forster . . . impossible," and then he began to lead me through one of them, *The city* I think, and: "But good – my dear Forster very good indeed – you have seen the point . . . good." '[23]

On one such occasion the Apuani and their followers burst in upon the two friends, some twenty in number (as Mr Basil Athanassopoulos, who was one of them, tells me). Cavafy was much annoyed, but kept his temper, introducing them to Forster in the most complimentary terms: this one was a poet, that one was a critic, another was a gifted short-story writer, and so on.

It cannot be denied that the Apuani and other young visitors

21. Letter to Alexander Singopoulos, 25 October 1918. Palladas was an Alexandrian epigrammatist of the fifth century A.D.

22. Forster, *Pharos*, p. 75.

23. Letter of E. M. Forster to the author, 6 August 1945.

came to the Rue Lepsius to mock as well as to admire. They were also attracted by the poet's generosity with his whisky. He was, however, careful not to give them the best quality. I have been told of his offering a drink to the artist Zacynthinos. The latter was about to help himself when Cavafy stopped him. 'That's the Palamas whisky,' he said (i.e. second-rate). 'As we're alone I'll give you something better.'

Nevertheless no league in Alexandria was durable – and perhaps durability is everywhere a rare thing in literary friendships. Vrisimitsakis was in the conspiracy that was intended to prevent Alexander Singopoulos from giving his famous lecture on Cavafy on 23 February 1918. This young man was not a man of letters, and it was rightly suspected that the lecture had been composed by the poet himself, who had chosen an intimate friend of his own to deliver it. An attack on Singopoulos was therefore an attack on Cavafy.

Vrisimitsakis formed the plot with two of his friends, Stamos Zervos and Sakellaris Yannakakis. The two latter lured Singopoulos into a bar an hour before the time of the lecture and made him drunk – perhaps he had stage-fright, and offered little resistance. Then they called a gharry to take him to the Ptolemy Club where the lecture was to be given. They placed him between them, and gave secret instructions to the driver, who whipped up his horse. They had intended to carry Singopoulos to the Nouzha gardens, a park some three kilometres out of town, and to keep him there until half an hour after the time appointed for his lecture. They had already got some way before their victim was aware of the trick. He leapt out of the gharry and had to make his way back on foot, arriving late and out of breath. When he came to deliver his lecture, it was with a shout, which was variously interpreted as due to drink, to nerves or to exaltation. In any case it was not a great success for, when the lecturer declaimed *What things are dangerous*, Madame Tsimbouki rose in indignation and left the hall ostentatiously on the arm of her gigantic daughter. Other people followed their example.[24]

Nevertheless, the lecture[25] is a document of the first importance. Four poems are analysed: *What things are dangerous* (30), *I*

24. Malanos, *Memoirs*, pp. 267–8.
25. Reprinted in *ET* 1963, pp. 614 ff.

went (40), *Far away* (43) and *Return* (37) and the poet's own interpretations are given. Of the first, we are told that the caution in the title is practical, not moral. Myrtías, according to Cavafy, chooses things that are 'dangerous', but not 'accursed', and that he will temporarily break off for a rest, sure of being able to return to a contemplative life when he wishes. 'It may be – I can't say definitely – Cavafy's opinion that only once in thousands of cases a Myrtías appears.' His case is contrasted with that of a young man in *Transit* (64); this poem shows not the beginning of a young life, not a whole life nor even a large part of it.

It is stated as Cavafy's opinion that the artist cannot discipline his life in youth, like the man of learning, the statesman and the merchant. Their activities 'do not need late nights and expense of vitality on physical pleasure – they need a clear head in the morning and the day that follows'. For the artist this disciplined life is impossible and would not be right. Cavafy does not mean that the artist should seek dissipation but that he should let himself go, as he says in *I went*: 'I let myself go completely.'

Far away is a memory of the time when he first began to set out on a life of pleasure: 'timid almost modest days' before 'the days and years that followed with their strong and passionate enjoyments'. It is contrasted with *Return,* which is altogether fleshly, or *One night* (53). Finally Singopoulos read *Candles* (6), and spoke of the poet's fear of old age.

This lecture was a singularly daring gesture, and a frank declaration of Cavafy's hedonism: there could no longer be any doubt about the poet's identification with his work, or that the poems analysed were autobiographical – and most people must have known that they were homosexual. Many people, especially those of the older generation, were scandalised. But 'Cavafy was chiefly anxious to attract the attention of the young towards his daring and unorthodox poetry'.[26] It seems a pity that Vrisimitsakis and his friends should have played their foolish prank.

More legitimate was the teasing to which Singopoulos was exposed after his one appearance as a man-of-letters. 'Why don't you write, Aleko?' he was constantly asked, by people who knew very well that he had never written. 'I must suffer first,' he used

26. Tsirkas, *Chronology.*

to say. 'Then let him cut his hand!' was a journalist's unkind comment.[27]

This year, 1916, was particularly productive. There are three poems on fictitious dead boys. Emis in *At the harbour* (74) was a Greek buried in Syria; the *Tomb of Lanis* (76) was in Alexandria, but *Aimilianos Monai, Alexandria, A.D. 628–655* (84) died in Sicily. Of these poems only the second is directly erotic. Mr Malanos informs me that there is no truth in the legend that the poem was named after one Karaolanis who began to receive Cavafy's poems at this time, and that Karaolanis was a most respectable person, although his two sisters ran a brothel in the Boulevard de Ramleh.

Aimilianos Monai, with his 'special panoply' of 'countenance and words and ways' donned to protect him from the wicked who might want to hurt him, is surely a 'mask' concealing the poet himself.

Caesarion (73) and *Aristobulos* (82) are erotico-historical poems about beautiful, ill-fated boys. In the former poem Cleopátra's son makes another appearance, in the beauty that Cavafy earlier bestowed upon him. His end is foreshown by a reference to Plutarch. 'As Caesar was determining with himselfe what he should do, Arrius said unto him :

Too many Caesars is not good.

Alluding unto a certaine verse of Homer that saith

Too many lords doth not well.

Therefore Ceasar did put Caesarion to death, after the death of his mother Cleopatra.'

Aristobulos was the young brother-in-law of Herod the Great, who unwillingly made him high-priest at the age of seventeen, to gratify his mother-in-law Alexandra, the 'First Princess'. The boy, who was of remarkable beauty, had a great success at the feast of Tabernacles, 35 B.C. Herod had him 'accidentally' drowned in a bathing-pool during a feast at Jericho. Here again is the drowned boy and the Mater Dolorosa : and when she is

27. Malanos, *Memoirs*, pp. 71–2.

alone, Alexandra's grief breaks out noisily, like that of the woman of Denshawi.

The setting is one that fascinated Cavafy, the Greco-Judaean court of the Herods, of which he had read in Renan or Josephus. It is, moreover, connected with Alexandria, for Alexandra 'was on friendly terms with Cleopatra, and tried to interest Antony in the fortunes of her children'.[28]

In the directly erotic poems of this year the blend of memory and desire brings to life again the physical pleasure of the past with an intensity that is probably unique in literature. In *Since nine o'clock* (81) the poet is haunted by a vision of his own youthful body; in *Under the house* (83) he walks by the 'infamous house' and feels again the violent sensations he experienced there in his youth. At *The next table* (78) he sees a boy of twenty-three or thereabouts (his sex concealed by the absence of pronouns) and feels that it was his body that he enjoyed nearly twenty-two years ago, for its every movement seems familiar. The greatest of these poems is the famous *Body, remember* (75).

> Body, remember, not only all the times you have been loved
> Not only the beds where you have lain down.
> But also those desires which for you
> Shone clearly in the eyes,
> And trembled in the voice – and some
> Chance accident brought them to nothing.
> And now, when all that is in the past,
> They seem very like those desires
> To which you gave yourself – how they shone,
> Remember, in the eyes that looked at you;
> How they trembled in the voice, for you, body, remember.

Seferis has rightly emphasised the union of feeling, learning and thinking in Cavafy's work, and applies to it Eliot's phrase about the later Elizabethan playwrights or the metaphysical poets: 'There is a direct sensuous apprehension of thought, or a recreation of thought into feeling.' In Cavafy's poetry it is not only the case that a thought is felt; the converse also is true – like that of Donne's Elizabeth Drury (though to very different

28. Mavrogordato, p. 103 n.

purpose) his body 'thought'. Whether he be ranked as a great poet or no, he has undoubtedly the right to be classed among the 'ultimate' writers, that is, those who have gone further than any others in the expression of some part of human experience. It is natural that he should be an elderly poet, for a body must at least have arrived at middle age before it can participate in 'the sense of the past'. When he said that the immediate impression was never his impulse to work, Cavafy certainly meant that neither public events nor private life immediately inspired him : probably this is the reason why so many of his poems were unacknowledged – they had not their origins far back enough in the past for him to feel sure of them.[29]

At the end of 1918 and the beginning of 1919 we have what is probably the only extant series of letters from Cavafy.[30] It is likely that his letters to his brothers were returned to him at their deaths, and that he destroyed them. Letters to other people are rare, and not very interesting; most of the time he had all his friends round him in Alexandria. Now his young friend Alexander Singopoulos was absent for some months, attached to a business house at Benha, at the head of the Delta. He made several short visits to Alexandria during this time, and the poet wrote to him nearly every day. The letters are affectionate, full of care for the health and comfort of the friend whom he misses so greatly, and of plans for his future. After learning about cotton at Benha – 'commerce is a great and fine thing' – Singopoulos is to return to Alexandria where his friend will get him a place with Benaki, and will help him to perfect his knowledge of French and English.

Such letters are too frequent and short to have literary quality; but Singopoulos liked his friend to write to him sometimes about his more serious interests. There are some observations about Leopardi, whom Singopoulos' friend Catraro[31] is

29. e.g. the wonderfully poignant *Half an hour* (Keeley and Savidis, pp. 48–9).

30. The correspondence with Forster was irregular.

31. Atanasio Catraro was later to pride himself on being the first to introduce Cavafy to the Italian public, but his translations (as Professor Pontani truly says) are ridiculous—e.g. (*The town*): Anima mia/perché soffrir/perché morir/cosi? . . . Un altro lido/no, non sognar/non sospirar/ mai più.

studying, and about D'Annunzio, whom one of Cavafy's visitors knew personally. Henri Massis, 'a highly cultivated man', has been brought to the house; he said the best French poet was Claudel.

More interesting are the passages about the ancient world.

'I've been reading lately – in translation – Suetonius. He's not of great value. His famous work is the biographies of the first twelve emperors of Rome. I've been reading that. It has the advantage of being anecdotal and one learns a lot or guesses it from what he says, about the social life of the time. One thing the student of imperial Rome should have in view is that the miserable situation in the capital doesn't at all imply the same situation in the state in general. For one thing, the slowness and difficulty of communications, and for another the good and orderly organisation of the different parts of the Roman state, often brought it about that a bad emperor, who did harm in Rome, did none in the provinces.'

Cavafy also records an interesting conversation with Valassopoulos about Greek studies in England, where for some years 'quiet but very important work' had been done on Greek texts. Headlam's 'marvellous edition' of the *Agamemnon* of Aeschylus was spoken of, and his early death lamented. Cavafy adds : 'As for the *Agamemnon*, I think I once spoke to you of a masterly translation of it by Browning, a great English poet of the last century. In that translation he has succeeded in the very difficult task of preserving the tone of the work, its poetical atmosphere.'

In *On board ship* (88) of 1919 we have the masculine pronoun again, and now for the first time attached to a personal memory of the poet's.

It's like him; but I remember him as better looking . . .

It professes to be a memory of the Ionian sea, and if it is autobiographical it must be about Cavafy's journey with his brother Alexander from Corfu to Brindisi on S.S. *Scilla* on 1 August 1901. Possibly the subject was the 'charming young man, M. Simopoulo', nephew of the Minister of Finance, whom they met on board, and possibly Alexander made the sketch which aroused the memory. The feelings behind this poem may be purely platonic[32] – and both the young man's station in life and Alexander's presence would probably have precluded any sort of adventure – but the masculine pronoun authorises us to identify the sex of characters in other poems in which it is not used. Not that we need any authorisation apart from the circumstances where they are seen (in the café or the tavern, or at the tobacconist's window), our knowledge of the poet's life, and the fact that he wrote no serious poetry that is certainly heterosexual.

To remain (86) is a vivid recollection of love-making long after midnight in the corner of a wine-shop, and the rapid stripping of lightly clothed flesh : 'The divine month of July was burning.' 'We', says the poet : and the vision of the other body has passed through twenty-six years to remain in this poem. Perhaps it is a memory of 1893.

The afternoon sun (90) is a touching and nostalgic poem, commemorating an affair of some duration (whether real or fictitious), and not a mere chance encounter.

> This room, how well I know it.
> Now it and the next one are to let
> As business offices. The whole house has become
> Offices for agents, merchants and companies.
> Ah, this room, how familiar it is.
> Here, by the door, was the sofa,
> And in front of it a Turkish carpet;
> Beside was the shelf with two yellow vases.
> On the right – no – opposite, a cupboard with a mirror.
> In the middle the table where he used to write,
> And the three big cane chairs.
> By the window was the bed
> Where we made love so many times.
> These wretched things must still be somewhere.
> By the window was the bed,
> The afternoon sun touched it half-way.
> . . . One afternoon at four o'clock, we had parted
> Just for a week . . . alas,
> That week became forever.

32. Malanos, *Cavafy*, pp. 96–7.

It is such a poem as this that has encouraged Marguerite Yourcenar to see a story behind the love-poems. It is not possible to follow her; there are too many stories – nor yet to acquiesce in her dislike for this and other poems where Cavafy speaks in the first person.

The two fictitious young men of 1919, the Alexandrian Jew Ianthes in *Of the Hebrews, A.D. 50* (85), and *Imenos* (87) of Syracuse in the ninth century, are further representatives of the Greek world in space and time. In each poem there is a kind of repudiation of conscience.[33]

This decade has been the decade of the greatest love poems; henceforward they will be few, and history will predominate. *Their beginning* (99) must however be mentioned: a poem of 1921 in which Cavafy reaffirms the importance of 'lawless pleasure' to his inspiration.

It is not always possible to separate the 'historical' from the 'erotic' poems, and even more difficult to isolate the 'philosophical' poems – indeed it is a thing only to be done for convenience, for as Marguerite Yourcenar says all the poems are historical (for the love poems are set in the past, even if it be a recent past) and all the poems are personal. Nevertheless it is easier to examine together, and apart from other work, the poems in which he creates what the same critic calls 'l'extraordinaire Orient gréco-syrien deviné (par quel miracle?) par Racine: Oreste, Hippolyte, Xipharès, Antiochus, Bajazet . . .'

The most interesting cycle of poems is that inspired by the kingdoms of Alexander's successors in Macedon, Syria and Alexandria.

The Battle of Magnesia (54) in 190 B.C. has undone Antiochus and the kingdom of Syria; but Philip of Macedon is not going to put off his (fictitious) feast because he hears of the downfall of another Hellenistic kingdom: seven years ago the Syrians had not been much affected when Macedonia fell to the Romans. The *Silversmith* (101) fifteen years later is trying to remember the form and features of a lover of his who fell in that battle, to reproduce them on the side of a bowl. The bowl is for Heracleides who shortly after went to Rome as ambassador of

33. An earlier form of *Imenos*, as a purely personal poem, is printed in the preface to *UP*.

Antiochus Epiphanes.[34] He was banished by Antiochus' successor Demetrius Soter in 162 B.C., and then supported the adventurer Alexander Balas who supplanted him.

The *Envoys from Alexandria* (80) had been sent on a (fictitious) mission to Delphi by the rival kings Ptolemy VI Philometor and Ptolemy VII Euergetes, presumably in 164 B.C. The priests did not know how to decide between the brothers, and were much relieved when a decision from Rome spared them the embarrassment. In 162 B.C. Ptolemy VI was expelled by his brother and went to Rome to ask the Senate to reinstate him. He came poorly attended, and *The displeasure of Seleucides* (56) – that is of the Seleucid prince, Demetrius Soter, then a hostage in Rome – was aroused at the sight of a brother monarch in such reduced circumstances. He 'hastened to meet him, with regal apparel and a magnificent horse, richly caparisoned. He was received with a smile, he must not spoil a calculated stage effect . . . he himself proceeded as he had begun, entered Rome a pathetic figure, and took up his lodging with a penurious Greek painter in an attic.'[35]

Unlike Philip of Macedon, Demetrius had a feeling of solidarity with another Hellenistic king. In Rome he was angered by the contempt for the Greek kingdoms that he sensed in his young patrician friends there, and his one ambition was to escape to Syria and to make it a great power once more. But when back in the East he found that 'the boys in Rome were right' – the Hellenistic dynasties were done for, and Syria was the land of Heracleides and Balas. In his complete disillusionment nothing was left but stoical courage – which indeed is all the Trojans had left them, or the Spartans at Thermopylae. The poem of which he is the hero – *Of Demetrius Soter, 162–150 B.C.* (89) – is one of the most interesting. Demetrius is the one almost heroic figure in an unheroic world, and he has an understanding that goes beyond his own personal problems to comprehend the collapse of his world. *Favour of Alexander Balas* (97) shows a spoilt lover of the adventurer who replaced Demetrius, a 'handsome genial youth of twenty-three', who 'fell under the dominion of mistresses and favourites'.[36]

34. Mavrogordato, p. 127 n.
35. Bevan, vol. 2, p. 189.
36. ibid., p. 313.

The two Roman poems are rather grim, the sinister *Theodotus*
(46) comes in with the severed head of Pompey. *Nero's term*
(77) is another ironical story about the Delphic oracle. It is
inspired by a passage from Suetonius, whom Cavafy was reading at that time. Philemon Holland has thus rendered it: 'But
sending one time to the oracle of Apollo at Delphi and hearing
this answer from thence that he must beware of the year seventy-
three, as who would say that he was to die in that year (of his
own age) and not before, and dividing no whit of Galba's years,
with so assured a confidence he conceived in his heart not only
long life but also a perpetual and singular felicity . . .' And so
Nero returned to Rome after the pleasures of Achaea and the
naked bodies, while Galba, aged seventy-three, was in Spain,
drilling the force that was to overthrow him.

The Byzantine poems are less interesting than those which
Cavafy was later to write. For all his Constantinopolitan
origins, Cavafy's imagination still moved less easily in that world.
He had rejected his early Byzantine poems as 'trash', but he was
later to return to that important part of the Greek past and
to make it his own – as he was to say: 'For me the Byzantine
period is like a cupboard with many drawers. When I want
something, I know where to find it, and to what drawer to have
recourse.'[37]

Manuel Comnenus (55), the emperor who ended his days
in the habit of a monk, may remind us of the dignified retreat
of *King Demetrius* (22). Cavafy always loved the forms of the
Orthodox Church (cf. *In church* (36)), with which he himself
was to die. *A Byzantine nobleman in exile, writing verses* (96)
is probably Michael VII. According to Gibbon 'his character
was degraded, rather than ennobled, by the virtue of a monk and
the learning of a sophist' – he is here as a contrast to Manuel I.
Anna Comnena (92) – 'Dizziness overcomes my soul, and tears
blind my eyes', she wrote, about her husband's tumour: but
Cavafy guesses that her only real grief was at the failure of her
plots against her brother John.

In this last poem Cavafy introduced untranslated phrases from
Anna's *Alexiad*, a practice he was to adopt in other historical
poems. Mr Malanos complains that this is behaving not like a
poet, but like the writer of an academic paper, and takes some

37. Sareyannis, p. 36.

passages from Suidas' Lexicon saying that they might be poems by Cavafy.[38] Seferis truly says that they might not, and cites Eliot: 'It is the sensuous contribution to the intelligence that makes the difference.'[39] Cavafy approaches Manuel I, Michael VII and Anna with sensibility, and a sensibility that is entirely his own – though as yet it finds fuller play outside the Byzantine period.

Two extremely interesting poems are about fictitious characters and their concern with poetry. In *Darius* (95) the poet Phernazes of Amisos in Cappadocia is preparing an epic about Darius in honour of his descendant Mithridates. But now news comes of war with the Romans – such a nuisance the work being broken off; Mithridates cannot be expected to have time for it now, and the poet himself may be in danger. All the same, his mind goes back to Darius.

The young men of Sidon, A.D. 400 is also, perhaps, a vindication of the art of poetry. An actor has given a recital of epigrams to five 'scented young Sidonians'. Finally he spoke the epitaph of Aeschylus, of whose 'tried valour' the 'Marathonian grove' could tell. One of the young men, 'fanatical for literature', rose in protest. Aeschylus should not have forgotten his tragedies, to boast only of having fought at Marathon. We cannot doubt that Cavafy sympathised with the young man, for the epigram (which we may hope is spurious) represents Aeschylus as the sort of 'public school' Ancient Greek who could have little appeal for him. Nevertheless the situation is not entirely well managed: the young man seems too decadent to win approval, even though the words put into his mouth might be the poet's own. It appears[40] that Cavafy was here trying to do two things: to represent the smart cosmopolitan world of Sidon, and to express his own convictions about poetry. His two purposes do not entirely cohere, and the poem is unsatisfactory – almost in the same way as *Thermopylae* – though here he has not allowed himself room enough for the development of his themes.

Demaratus (100) is also difficult: a character of the dethroned king of Sparta who went over to the Persians and served Darius and Xerxes. Cavafy, commenting on this poem, said:

38. Malanos, *Cavafy*, p. 153.
39. Seferis, *Greek Style*, p. 138.
40. Malanos, *Cavafy*, p. 346.

'The poem shows that Demaratus is not a traitor. Deep down in his conscience he rejoices when he learns that the Greeks are winning.'[41] But his mixed feelings bring too much confusion into the poem, and it fails to show this. The *Melancholy of Jason, son of Cleander, poet in Syria Commagene, A.D. 595* (102) is a cry against age :

> The ageing of my body and my beauty
> Is like a blow from a frightful knife . . .
> It is a blow from a frightful knife –
> Bring your drugs, Art of Poetry,
> Which make – for a little – the blow not to be felt.

41. ibid., p. 351.

X   The Last Years

In December 1921 Cavafy informed his superiors that 'for personal reasons' he did not wish to renew his contract, which expired at the end of the following March.[1] His immediate motive was a wish to profit by the compensation offered by Saad Zagloul to government employees retiring at that date (an offer made with the object of ousting British officials, though other nationals also benefited by it). Moreover he had now put aside enough, and had gained enough upon the stock exchange to afford to retire on a pension.[2] Christopher Nomikos had offered to place his money for him in an annuity, which would have made him considerably better off; he refused, saying superstitiously, that it would be just like his luck to die at once, and lose by the speculation.

'At last,' he said, on leaving the office, 'I'm free of this loathsome thing.' Henceforth his life centres more and more on his flat.

At the end of 1907 he and Paul had moved from the Rue Rosette to the second floor of 10 Rue Lepsius, a street which owed its name to a distinguished German Egyptologist. Years later he said to Yanko Pieridis: 'When sixteen, no, eighteen years ago, I took this house with a friend [the scandalous Paul was never named] I didn't expect to stay long. Then my friend went away and I kept it for myself, but I always had it in mind to leave . . . Years passed without my taking a final decision. Shall I leave, or shall I put in electric light?'[3]

The Rue Lepsius, indeed the whole quarter, called 'Massalia', was very ill-famed, but respectable people had always lived in Cavafy's house, and in 1910 the funeral of a highly esteemed lawyer started from there. Forster makes no comment, and it

1. Tsirkas, *Chronology*.
2. Peridis, p. 59 n. 2.
3. Pieridis, p. 19.

may have been after his time in Alexandria that a brothel was opened on the ground-floor. I have been told of 'an important English Sir' (unidentified) who called to see Cavafy, and was very much surprised at what he saw when he tried the wrong door. 'The whores looked out of the windows, and called to passers-by,' I have been told by an old Alexandrian. 'We called it the "Rue Clapsius".'

They were civil to Cavafy. 'Poor things!' he said, to a friend who had accompanied him to his door one night. 'One must be sorry for them. They receive some disgusting people, some monsters, but' (and his voice took on a deep, ardent tone) 'they receive some angels, some angels!'[4]

It was an old Greek quarter: opposite was the Greek hospital and round the corner was the patriarchal church of St Saba, whose evening bell was a familiar sound to the poet's visitors. He was fond of saying: 'Where could I live better? Below, the brothel caters for the flesh. And there is the church which forgives sin. And there is the hospital where we die.' Sometimes he would say: 'I'm the spirit, below me is the flesh', and sometimes: 'Alone up here, hero and victim.'

In the streets he would walk slowly, his hands in his pockets, looking in at shop-windows, ill-dressed (sometimes in a filthy old waterproof) and often talking to himself. If he met a well-informed person, he might stop him and question him about some historical problem. If he met a bore he would ask him which way he was going, in order to say at once that 'unfortunately' he was going in the opposite direction.[5] He was never in a hurry, frequently he would stand still: 'A Greek gentleman in a straw hat, standing at a slight angle to the universe',[6] perhaps with arms extended and the hat slanting to the back of his head. Generally he wore great round glasses in a tortoiseshell frame. He tried to look younger than his years (and liked to be styled 'middle-aged'), he frizzed his hair, and dyed it after some prescription of his own. For as long as he could, he took care of his skin – and he always insisted that in any sketch of him the wrinkles should be left out. His face, one observer tells us, was not that

4. Pieridis, p. 18.
5. Ouranis, p. 130.
6. Forster, *Pharos*, p. 75.

of an old man trying to keep youthful, but that of 'a boy who had aged'.[7] Latterly he was rather bent.

In the shops he was difficult, hard to please. He was known all over the town and to almost every waiter, for he liked to try new cafés and restaurants, and to study their customers. He would get into conversation with merchants and brokers and people of every class and trade. He was fond of drinking raki, standing at low bars where he could besiege his neighbours with questions, designed to make them bring out the interesting word or phrase. But he was interested in other things as well as language : he liked to know all about everybody. Gaston Zananiri spoke of going out with him at night to places full of out-of-work youths, playing cards, dominoes or backgammon. In a tavern he said : 'Truth comes from the mouths of babes . . . and of drunkards.'

Between five and seven o'clock he was generally at home to any friends who cared to call. Mirgani or one of his successors, Achmet or Aly, opened the door, or more often Cavafy himself. 'I found myself sunk in shadow,' said Costas Ouranis. 'The passage was a current of shadow and the servant himself glided like a ghost. The little, dim light that came from a neighbouring room made the shadow still more mysterious. I had the impression that I was in the apartment of the hero of a fantastic tale of Hoffmann.'[8]

Paul had spoken with loving nostalgia of their charming intérieur, the green hall, the red salon, the mauve dining-room. It is likely that he had much more visual sense that Constantine, and that after his time the big salon, at least, had been allowed to fall into considerable disorder.

In the hall was a long bookcase; Cavafy was never a bibliophile and there were not many books : only some three hundred, not at all representative,[9] and many odd volumes. If the talk fell on one of his books, he would come with a candle and look for it.

7. Ouranis, p. 128. Unlike his brothers Paul and John, Constantine had abandoned the moustache he wore at one time. I have seen one photograph of him (probably c. 1895) with a beard.

8. NE, 1933, p. 774.

9. Sareyannis, p. 35. The account of the flat and of Cavafy at home is derived from the pages of Sareyannis, Pieridis, Ouranis and Mr Malanos, and from private communications from the latter and from Mr Basil Athanassopoulos.

From the hall ran a passage. On the left was the little red salon, which was more formal and was reserved for his more important visitors. Here was his better furniture. His niece – who was presumably received there with her mother – speaks of family things : old carved wood, lustres of pierced copper, little tables inlaid with mother-of-pearl, silk cushions embroidered with birds and flowers, and marble tables supporting porcelain lamps. The red salon had a balcony, where he sometimes went out to see the life passing below, and perhaps to get a glimpse of the whores' angel visitants.

The larger salon into which it opened (as did the dining-room) might flatteringly be called 'Arabian', for there was a lot of oriental-looking furniture. Those who only saw it in a dim light have supposed that it contained objects of value. Sareyannis, who found himself alone there one morning, has given the truest account of it : he was astonished to find that it was so shabby.

Left of the door was a divan, and between the divan and the window the old arm-chair where the poet used to sit; opposite was another, for a friend or for a new visitor upon his probation. There was a small table, and there were other chairs here or there. Further back were bare velvet arm-chairs, a black desk with gilt ornament, folding-chairs like those in colonial bungalows and every sort of rubbish crammed in haphazardly. There were oriental carpets of every sort, shelves on the walls bearing a Tanagra girl, and vases in the worst taste of 1900. A worn Chinese weave, gift of some travelled relation (perhaps Sevastie), hung on the far wall, and there were old Indian and Bokhara stuffs on the divan and at the windows. The whole room looked like a rather inferior junk shop; there was hardly anything of quality in it except a console, an old family piece, at the back of the room, and a Venetian mirror above it. On the console were photographs of bearded men, presumably relations. 'Young men of thirty to thirty-five,' Cavafy commented. 'Not more. Thirty-five years ago a man of thirty called himself old, while today he's scarcely begun to live. Bathing and sport, you see, have made this change.' There were family portraits (no doubt, exceedingly bad) and other pictures all over the walls.

Like a photographer, Cavafy was continuously adjusting the light; he himself invariably sat in shadow, timidly avoiding the eyes of others while yet examining them closely. He would get up and open or shut or half-shut the shutters in different parts of the room, or half-draw the curtains. He would light or lower the petrol lamp, though he usually preferred candles. He would light or snuff a candle or two, sometimes adding another if a beautiful face appeared in the room.

All the time he was gesticulating. He would put a half-cigarette in his holder, light a match and wave it about in the air; often a second was needed. This was partly to change the conversation. Perhaps the half-cigarette was a dramatic device as much as an expedient adopted for reasons of hygiene or economy.

A tray was brought in with ouzo, masticha and whisky: 'Or would you rather have beer? I'll send the boy for some.' Red glasses were brought out for favoured visitors, or for the beautiful. A variety of *mezedhes* was offered with the drinks: little bits of meat, quarters of hard-boiled egg, cheese and olives. The latter were used to stop the mouths of the over-talkative: 'Have an olive?' He got rid of visitors by saying: 'In five minutes I'm going to my friend Benaki's. Stop if you like: I'm going.' And out he went, but slipped back again as soon as the bore was out of the way.

This was the centre from which he organised his literary reputation, whence he would :

> Like Cato give his little senate laws
> And sit attentive to his own applause.

He said of Xenopoulos, whom he admired, and who had been the first to write about his work: 'What a mania he has for replying to everyone! What a fearful thing! He has an answer ready for every criticism made of him. He looks after his reputation (and he's quite right) but how he exposes himself!'[10] Cavafy, who lost his sleep if the silliest young literary aspirant printed two sentences against him, put up other people to defend him.

He wished to be written about, no matter by whom. 'Most people,' he said, 'when they read an article about someone in a newspaper, see a signature, a name at the end. But the reader will never try to find out what sort of a name it is, and if it has or

10. Alithersis, p. 18.

hasn't a place in letters, if it's competent or not. What the reader will remain is what is written in the article.'[11]

He would urge the young to write about him in this way: 'It's not worth your while to write about an established poet. Why not write about Cavafy? Yes! Because if Cavafy's work doesn't survive you won't lose anything! Who remembers the critic when the work doesn't last? But if the work lasts – oh, then everyone will say that first X, or among the first X saw and understood! And what a critical spirit he had!'[12]

He did not, however, encourage creative writing, and it has been suggested that he was afraid of rivalry. When Mr Basil Athanassopoulos remarked that there was no more literary movement in Alexandria, he said: 'And if there's no literary movement here, Alexandria doesn't lose anything. Perhaps it's all for the best. Those young men could have devoted themselves to commerce.'[13]

Mr Malanos published a letter in a newspaper, 27 November 1926: 'Until today I have never written a hostile article against Mr Cavafy's work. All I have written are some articles against his tactics as a *teacher*. I think I had a profound obligation to enlighten by every means in my power the poet's youthful victims who by flattery and praise insensibly became blind instruments of his pursuit of applause.' Peridis declared that he had not found anyone thus corrupted, but Mr Malanos produced the example of Vrisimitsakis, whom Cavafy had called 'the strongest intellect of modern Greece',[14] and added that he could name six more. He records Cavafy as saying: 'I don't understand affection and hatred except as affection and hatred for my work.'[15]

Nevertheless Cavafy seems to have had little interest in his reputation abroad. Forster's letters on the subject to Valassopoulos show the poet's lack of collaboration with his efforts: he had interested T. S. Eliot (then editor of *The Criterion*) and the Hogarth Press, and Heinemann was making advances. Forster wished Valassopoulos (whose translations he over-

11. Malanos, *Cavafy*, p. 96.
12. Alithersis, p. 12 n.
13. Malanos, *Cavafy*, p. 36 n.
14. Peridis, pp. 130–1 and 130 n.; Malanos, *Cavafy 2*, p. 98.
15. Malanos, *Cavafy*, p. 46.

estimated) to make a complete version. In a letter of 8 January 1928 he said that he was in agreement with Cavafy that if the erotic poems were to be done there must be no 'softening'. I am privately informed that Valassopoulis was very much scared at this idea, and in any case he disliked the erotic poems. This may have been a contributory cause to the failure of the scheme; but Valassopoulos told Peridis that Cavafy did not regard his work as ready for a definitive edition, and in any case he naturally did not wish a translation to precede an edition of the original text.[16] A few poems were in fact published in English periodicals, the only poems for which Cavafy ever received any cash payment. He might rightly mistrust translations: his brother John's English versions were tediously prosaic, Cataro's Italian versions were absurd, and a French writer had rendered the praetors in their togas in *Waiting for the Barbarians*, as 'coiffés en toques'.[17]

There was never anything like a *salon* in the Rue Lepsius. People dropped in as they wished, and introduced their friends, if they were likely to be agreeable to the poet – and if they were not, they soon found out. He was timid about meeting new people, and would not speak to anyone who had not been properly introduced. Once Pieridis wrung his unwilling consent to receive a Greek actor – who was not young enough to please – and prompted his friend on the way upstairs. Cavafy (who did not examine him closely) was delighted that he appeared to know his work. 'But how could I not know *The god leaves Antony, Ithaca, The Town?*' said the actor, who had just learned the names by heart. The red glasses were ordered.[18]

Once a week there was a family visit: Marie Cavafy (Aristides' widow) came with her daughter Haricleia to pass an afternoon. 'Hari is coming tomorrow,' he would say (as Mr Basil Athanassopoulos tells me), and his younger friends felt that they had better not show themselves. With the two women of his family he was the 'archon', the 'protoclassatos'. He liked talking of past family glories as the black beads of his *kombolöi* slipped between his long fingers. When he spoke of more ancient history his niece's attention strayed, and her mother dozed. When he gave Haricleia some of his poems on *feuilles volantes*, Marie

16. Peridis, p. 112
17. Pieridis, p. 47. Cavafy himself made some translations.
18. ibid., p. 41.

snatched them away from her. If any young intellectuals came in he broke off his English or French conversation to talk to them in Greek, and offered the young people raki and cheese and olives.

People on both sides of his life were aware of his interest in other worlds than their own. He took pride in belonging to more worlds than one, and in showing each off to the other. Mr Malanos tells us how he liked to talk of his social life: 'Beginning: "Tomorrow evening I'm invited to Antony Benaki's" . . . or "Timo, try some of this masticha; it's from Chios, Mme Delta sent it me", he went on with a whole conversation which often left most of the company that was not *mondain* cold – for there were people from the smart world there too. Once or twice I happened to meet Antony Benaki at his house, and once the diplomat Spyros Constantinides . . . With them he positively flashed with happiness. And in fact, at such minutes, we the rank and file of his friends had the impression that these people entirely robbed us of him, and forever.' He liked returning to his old world: 'He thirsted for information about everyone and everything. He hadn't forgotten any of the people of that older world. He knew each one's family tree . . .'[19]

It is not difficult to remember anything in which one has once been interested, and Alexandrian family trees are not long. Cavafy also remembered the first steps in literature of his young friends. Moreover, he himself was capable of teasing snobs on occasion. 'My dear B.', he said to a smart young man of slender literary pretensions, 'I'm deeply grateful to you for coming to-day. For days I've been tortured by a doubt. Only you can resolve it . . . Tomorrow evening I'm invited to dinner at Antony Benaki's. And without you, dear B., I should have made myself ridiculous, absolutely ridiculous. I've forgotten how to go into the world! I've forgotten how people eat! Once, I remember, when people ate soup, they used to put the spoon into their mouths by the point. Then you were only supposed to eat out of the side of the spoon. My dear B., what's the correct thing today? Only you know, only you can tell me. These things are important, but very important. Often our happiness hangs on them.'[20]

19. Malanos, *T.*, p. 35.
20. Sareyannis, p. 39.

He was now more or less alone in the world. There was a degree of coldness in his relations with his brother John. Their niece Helen (Alexander's daughter) has suggested that the reason for this was Constantine's wish to bestow her and her handsome dowry on Alexander Singopoulos as a way of providing for him by marriage – a plan of which John disapproved.[21] Moreover John, who retired in 1919, was in bad health, and spent much of his time in the warm dry climate of Helouan. Haricleia, their niece, wrote thence on his account to Constantine in November 1919, urging him to join them there if things looked bad in Alexandria – things often look bad in Egypt. Somewhere in the offing was 'Mme D.', presumably John's mistress, and his family were trying to make a breach between them.

In January 1920 John wrote sadly: 'A man's soul is sometimes wont to bring him tidings – and my soul announces that my life is over, and what appals me is the meagre result I have to show for the many years I have lived . . . but don't let me sadden you: *you* are my brother, and that is no small thing, for I am proud of you and your work, and I do my best to make the value of that work known among my small circle of English acquaintances.' A month later Paul's death left them as the sole survivors of a family of seven.

John was as prodigal as Constantine was parsimonious, and infuriated his brother by his extravagances. A special compartment on the train that brought him and his niece back from Helouan and cost £30 particularly annoyed Constantine, who was vexed to see them getting out of it with great bunches of flowers presented by the station-master at their departure. A discussion raged, John continuing in English and Constantine breaking into Greek.

John now lived in Alexandria with his niece and her mother. He was attacked by palsy, and Constantine frequently visited him. When he died in February 1923, and friends had gathered at the house before the funeral, Constantine kept leaning over the open coffin and crying: 'John! John!' into his dead brother's ear. He told those standing by that he wanted to be sure that John was dead, and was not to be buried alive.[22]

21. *NE*, 1 August 1972, p. 1068.
22. Malanos, *Cavafy*, pp. 147–8.

A few days later he was crying out against 'injustice' and threatening to contest John's will. He had left the greater part of his property to a foreign woman[23] (presumably 'Mme D.'), some thirteen thousand to his niece Haricleia (who was in part dependent on him), and only one thousand pounds to Constantine – who was, however, quite adequately provided for, and need hardly have cried out that he was 'disinherited'. A coolness ensued between him and his niece; when he drew up his own will in the following June he left her only £200. He left £700 to his other niece, Helen, whom he believed to be very well off. The rest of his estate, including some diamonds, was left to his friend Alexander Singopoulos.[24]

Nevertheless, though grief had for a moment given place to anger, his sorrow for his last and surviving brother was sincere and great. Rika Singopoulos tells us that at the funeral of George Petridis, when his brother Paul cried with heart-rending sobs, Cavafy tenderly stroked his shoulder saying : 'I sympathise with you, poor Paul. Believe me, no one but I can understand your terrible grief. Remember, I have lost five brothers.'[25]

In 1924 there occurred one of the most disagreeable episodes in the poet's life, and the cause was utterly trivial. Early in that year he circulated his poem *Before time should change them* (112): it is about the parting of two lovers, one of whom has to go to Canada or New York. Cavafy naturally printed the word 'York' in Greek with a smooth breathing for it is not pronounced 'Hyork'. A journalist observed that in this he differed from Socrates Lagoudakis, who used a rough breathing. Lagoudakis, an eccentric and self-important journalist, began to attack Cavafy in his weekly column; his attacks became increasingly more virulent, and were not confined to the poet's work, but extended to his personality, and he was denounced as 'another Oscar Wilde'. It seemed that a dangerous and unpleasant law-suit was almost inevitable.

A number of the poet's friends then published a protest : 'not so much against Lagoudakis as against a section of the press which

23. Peridis, pp. 114–15.
24. ibid., p. 115 n.
25. No doubt he said 'six'. Rika Singopoulos is sometimes curiously inaccurate, and she seems to have forgotten the existence of George.

permits him to insult in his column a man whose literary value, whose fine manners and mild nature have not only offended no one, but have earned general respect and sympathy.'[26]

On the same day Lagoudakis was to give a lecture at the Aeschylus Club. Many of Cavafy's friends gathered there at the hour, and shouted: 'Down with the libeller!' The directors of the club were so unwise as to order an attack to be made on the demonstrators, and Mr Malanos received an honourable wound on the occasion.

He was, in fact, having a coolness with the poet at that time, but next day as he was walking in the street he felt an arm embrace him from behind, and heard Cavafy say warmly: 'Timo, I always knew you were a dog!'[27] (i.e. faithful).

Nevertheless he was not very ready with his sympathy when another poet was in difficulties in 1925. Costas Varnalis had been suspended for six months by the Ministry of Education on account of his work *The Light that Burns* (issued three years earlier under a pseudonym). Stephen Pargas, the editor of *Grammata*, tried to get up a protest on his behalf in Alexandria like that which had been made in Athens. Cavafy's signature, of course, was wanted to head the list.

Mr Malanos offered to approach him. He called about four o'clock and found Cavafy playing chess with his friend. He took the document, read it with care, and refused to sign: he had never cared for Varnalis' revolutionary poems. 'Mr Cavafy,' said his visitor, 'Varnalis is one of your sincerest admirers; how will he take the absence of your name from the protest?' And in fact Cavafy went to *Grammata*, to read the document again, and paid great attention to the signatures that had already been procured. He looked at it yet a third time and suggested several amendments, and only signed it after a fourth reading.[28]

It was shortly after this time, as Mr Malanos tells us, that he cherished for a while the idea of being Cavafy's Eckermann, but he received too great discouragement from the poet who, rather than answer his questions, made him ask questions of himself. Cavafy hardly seemed to require an Eckermann, for he really only wanted to talk about his own work; and even

26. Malanos, *Memoirs*, p. 208.
27. ibid.
28. ibid., p. 165.

then he liked to keep his secrets to himself: 'You're a poet,' he said, 'and you know.'

Littera scripta manet: a few fragments of his table talk have been recorded, and they are in no way extraordinary. It is always natural to entertain some scepticism about past conversation and dead talkers, and – having perhaps never heard any very remarkable talk oneself – to suspect that their brilliance has been very much exaggerated. Yet it seems certain that Cavafy was a great virtuoso, and his highest praise comes from Mr Malanos, whom some people have seen as the Devil's Advocate.[29]

'The truth is he was an enchanting talker. But a talker who exploited his rare charm to create affection for his work. What chiefly interested him when he talked was the meandering development of his theme, that is the playing with words, from which of course his ostentatious vanity was not absent. By this I don't at all wish to disparage what he said; I mean only that its originality was elsewhere. And in fact what attracted the attention of his hearers was his tone, was his art in handling his theme, was his rhetorical figures. It is all this that makes me think that, perhaps for the first time, a modern Greek was speaking our language with the art and grace of the conversationalists of antiquity.'[30]

In 1926 the dictator Pangalos awarded Cavafy the order of the Phoenix, which he bestowed at the same time upon a Spanish

---

29. 'His character, as Mr Malanos saw it, was very unpleasing; he found him self-centred, sly, secretive and jealous, always wearing a mask and playing a part, with never anything in his mind but his own self-interest. How far it was fitting to write such a study when the poet was suffering greatly in his last illness is perhaps hardly the business of the reviewer to discuss, but it would be unfair to pass over the fact that I have talked to not a few of Cavafy's acquaintances, and have never found anyone who had not the warmest remembrances of his personal charm: none of them saw any trace of the detestable poseur described by Mr Malanos.' – R. M. Dawkins, *JHS*.

'Perhaps' it would have been better if the reviewer had attended to his business. Mr Malanos' study was begun in 1926 when the poet was in good health and at the height of his celebrity. Most people who have written about Cavafy have seen every trace of the poseur; but neither they nor Mr Malanos found him detestable. It is fair to say that Professor Dawkins was reviewing the first edition; the book has since been somewhat toned down.

30. Malanos, *Memoirs*, p. 152.

dancer, Aurea. This was not unnaturally the occasion for many ribald jests and caricatures. Some people urged Cavafy to return the decoration, but he said: 'It was awarded to me by the Greek state, which I love and reverence. To return the decoration would be an insult on my part to the Greek state, and therefore I am keeping it.'[31] He was in the right, for Aurea was a great artist, and Palamas wrote a poem to her.

A favourite haunt of literary Alexandria, and one much frequented by the poet, was the bookshop *Grammata* in the Rue Debbane. It was run by Stephen Pargas (alias Nikos Zelitas) and his wife. She used to be shocked when Alexander Singopoulos called there for Cavafy and said: 'Get up, old man; let's be going.' She thought it an unkind insistence on the age that he wished to conceal.

She and her husband knew the poet well, and she records how once he came to their house after ten o'clock at night to give Pargas a poem that he had just finished: 'I brought it to you now, Niko, so that I can go to sleep in peace.' And on another occasion: 'Take it, Niko, it's burning my fingers.'

Cavafy would bring poems to the bookshop for Pargas to post for him, and he would chat and exchange news (gaining by the exchange, for Pargas was a publicist as well as an editor): 'Nothing escapes us, Niko; if anything happens on earth or even on Mars, we'll hear of it, either you or I.'[32]

Sometimes at night he went to the Rue Missala to the Billiard Palace to find the editor Sotiris Liatsis when he wanted to beg a notice in the *Tachydromos* or for a chat: he was fond of the ash-grey 'literary cat' (as he called it) belonging to the establishment. Sometimes he visited the Café Al Salam in the same street. An unnamed correspondent informed Mr Malanos[33] of Cavafy's visits to the latter from 1929 to 1931. There he got to know three boys, Spyro, George (who was book-keeper at a café in Ibrahimieh) and Toto, a motor mechanic. He used to take them to his house, and he tipped them: they told Mr Malanos' informant and his friends that this was merely out of kindness, but they hardly expected to be believed, and they were not. Toto was Cavafy's favourite, and the respectable clients of the café

31. Tsirkas, *Chronology*.
32. Malanos, *Memoirs*, pp. 416–17.
33. ibid., pp. 296–8.

were much amused when the poet looked in and asked if he were there, and went away at once if he were not. It was conjectured that Toto became a regular visitor to the Rue Lepsius, and this was why Cavafy's visits to the café later became infrequent.

Yet it may have been the wish for company as much as for sex that drove Cavafy to the Al Salam. Rika Singopoulos insists on his fear of loneliness. She herself did much to alleviate it. After her marriage with Alexander Singopoulos in July 1926 they lived on the floor below the poet. At first he had been opposed to this marriage, and wept at the wedding; but he found in her a very faithful friend both to himself and his work. It seems to have been one of those happy intellectual friendships that often exist between a homosexual man and a very superior woman. Posterity, however, may reproach her for her dilatoriness in writing down her recollections, her over-confidence in her memory, and her slapdash methods; she often makes obvious mistakes. Her evidence, however, is always that of a loyal friend and a (would-be) truthful recorder. For some years she edited *Alexandrini Techni*, which was supported by Cavafy, and was virtually his organ. She looked after his work, and her husband was his nurse if he were ill. After his death it was they who brought out the first edition of his works; and it was to her above all that he turned in his last illness,

In 1922 occurred the Asia Minor disaster, and the destruction of Smyrna, which left a million and a half Greeks without homes. We do not know how much Cavafy was affected by this tragedy. It has been suggested to me that he wished to appear more unmoved than he really was, because his younger friends were anti-nationalistic. As a Constantinopolitan and an Alexandrian he must have felt twice over that it was a kindred city that had suffered : but whether he viewed this suffering with the indifference of his Philip or the sympathy of his Demetrius we shall probably never know. He told Mr Malanos that he had been deeply moved by the Balkan war of 1912–13; yet it was unimportant to his writing self, for it left no trace on his work. It is still a matter of dispute whether he were on the side of Venizelos or of Constantine I when Greece was divided between them; it cannot therefore be important to discover which side he took (if any).

If it had mattered to him, he would have let us know. He had friends on either side.

George Seferis, to whom the disaster of 1922 was the worst thing that could happen, wished to see the contemporary feeling of despair in a poem which Cavafy published in 1922, but some months before the event: *Who fought for the Achaean League* (105).

> Brave men were you, who fought and fell with glory,
> Not fearing those who conquered everywhere.
> Blameless, if Diaios and Critolaos were to blame.
> Whenever the Greeks wish to boast,
> 'Such men our nation turns out,' they will say
> Of you. So marvellous shall be your praise.
> Written in Alexandria by an Achaean
> The seventh year of Ptolemy Lathyros.

The publication of the poem preceded the Smyrna disaster; it was, however, composed in this year of crisis.

Fortunately we know for certain what his attitude to it was: Mr Bryn Davies, then professor of English at Fuad I University, Cairo, wrote me the following note (25 November 1948).

'When I was talking to Cavafy in 1930 I had just had the poem about the Achaean League translated to me, and had been told that it had a special significance in view of what happened in 1922. It was this, he said, he could not understand and evidently, from the very detailed account he gave me of the Achaean League, he had actually been thinking in terms of what he called an entirely futile and inexplicable revival, with no relation whatever to modern events at all. What struck me at the time was that he spoke of the Achaean League as though it was a purely contemporary event.'

This is no isolated testimony, for Sareyannis wrote: 'Many Alexandrians will remember his indignation when he heard it said that [this poem] was inspired by the Asia Minor disaster, that he himself and the Athenian men of letters were the subject of *A Byzantine nobleman in exile writing verses* (96) and Malanos of *Understood not* (137) etc. Cavafy did not want his poems to appear linked with definite actuality ...'[34]

34. Sareyannis, p. 121.

It is therefore an error to see (as Seferis did) the two last lines
as a deliberate connecting link between the events of 146 B.C.
and those of 1922. the seventh year of Ptolemy Lathyrus
(109 B.C.) being the period when 'omnipotent Rome is all the
time drawing its web closer round the pitiful kingdom of the
Lagids', another date in the decline of the Hellenistic world.[35]
Cavafy was merely giving distance and time to the defeat of the
Achaean League as he had done to the battle of Magnesia. It is
this detachment that gives his poems a universality which
entitles the reader to apply them even to events that happened
after their author's death, and Mr Malanos could apply the lines
on the Achaean League to the fall of Crete in 1941 with as much
right and greater appropriateness. Moreover the unnamed
Achaean who celebrates his countrymen years after the event,
out of the way in Alexandria, and does not venture to name the
Romans, is a typically unheroic figure, fit to be Cavafy's mouthpiece.[36]

And yet, disagreement with Seferis about the origin of the
poem only brings one into closer agreement with him about its
impact. 'It is no visual reminiscence, no reference to a vague
mythology, no thematic treatment by the artist of "the beautiful"
as seen in an icy and solitary piece of sculpture. Diaios,
Critolaos, Philip, Demetrius, Ptolemy Lathyrus, the Achaean
are inside us, and inside us now; each of them could be you and
I and everybody who has some consciousness of the evil and of
the calamity.'[37]

In Cavafy's poetry the past is always present, and the present
(or rather the recent) is involved in time past. In *Days of 1909,
1910 and 1911* (140) he writes of a poor boy working in a
blacksmith's shop who prostitutes himself for a dollar or
two:

> I ask myself if in ancient times
> Great Alexandria had a lovelier boy.

Seferis commented: 'One is never quite sure when one reads
him whether a youth who works in a blacksmith's shop in con-

35. Seferis, *Greek Style*, p. 130.
36. Sareyannis, p. 96 n.
37. Seferis, l.c., p. 131.

temporary Alexandria will not turn up in the evening at one of
those dives where the subjects of Ptolemy Lathyrus are holding
their revels.'[38] But the poem was printed in 1928 : if he were still
alive (and he was likely to have been destroyed by misery and
debauchery) the beauty of the blacksmith's boy must by then
have been as much a thing of the past as that of any of Ptolemy
VIII's subjects. Only the immortals are eternally beautiful; one
may imagine *One of their gods* (62) – Hermes, Apollo or
Dionysus – among the 'angels' entertained on the ground floor
of 10 Rue Lepsius.

   This poem and others, especially *Days of 1908* (153) where
the hero peels off a shabby cinnamon-coloured suit and mended
underclothes to reveal a faultless body, show the poet's aware-
ness of extreme poverty – of which no inhabitant of Egypt could
well be unaware – and his compassion with it. But this is nothing upon which a theory can be built. Rika Singopoulos noted
that he had a liberal hope for social progress and the gradual
redress of injustice, but that he was hostile to any sort of
violence – a thing to which his constitutional timidity must in
any case have opposed him. Mr Savidis[39] calls attention to the fact
that some 'political' poetry of later date has been influenced by
Cavafy, but agrees that it is an accident of chronology that
'political' poetry was in fashion at the time when his influence
was beginning to make himself felt. Most of it owes nothing to
him, and his muse was in no way 'engaged'.

   Cavafy was 'political' in the sense that for him what he read
in Renan or Polybius or Bouché-Leclerq was as 'actual' to him –
as much 'news' – as anything he might read in the *Tachydromos*
or the *Egyptian Gazette*. We may imagine a detached but intensely interested reader of the newspaper (as it were) of 146 or
149 B.C., above all a defeatist. No doubt his sympathies were,
to some extent, with the Hellenistic kingdoms; but like
Demetrius Soter, he knew that their day was over. He preferred,
we may suppose, Alexandria and Antony to Rome and Octavius;
but his preference was not much more than local patriotism, and
an inclination towards the losing side.

   Victrix causa deis placuit, sed victa Cavafi.

38. ibid., p. 173.
39. Savidis, *DL*, p. 8.

As Forster said, his Hellenism consisted mainly in a proud know-ledge of 'the influence that has flowed through the ages'. Know-ing that 'captive Greece tamed her fierce victor', he might not think her captivity of the first importance.

In *A township of Asia Minor* (125) the townsmen were 'com-pletely indifferent whether the ruler of the world was called Antony or Octavius',[40] and Cavafy completely understood their indifference to a struggle which could in no way benefit them. Equally well could he understand the poor young man in Antioch, ready to sell his services to any one of the three power-ful men who might pay for them – 'all three of them do Syria the same amount of harm'. *They ought to have thought* (149) – the Gods ought indeed to have thought of creating a fourth and honest man; then it would have been a pleasure to serve him.

As far as we know, Cavafy regarded the present with the same indifference and the same cynical disbelief as the past, but with much less interest, for it lacked coins, inscriptions and historians. The chief thing it could do for him perhaps (since history repeats itself) was to throw light on the past and of course it provided living witnesses.

In any case, Cavafy is never a partisan in politics or in religion. One may imagine him, unlike the priests of Delphi, trying to come out on the side of the vanquished. But an individual on any side may awaken his sympathy. He cares as much for the old heathen servant praying to her idol, as for the fevered, love-sick Christian boy Cleitus (122) for whom she prays. He feels as much for the Christian boy mourning his father, *Priest of the temple of Serapis* (128), as for the pagan boy who rushes from the house where Christian priests

> Made prayers and fervent supplications to Jesus
> Or to Mary (I don't know their religion well) –

for the soul of his dead friend *Myris* (143).

The Julian poems well illustrate this balance: the cycle begins with *Julian at the Mysteries*[41] of 1896, and ends with the last poem of the canon *On the outskirts of Antioch* (154) which was unprinted at his death.

40. Mavrogordato, p. 154 n.
41. Keeley and Savidis, pp. 2–5.

The first poem, originally entitled *Julian at Eleusis*, is probably based on a note of Gibbon's: 'When Julian, in a momentary panic, made the sign of the cross, the daemons instantly disappeared . . . Gregory supposes that they were frightened, but the priest declared that they were indignant. The reader, according to the measure of his faith, will determine this profound question.'[42] The tale is here related by a credulous Christian, but Cavafy's feeling in the matter must have been that of Gibbon: amusement at both explanations.

It cannot be supposed that he was near to sharing the viewpoint of fourth-century Christians, greatly as he admired St Gregory of Nazianzus – indeed he spoke once of having left several poems unwritten for want of a copy of Gregory.[43] Nevertheless the fact that he (ironically) makes the Christians the narrators of the Julian poems does not mean that he had any greater liking for the other side. Julian was a pedantic prig, and his artificially reconstituted paganism was puritanical and austere. Cavafy accepts both Julian and Gregory as part of the Greek past – but on the whole his sympathies are likely to have been with the easy-going citizens of Antioch (106) who had never suffered any inconvenience from Christ or from the Christian emperor Constantius, and were irritated by the bearded, kill-joy Julian. For Cavafy had no Swinburnian sentimentality about the Apostate, and 'the great king's high, sad heart'; he knew that he was a bore, and perhaps the only thing that he tolerated in him was the fact that his was a lost cause.

Other poems extend the frontiers of the Hellenistic world: there is an epitaph on the ruler of the little kingdom of Commagene (107) on the Euphrates; there is a prince from Western Libya (141) visiting Alexandria and proud of his Hellenism, but hardly daring to open his mouth because of his bad Greek; there are the Jewish sovereigns, *Alexander Jannaeus and Alexandra* (145). They make a splendid progress through the streets of Jerusalem: the work of the Maccabees has established the independence of their country.

> The King Alexander Jannaeus
> And his consort the Queen Alexandra

42. cit. ibid., p. 6.
43. Malanos, *Cavafy*, p. 123.

In all respects equal to the Seleucids.
Good Jews, pure Jews, faithful Jews – above all.
But, just as circumstances required,
Also conversant with the Greek speech;
And having relations with Greeks and with
Greek-mannered monarchs – but as equals, and no mistake.[44]

They were more thoroughly hellenised, no doubt, than the
prince from Western Libya, or than the other 'minor kings' at
whom the Alexandrian philosopher laughs in *Return from
Greece*[45] – an unpublished poem of 1914. And this Alexandrian
admits that Greece has been a bit too much for him. He has
Asiatic feelings, and is no more purely Greek than those in whom
'a bit of Arabia shows through'. No doubt he is another mask,
imperfectly concealing his author.

Seferis, who particularly admired the poem about Jannaeus,
saw here the 'deception' that he found characteristic of Cavafy :
'The conquest, the great Diaspora, the endless agony of the Jews
are there, muttering in their sleep, as if dreaming of Alexander
Jannaeus and of his Queen and of the great Judas Maccabeus
and his four illustrious brothers, all of whom will dissolve just
like dreams as soon as, in a very few years, Destruction awakes.'[46]
It may be so; but this looks more like a romantic meditation upon
a theme from Cavafy than criticism. Cavafy may perhaps have
been living for the moment in Jannaeus' day of triumph.

In Sparta (139) and its sequel *Come, O King of the
Lacedaemonians* (146) take us to Sparta in the third century
B.C. But the story of Cleomenes and his noble mother
Cratesiclea is bound up with Alexandria. Ptolemy III Euergetes
had promised to help the Spartan king against Macedonia and
the Achaean league if he would send his mother and children to
Egypt as hostages. Plutarch (here quoted in North's version)
tells the story : 'So he was a long time before he would for shame
make his mother privie unto it . . . When she heard it, she fell a
laughing, and told him : "Why how cometh it to passe that thou
hast kept it thus long, and would not tell me ? Come, come," said
she, "put me straight into a ship, and send me whither thou wilt

44. tr. Mavrogordato.
45. Keeley and Savidis, pp. 38–9.
46. Seferis, *Greek Style*, pp. 148–9.

that this bodie of mine may do some good upon my country, before crooked age consume my life without profite." ' When she was about to sail from Taenarum 'she took Cleomenes aside into the temple of *Neptune*, and embracing and kissing him, perceiving that his heart yearned for sorrow of her departure, she said unto him: "O King of LACEDAEMON, let no man see for shame when we come out of the temple that we have wept and dishonoured SPARTA: for that only is in our power: as for the rest, as it pleaseth the gods let it be." '

There are three Byzantine poems issued during the last period. *John Cantacuzene prevails* (114) is a poem about the clash of disloyalties: the Byzantine nobleman who speaks only wishes he had chosen the winning side. *Anna Dalassina* (129) is a noble mother, worthy to stand beside Cratesiclea. *Of coloured glass* (117) is the most interesting of these poems: here the deceptive pomp of Alexander Jannaeus and Alexandra is absent.

A detail much moves me
At the coronation at Vlachernae of John Cantacuzene
And Irene, daughter of Andronicus Asàn.
As they had only a few precious stones
(The poverty of our poor empire was great)
They wore artificial ones. A lot of little bits of glass,
Red, green or blue. In my eyes
They have nothing humble or undignified
About them, these little bits
Of coloured glass. Rather they are like
A sorrowful protest
Against the unjust misfortune of the crowned.
They are the symbols of what should have been,
Of what on all accounts should have been
At the coronation of a Lord John Cantacuzene
And a Lady Irene, daughter of Andronicus Asàn.

'Three emperors and three empresses were seated on the Byzantine throne,' says Gibbon. 'During the last troubles, the treasures of the state, and even the palace had been alienated or embezzled: the royal banquet was served in pewter or earthenware; and such was the proud poverty of the times that the absence of gold and jewels was supplied by the paltry artifice of glass and gilt leather.'[47]

Cavafy had now learned in what drawer to search if he wanted anything out of the cupboard of Byzantine history, and he spoke warmly of the Byzantine historians: 'They're neglected. One day they'll be discovered and their originality will be admired. They cultivated a kind of history that has never been written before or since. They wrote history dramatically.'[48]

Many of the last love poems are sad. In some of them, perhaps, we may guess at a personal experience. *A young artist in words in his twenty-fourth year* (134) is tortured by 'halved enjoyment': his friend allows himself to be kissed, and more, but does not really enjoy it. One may even imagine that *Desperation* (110) tells the end of the same story: the lover has lost his friend, who is determined to forsake 'the lust that is branded', and he vainly seeks to find him again in the arms of other boys. *The twenty-fifth year of his life* (121) recalls *Days of 1903* (70): the agonised longing for a stranger, once met and not to be found again. The boredom of the young man *In the dreary village* (120) who enjoys the longed-for love in a dream, may be a sympathetic recollection of the life of his friend in Benha.

Other poems may have been inspired by people whom Cavafy knew: the wretched poverty of the blacksmith's boy (140) or of the boy in the cinnamon-coloured suit (153) has already been mentioned. Perhaps he had enjoyed the confidence or had even employed the services of the young man in *Days of 1896* (133), who was ruined, and sometimes acted as a pimp, but yet in all his degradation retained a moving beauty.

Two fictitious lovers are parted *Before time should change them* (112), for one of them has to go to America to work. Another couple is parted by death. The survivor lays *Lovely flowers and white* (147) on the dead boy's cheap coffin. Three months ago his friend had deserted him in favour of an admirer who had promised him two suits and some silk handkerchiefs – they were too poor, he said, to go about together. The forsaken lover worked hard, raised twenty pounds and got back his friend –

47. cit. Mavrogordato, p. 145 n.
48. Sareyannis, p. 36.

who had been deceived by false promises and, anyway, loved him. But now he is dead : we may imagine him lying in his one new suit (all he managed to get out of his new admirer) in his cheap coffin. The white flowers suit his beauty and his age of twenty-two : for those of riper years (as a Greek undertaker once told me) purple flowers are more appropriate. The matter-of-factness of the poem adds to its poignancy : one can well believe that Cavafy had 'verified' the details. I have heard of a German woman who paid for Greek nationality with two suits, made for the husband from whom she parted at the church door; and of a Turkish boy who said to an Englishman, pointing out two Americans : 'Let's each take one of them ! They've got dollars !'

The survivor has to go on business to the café where he went with his friend : 'A knife in the heart.'

The poems about fictitious boys of the ancient world are sad too. A young man wastes his life *In the taverns* (123) of Beirut. Tamides has left him to go with the Prefect's son (an advantageous liaison) and Alexandria has become intolerable. *The illness of Cleitus* (122) is as much due to his desertion by the young actor whom he loved as to the fever that is ravaging Alexandria. *Myris* (143) is dead, and his pagan friend feels that he has lost him a second time.

> I felt that, as a Christian, he was united
> With his own people, and I had become
> A stranger, a complete stranger; I felt already
> A doubt approaching : perhaps I had been mocked
> By my passion for him, and I always was a stranger –
> I rushed out of the frightful house,
> I ran quickly before it was snatched away and altered
> By their Christianity – the memory of Myris.

In a city of many religions, like Alexandria, Cavafy may have 'verified', indeed have lived this poem, and most painfully. A friend of his once told me that it exactly expressed his own feelings at a Jewish funeral.

Cimon son of Learchus, aged twenty-two, student of Greek literature in Cyrene (138) hears of the death of his cousin Marylos, mourned by his lover Hermoteles.

> His untimely death
> Has done away in me every bit of resentment . . .
> Every bit of resentment with Marylos – although
> He stole from me the love of Hermoteles.
> So that if Hermoteles should want me back again
> It won't be at all the same thing. I know
> What a sensitive nature I have. The image of Marylos
> Will come between us, and I shall imagine
> I hear him saying : 'Well, now you're satisfied;
> Now you've got him back, as you wanted, Cimon;
> Now you've no longer any reason to slander me.'

Nevertheless *Twenty-three to twenty-four* (132) is the most triumphant of the love poems. The long vigil of four hours in the café, where the boy has mechanically turned over newspapers, has spent all his money on coffee or brandy, has smoked all his cigarettes, has a happy ending. His friend arrives at last, almost beyond hope with sixty pounds won at a gambling house. They go together to a 'house of ill-fame' – probably that in the Attarine quarter – and for once it is the scene of mutual and unbought love.

Temethos of Antioch, A.D. 400 (118) is an extremely interesting poem, for Temethos, like Cavafy himself, is a maker of masks. At this late period, the very end of paganism, he has written a poem entitled *Emonides*, named after a (fictitious) lover of Antiochus Epiphanes (175–164 B.C.), but in this poem he expresses his own passion.

> We the initiate,
> His close friends; we, the initiate
> Know for whom the lines were written.
> The ignorant Antiochans read 'Emonides'.

According to the Magic Prescriptions (152) is a last cry against devouring time. Seferis (though his application of this poem to the myth of the resurrection of a dead god is an example of the embarrassing way in which he sometimes abandons criticism in favour of vague poetical monologue) speaks of it as one of the most beautiful passages in the Greek language.[49]

49. Seferis, *Greek Style*, p. 158.

'What extract can be found from herbs
  Of magic?' said an aesthete.
'What extract made after the prescriptions
  Of ancient Greco-Syrian sorcerers,
  That for one day (if for no longer
  Its power lasts) or even for a little
  Can bring me back my three and twenty years,
  My friend at his two and twenty years, can bring
  Me back – his beauty, his love.

  What extract can be found, made after
  The ancient Greco-Syrians' prescriptions
  That in accordance with that return
  Can bring back too our little room again.

Up to his last days Cavafy was writing, and it is said that while on his deathbed he asked Rika Singopoulos to look up a reference in the municipal library that he wanted for his last poem.[50]

When his friend Antony Benaki went to settle in Athens, he tried to persuade Cavafy to move, but he steadfastly refused to leave Alexandria. 'Mohammed Aly Square is my aunt,' he used to say. 'Rue Cherif Pacha is my first cousin and the Rue de Ramleh my second. How can I leave them?'

He could not, nor could he leave the tradition to which his city was heir, and it was he who had claimed this heritage for it. He was the last and greatest Alexandrian. 'It was not, as has been thought, the Alexandrian period that was his source of poetical inspiration. It was Cavafy who enriched it with his poetry.'[51] His was the really new work of art whose arrival, as Eliot would have said, altered the whole existing order of the Hellenistic past.

In 1930 he received a visit from Marinetti: the dialogue has been recorded.[52]

MARINETTI: 'And you, Cavafy, are a futurist . . . You're a man of the Past, Poet, but up to a certain point. I can see you haven't been impressed by the beauty of machines (motorcars, for instance) and that you still use verbs and commas and

50. Sareyannis, p. 50.
51. Ouranis, p. 136.
52. Catraro.

full stops, and despise electric light. All that has no great importance. You're a man of the past in form, but from what
I can discover in your poems, I come to the conclusion that
you are a futurist. You have universal ideas, you recreate old
times perfectly and enchantingly in our own time; in short,
you have broken with the rotten poetic world of the tearful
romanticism of the nineteenth century and its themes – which
were fit for a barrel-organ. Do I understand you, or am I
mistaken?'

CAVAFY: 'Your idea is really wonderful, dear Marinetti. But
it seems to me that I am far from futurism.'

MARINETTI: '. . . Whoever is in advance of his time in art
or in life is a futurist.'

Cavafy had been suffering for some time, and in June 1932
cancer of the throat was diagnosed. Alexander and Rika Singopoulos with the help of other friends persuaded him to let them
take him to Athens for consultation and treatment. He went
early in July, staying first at the Hotel Cosmopolite. There he
received visits from many Athenian men-of-letters both before
and after his operation. Mr George Katsimbalis visited him, in
connection with a bibliography that he was preparing. 'Take care,
Katsimbalis,' he managed to say, 'to put a title to it that says
there's lots, lots more about Cavafy, and that your bibliography
isn't exhaustive . . . Yes, put something like "From the bibliography of Cavafy" or something like that. For God's sake don't
write that it's the whole Cavafian bibliography for there will be
a danger that you may be exposed and blamed for not knowing
all the rest that has been written about Cavafy. And there's lots
more, Katsimbalis.' Mr Katsimbalis chose for his title 'Sketch for
a Cavafian Bibliography'.[53]

At first he could speak only a little and in whispers. At the
Red Cross a tracheotomy was performed, after which he could
not speak at all; for the remainder of his life he communicated
with others by pencilled notes. He had said to Rika Singopoulos:
'All old people have something. One loses his eyesight, another
his hearing. I'm going to lose my voice – I should think myself
lucky.' But to his friends the loss of that marvellous voice, so
subtly controlled, was the loss of the greater part of himself. For

53. Katsimbalis, p. 3.

aesthetic reasons he refused to have the metal larynx which might
for a brief time have prolonged his life.

He went to a clinic in Kifissia for his convalesence; there he
disliked the view of the mountains from his room. 'They bore
me,' he said. He was glad to return to his hotel in Omonoia;
thence on at least one occasion he slipped away from his admirers to make a rapid walk in the neighbouring streets at the
hour of the evening bustle. During his illness he would only
read detective stories; he had just discovered Simenon. In
October he returned to Alexandria.

In the spring his condition became worse. 'Once,' wrote Rika
Singopoulos 'in all his dreadful illness Cavafy wept. It was the
day when he was to go into hospital. We brought a little suitcase
for him to take some papers with him [he took the two folders of
his poems] and a few bits of clothing he wanted. When he saw the
suitcase he was overcome with tears. We tried to calm him at
this heart-rending moment when he was leaving his house for
ever. He took the block and wrote : "I bought this suitcase 30
years ago, in a hurry one evening, to go to Cairo for pleasure.
Then I was young and strong, and not ugly.'

Like a man long prepared, like a man of courage . . .
quotes Rika Singopoulos, who says that his attitude to death was
'heroic, admirable, Christian'. Mr Malanos tells us that he was
afraid, that he wept and clung to the friends who visited him in
hospital, and did not want them to leave him. We must believe
both of them. What or how much Cavafy himself believed we
hardly know; we are told that he always wore a cross round his
neck, no doubt that given to him by Amalia Pittardis at his
baptism. We know that on Good Fridays he used to wait in the
street, hat in hand, for the emergence of the beautiful and
touching funeral procession of Christ from the patriarchate. We
do not know if this was only a love of Greek forms, or if he had
any religious conviction. A long time ago John had written to
him : 'I am right glad to note that we are *d'accord* as regards
religion. Atheism is most deplorable, and I am positively con-
vinced that no man hath ever reaped any advantage through the
acceptance of this absurd and at the same time obnoxious
theory' – but that was fifty years ago. We may, however, be
reasonably certain that Cavafy was not enough of a materialist
to be without fear of the unknown.

When the patriarch came to the hospital he at first refused to see him, for the visit had been arranged without his knowledge; then he consented, and apparently received the last sacraments with contrition.

After a long agony, he died at two o'clock in the morning of 29 April 1933, his seventieth birthday. His funeral service took place on the afternoon of the same day at St Saba, and his body was laid in the family burial-place in the Greek cemetery. It may be hoped that it may lie there in peace, but the cemetery is now threatened : it occupies a site most eligible for building. In any case, the idea of translating his remains to Greece must be deplored. He was an Alexandrian of the Alexandrians. Rue Cherif bore him, Massalia undid him, Chatby holds him. And if Chatby should relinquish hold, we must wish that another resting-place may be found for him in his great city, not too far from the dust of Antony and Cleopatra, and of the great Alexander.

Appendix

Fragments of Table Talk

On the Greek Langage

'My dear! That που how unmanageable it is! It appears all the time. πὸυ with grave, π̂ου with circumflex! And how ugly it sounds with frequent repetition! Poor Flaubert tried to get rid of two *que* that were near together in a phrase, since he fancied they offended his ear. And he worked for days!

Imagine what he would have gone through with our πόυ! For that reason I say that the participle which is disappearing is destined to return and to live, to save us from all these cacophonous πόυ!'

Mistriotis had said half the language was to be thrown into the sea; Psycharis had said the other half was to be thrown into the river.

'All that is absurd. We must study our language since we don't know it. What hidden treasures it contains, what treasures! Our

54. Komis, p. 12.

thought ought to be how we are to enrich it, how to bring to light what it has hidden in it.'[55]

On Versification

'My dear, why should I take this pointless trouble? Perhaps you think Poetry is something technical, and that it doesn't live the natural life of every Art? You'll say: "What about the Verse?" But doesn't that exist in our conversation? What is most of our talk but verse, and iambic verse? Observe, and you'll perceive it yourself. Why then shouldn't I prefer the iambic, and exclusively the iambic?

Many people have made your remark to me, my dear, and they have added: "Why don't you use rhyme, Cavafy?" But they're wrong. For their question ought to be addressed to poets before my time who, good souls, didn't use it either, though rhyme was the established thing in their day.'[56]

On Literature

Several friends were speaking of Omar Khayyam, and one of them (probably Polis Modinos) admired as a beautiful image:

The flower that once has blown forever dies.

CAVAFY: 'What's beautiful about it? Every flower will fade. That's what happens, and is what we see. It's superfluous for the artist to take it up. The visible is seen with a little observation. Art is what the artist invents.'[57]

'If a story that should be told in fifty pages is written in thirty it will be better . . . that is, the artist will leave something out, but that's not a fault . . . But if he gives it in a hundred pages it's a fearful fault.'[58]

'The adjective weakens speech and is a weakness. For something – a landscape – to be given in many epithets is nothing . . . Art

55. Sareyannis, p. 42.
56. Komis, p. 17.
57. Alithersis, pp. 40–1.
58. ibid.

is to give all that only with substantives, and if an epithet is needed it must be the fit one.'[59]

On Ancient Egypt

'I don't understand those big immobile things.'[60]

59. Alithersis, pp. 40–1.
60. Sareyannis, p. 45.

Afterword

E. M. Forster, returning after several years' absence to Alexandria, promptly lost his way at the (then) new railway-station. One can imagine the hot wind swirling into his mouth dust that may once have been part of the great Alexander. 'Why may not imagination trace the noble dust of Alexander till he find it stopping a bung-hole?' And what bung-hole would be secure against a khamsin? Perhaps Alexandrians still wipe their eponymous hero from their noses, or comb him from their hair.

There is a persistent legend that his body lies, lapped in gold, deep under the mosque of the Prophet Daniel in the middle of the town. Cavafy told another story to Mr Bryn Davies: 'The truth of the story of the dragoman of the Russian embassy is this. In 1853 among the Greek people of Alexandria, for they were and are a people not a community, now of 55,000 then of three or four thousand, a hundred or perhaps two hundred families, was a merchant called Kirritchi. Mr X is – am I right? Yes, his grandson. This merchant one evening had some business at Moharrem Bey. He was in the habit of taking three or four more and when he reached the house of his client he found he had to wait for him. It was then that he said he went down some steps and saw a glass coffin and inside the coffin Alexander the Great. His more sceptical neighbours suggested Kirritchi had dreamed it all; he was a man of some culture; he read Greek, and it is not impossible he may have done so.'

Cavafy had probably a treasure of Alexandrian lore that has never been fully exploited. He also told Mr Bryn Davies about Néroutsos, a philosopher and archaeologist (d. 1885). 'I went to see him as a young man. Everybody went and made use of his conversation . . . His appearance – a long green coat and a pointed hat – a magician. He knew Alexandria and went about in a closed cab. Said "the Hippodrome, you will find it in such and such a place" – and they did!

Between Forster's visits Alexandria had changed, at least beyond his immediate recognition: he spoke nostalgically of quiet little restaurants by the Mahmudieh canal, long vanished. But to him the climate always seemed marvellous. It is true that it boasts of a 'European' climate; that is to say, instead of having the beautiful Egyptian winter of Cairo, it is wet. In early spring, violent winds unhasp window shutters and send them dangerously hurtling to the street below. After a beautiful April (perhaps), summer sets in and a mephitic damp rises in the evening from the sea. Not even a handkerchief comes back completely dry from the wash, and asthma grips the throat. Few Alexandrians care to sit out-of-doors at night.

Though an Anglo-Egyptian Gezira child, I had never visited Alexandria until May 1941, when I went to say goodbye to George Seferis, who was posted to South Africa. With Nanis Panayotopoulos (another dear friend since dead), we walked round Cavafy's quarter, Mr Malanos our guide, in the bomb-inviting moonlight.

'Here he lived,' said Mr Malanos, outside the house in the Rue Lepsius. 'Here he died,' and he indicated the former Greek hospital, then the Fleet Club. 'Here they read the service over him', and we were by the door of St Saba.

When I returned a few months later to live and work in Alexandria, Cavafy seemed the *genius loci*. There were still the three streets of Forster's books: the Rue Cherif Pasha (where Cavafy was born), long since 'too shoppy to be genteel'. The Boulevard de Ramleh (where he lived with his mother) had long since gone down. The Rue Rosette, where he and Paul had lived, still went on for ever, and was still dull. Thirteen hundred years ago the conquering Arabs had laid low the marble colonnades, the gates and the palaces described by Achilles Tatius and resurrected by Anatole France in *Thäis*. It is no affectation to say that only the great past of Alexandria made it tolerable to live there – and only Cavafy connected the great past with the contemporary world.

In wartime Alexandria many things had come into being that he knew nothing of, but I saw little cafés where I think he had gone, and ate in a small Greek restaurant where he sometimes went. 'What did he like to eat?' I asked, and was told: 'Dates.' One bookshop held memories of him. I came to know many of his friends and acquaintances (not always friends of each other).

People told anecdotes of him, drew caricatures of him on cigarette boxes, imitated his gestures, and tried to imitate his voice, though they owned it to be inimitable. Alexander Singopoulos showed me some of his furniture and remains of his library. I heard a lecture on him in French by his friend Gaston Zananiri : a retired actress, now married to a 'protoclassatos', smirked at her friends, and read *Myris*.

When I had to take the Ramleh tram to the depressing suburb where I lived, I could imagine Cavafy, under the palm trees that clacked in the wind, looking to see if any beautiful face were lit by the 'to-fro tender tram beams' that alone illuminated the black-out, and following with his blessing the dubious couples that slipped away into side streets.

The city is going to follow you, and so I found. Transferred to Cairo (so infinitely more beautiful, so much dearer to me), Alexandria always haunted me. In 1948 I had the honour to be invited to give the English lecture in the celebrations of Cavafy's fifteenth anniversary : Mr Malanos had spoken in Greek, M. René Etiemble in French, and an Egyptian official had spoken in Arabic when he unveiled the plaque on Cavafy's house.

That same spring, walking between the splendid herbaceous borders of Nimr Pacha at Meadi, Sir Walter Smart had said to me : 'If you're going to write an Alexandrian novel, it must centre round Cavafy.' This was the 'little germ' of *Unreal City*, in which I imagined Cavafy as living in the city I knew, where he still seemed to live.

Five years later I saw Alexandria for the last time, from the air. Since then it has been further 'transwogrified' (if one may coin the word); there is a bazaar in Cavafy's Rue Cherif, and his very bones are threatened.

Unreal City – for all its materialism and its hideousness, yet one of the cities of the soul. There I have known the misery and nostalgia of other exiles, 'stretching out our hands with love for the other shore'. But 'good things have not held aloof' : friendship, work and happiness – though later there followed illness, danger and extreme grief. In five years, I feel, I have taken out in experience my citizenship of no mean city, and am bold to say *an Alexandrian is writing about an Alexandrian* : Ἀλεξανδρινὸς διὰ Ἀλεξανδρινὸν γράφει.

Bibliography

Unpublished Sources

I. Manuscripts of the poet's and collections made by him

  1 A manuscript genealogy and other notes on family history, in English.

  2 Notes and letters referring to his position in the Third Circle of Irrigation, in English.

  3 Notes on Gibbon, *c.* 1897.*

  4 Theatre programmes etc.: souvenirs of his journey in France and England with his brother John, 1897.

  5 Notes chiefly referring to his mother, and a rough journal of the days immediately preceding her death, in Greek and English, *c.* 1899.

  6 Notes about the last illness of his brother Alexander, mostly in Greek, 1905.

  7 Miscellaneous scraps, mostly in English, including the 'confessions',* his betting book, etc.

  8 Letters to Alexander Singopoulos, in Greek, 1918–19.

II. Letters addressed to the poet

  1 By the 'three friends': Mikès Ralli, Stephen Schilizzi and John Rodocanachi, in English, 1882–5.*

  2 By his brother John, 1882–5* – and a few of later date; in English (with one or two in Greek).

  3 By his mother, in Greek, 1895–7.*

  4 By his brother Paul, in Greek, 1908–19.

III. Miscellaneous papers, including a few family letters, Haricleia Cavafy's cookery receipts, her visiting list and a list of her jewellery, etc. Album of invitations received by Paul Cavafy, 1883–97, and other small items. Notes by Rika Singopoulos.*

All these are in the possession of Mr George Savidis, by whose great kindness I have been able to use them. I have tried to make my references to these documents as precise as possible, so that they may be easily verifiable when these papers have been calendared and catalogued.

* Used also, to a small extent, by Michael Peridis.

I have examined the Album of Aristides Cavafy in the Benaki Museum, Athens. By the courtesy of Mr Robert Rowe of Gonville and Caius College I have been allowed to read photocopies of Cavafy's letters to E. M. Forster. I undertook not to transcribe them, and they were not much to my purpose.

Printed Sources

Alithersis: Γλαύκου Ἀλιθέρση, Τὸ πρόβλημα τοῦ Καβάφη (Alexandria, 1934)

Baud-Bovy: Samuel Baud-Bovy, Poésie de la Grèce moderne (Lausanne, 1946)

Bevan: Edwyn Bevan, The House of Seleucus (London, 1902)

Bowra: Maurice Bowra, The Creative Experiment (London, 1949)

Catraro: Atanasio Catraro, Ὁ φίλος μου Καβάφης n.d.

Cavafy, Prose: Κ. Π. Καβάφη, Πεζά: Παρουσίαση, σχόλια Γ. Α. Παπουτσάκη (Athens, 1963)

Cavafy, U(npublished) P(oems): Κ. Π. Καβάφη, Ἀνέκδοτα Ποιήματα, 1882–1923, φιλολογικὴ ἐπιμέλεια Γ. Π. Σαββίδη (Athens, 1968)

Cavafy, U(npublished) Prose: Κ. Π. Καβάφη, Ἀνέκδοτα Πεζὰ Κείμενα, εἰσαγωγὴ καὶ μετάφραση Μιχάλη Περίδη (Athens, 1963)

Cromer: Earl of Cromer, Modern Egypt, 2 vols (London, 1908)

Dalven: Rae Dalven, The Complete Poems of Cavafy (New York, 1961)

ET: 'Επιθεώρηση Τέχνης

Forster, Alexandria: E. M. Forster, Alexandria, a History and a Guide, n.d.

Forster, Pharos: E. M. Forster, Pharos and Pharillon (London, 1923)

Genealogy: N.E. May 1948, pp. 622–9.

Halvatsikis: Μανώλη Χαλβατζάκη, Ὁ Καβάφης στήν ὑπαλληλική του ζωή (Athens, 1967)

JHS: Journal of Hellenic Studies

Katsimbalis: Γ. Π. Κατσίμπαλη, Βιβλιογραφία Κ. Π. Καβάφη (Athens, 1943)

Keeley and Savidis: Edmund Keeley and George Savidis, Passions and Ancient Days (New York, 1971)

Komis: Ἀντώνη Κόμη, Κ. Π. Καβάφης (Corfu, 1935)

Lehonitis: *Γ. Λεχωνίτη, Καβαφικὰ Αὐτοσχόλια* (Alexandria, 1942)

Malanos, *Cavafy: Τίμου Μαλάνου, 'Ο Ποιητὴς Κ. Π. Καβάφης* (Athens, 1957)

Malanos, *Cavafy 2: Τίμου Μαλάνου, Καβάφης 2* (Athens, 1963)

Malanos, *Memoir: Τίμου Μαλάνου, Ἀναμνήσεις ἑνὸς Ἀλεξανδρινοῦ* (Athens, 1971)

Malanos, *Τ: Μανώλη Γιαλουράκη, 'Ο Καβάφης τοῦ κεφαλαίου ' Τ', συνομιλίες μὲ τὸν Τίμο Μαλάνο* (Alexandria, 1959)

Mavrogordato: John Mavrogordato, *Poems by C. P. Cavafy* (1971 edition)

N.E.: *Νέα 'Εστία*

Ouranis: *Κώστα Οὐράνη, Δικοί μας καὶ Ξένοι* (Athens, 1955)

Peridis: *Μιχάλη Περίδη, 'Ο Βίος καὶ τὸ "Εργο τοῦ Κωνστ. Καβάφη* (Athens, 1948)

Pieridis: *Γιάγκου Πιερίδη, 'Ο Καβάφης συνομιλίες, χαρακτηρισμοί, ἀνέκδοτα* (Athens, 1943)

Pontani: Filippo Maria Pontani, *Costantino Kavafis Poesie* (Verona, 1961)

Radopoulos: *Ραδ. Γ. Ραδοπούλου, Εἰσαγωγὴ εἰς τὴν ἱστορίαν τῆς ἑλληνικῆς κοινότητος Ἀλεξανδρίας 1830–1921* (Athens, 1928)

Sareyannis: *Ι. Α. Σαρεγιάννη, Σχόλια στόν Καβάφη* (Athens, 1964)

Savidis, *Bibliography: Γ. Π. Σαββίδη, οἱ Καβαφικὲς 'Εκδόσεις (1891–1932)* (Athens, 1966)

Savidis, *DL: Γ. Π. Σαββίδη, 'Ο Δραστικὸς Λόγος τοῦ Κ. Π. Καβάφη* (Athens, 1972)

Seferis, *Essays: Γιώργου Σεφέρη, Δοκιμές* (2nd ed.) (Athens, 1962)

Seferis, *Greek Style:* George Seferis, *On the Greek Style, Selected Essays in Poetry and Hellenism*, trans. Rex Warner and Th.D. Frangopoulos (London, 1966)

Storrs: Ronald Storrs, *Orientations* (London, 1945)

Tsirkas, *Chronology: Στράτη Τσίρκα, Κ. Π. Καβάφης, σχεδίασμα χρονογραφίας τοῦ βίου του* (Athens, 1963)

Tsirkas, *Epoch: Στράτη Τσίρκα, 'Ο Καβάφης καὶ ἡ 'Εποχή του* (Athens, 1958)

Tsirkas, *Politikos: Στράτη Τσίρκα, 'Ο πολιτικὸς Καβάφης* (Athens, 1971)

Yourcenar: Marguerite Yourcenar, *Présentation critique de Constantin Cavafy* (Paris, 1958)

Index